# ASTROLOGY ALIVE!

'Astrology Alive! conveys both the excitement and the potential of experiential astrology. Taking the reader beyond a traditional intellectual understanding of astrological principles, Barbara draws on a wealth of professional and personal experience to show how signs, planets, houses and aspects can be directly felt, experienced and expressed.

'Presented in a clear and inviting style, it serves not only as an invaluable resource manual for students, teachers and practitioners, but also offers a genuine path for self-exploration and therapeutic healing.

'This is a warm and sensitive book. Take it to heart, try out the exercises and techniques it recommends, and your understanding of astrology — and of yourself — will multiply a thousandfold.

'In Astrology Alive! Barbara Schermer does exactly what her title suggests — she brings the astrological chart to life in a way that few other writers have done. It seems destined to become the classic textbook on experiential astrology. It certainly deserves to be.'

HOWARD SASPORTAS

## ERRATA

Page 20: The fourth paragraph should begin:

Scene Six: A young woman contemplates the kaleidoscopically colored circle of

Pages 46 & 110: Rebecca's Chart and Sandi's Chart have been transposed in error.

Barbara Schermer

# ASTROLOGY ALIVE!

*Experiential Astrology, Astrodrama, and the Healing Arts.*

## BARBARA SCHERMER

THE AQUARIAN PRESS

First published 1989

British Library Cataloguing in Publication Data

Schermer, Barbara
Astrology alive: experiential astrology,
astrodrama and the healing arts. —
(Aquarian new directions in astrology
series).
1. Astrology
I. Title
133.5

ISBN 0-85030-703-1

The Aquarian Press is part of the Thorsons Publishing Group,
Wellingborough, Northamptonshire, NN8 2RQ, England

Typeset by Harper Phototypesetters Ltd, Northampton
Printed in Great Britain

1  3  5  7  9  10  8  6  4  2

# ACKNOWLEDGEMENTS

I am not one of those who dashes out of the movie theater just as The End flashes up on the screen. I often keep my seat as the lights come up and watch the parade of credits, marveling at the number of people it takes to make a film. And now, having written *Astrology Alive!*, I look back with wonder at how many people it has taken to truly make a book. To the many who helped me, I offer these 'credits' — and my sincere gratitude.

Shellyji for sharing his deep yogic wisdom and Scorpionic humor — and his abiding faith in me.
Kriyananda for teaching me to stand on my own two feet.
My father who taught me strength through his gentleness.
Jeff Jawer for the support, encouragement, and inspiration of a colleague and friend.
Clay Bodine, Noel Tyl, Paula Walowitz, and Rick Tarnas for their editing suggestions, sensitive feedback, and sound advice.
Eileen Campbell for being willing to publish this author's first book.
My friend, storyteller Marcie Telander, for her charming tale of Tamlaine.
Bobby Skafish and Dixie Sue Botari for helping me find appropriate planetary music.
B. J. Johnson for her superb illustration of the Kriya Yoga chakra system.
Greg Vlamis for his cosmic connection.
Michael Cox for writing to me out of the blue to suggest I write this book.
My colleagues and friends, Margie Nicholson, Debra Trimmer, Moira Canes, Mary Ellen Glass, Jamie Binder, Betsey Means, Susie Cox, Anne Trompeter, Carl Fitzpatrick, Tom Brady, Ramona Lucero, Marti Beddoe, and my mom and family who gave me their encouragement, good ideas, and in two cases, allowed me to share their personal stories.
Most of all, I wish to thank my husband, Bob Craft, for his consistent and loving support of me and my work, especially in my moments of frustration and doubt; for his taming of the beasts that invade every computer and word processor and for his reading and commenting with care upon every chapter, sentence, and word in the book.

## Dedication

To Shellyji and those who preceded him;
to Kriyananda and those who follow him.

# CONTENTS

## Book I

# BOOK II: RESOURCE WORKBOOK

# BOOK I

# INTRODUCTION

In the beginning, astrology was *alive*. Life and especially that aspect of life we call *mind*, is shaped by the recurrent patterns of relationship between the living and the surrounding world.[1] As humankind evolved it was always in the context of an existence upon a whirling sphere, cyclically exposed to sun, moon, planets, and stars, and interactive with them. Thus we may truly say that the patterns of heavenly movement are inherent in life, in mind, and in humanity. And as men and women further regarded the stars as their wandering companions, the diverse regularity of the heavens continued to inform them of the subtleties of pattern, as they in turn laid upon the stars a template revealing the qualities of emerging mind.

Human life at the beginning was not separate from creation. The stars must have been an intimate part of day to day life. Yet so little remains to inform us of our ancestors' earliest attempts to grasp the heavens. Did they climb mountains to place themselves closer to the stars? Did they pile up bricks or stones to mark their course through the skies? We know that they did so as much as 4000 years ago in ancient Mesopotamia, and at least by 1500 BC at Stonehenge — and who can say how long the Great Medicine Wheel, with its precise astronomical alignment of stones, has stood high in the Bighorn Mountains of Wyoming? In any event we are safe to assume that in the splendor of the dark, quiet nights, gazing into the starry vault, early man was transported; lifted to the realm of the gods. Many centuries later the Roman poet Manilius (first century AD) captured what early men and women may have felt:

> Those moonless nights when even stars of the sixth magnitude kindle their crowded and gleaming fires, seeds of light amid the darkness. The glittering temples of the sky then shine with torches more numerous than the sands of the seashore, than the flowers of the meadow, than the waves of the ocean, than the leaves of the forest. If nature had given to this multitude powers in proportion to its numbers, the ether itself would not have been able to support its own flames, and the conflagration of Olympus would have consumed the entire world.[2]

And later yet (c. 150 AD) Ptolemy wrote, 'Mortal as I am, I know that I am born for the day, but when I follow the serried course (of the stars), my feet no longer touch the earth; I ascend to Zeus himself to feast me on ambrosia, the food of the gods.'[3] Even with the refinements of Greek and Roman civilization, humans remained close to the earth beneath them, the stars above. Men and women had a relationship to the natural world, and their contemplation of the heavens was a vital, primal communion which brought meaning to life.

Today, we can see that we have lost touch with this primal experience. And astrology, child of this union of the contemplative urge with light from the heavens, is in danger of losing its primal vitality by becoming too abstract, theoretical and analytical. Brain researchers have made us aware in the last few years that we have not one brain but two, with, to risk over simplification, an analytical, verbal, rational left hemisphere and an intuitive, visual, holistic right one.[4] Our culture's traditional way of educating has cultivated and encouraged the left brain, touting abstraction while ignoring the development of our intuitive, imaginative right brain. Math, science, and verbal skills are taught at the expense of art, music, and creative expression. Although enlightened educators have responded of late in recognition of this fact, such programs are the first to go when funds are cut.

It is important to point out that many of us do not learn well with words or abstract symbols, but depend on that part of the brain that 'paints pictures.' Numerous studies have confirmed the fact that vividly experienced imagery, imagery that is both seen and felt, can substantially affect the brain waves, blood flow, heart rate, skin temperature, gastric secretions, and immune response — in fact, the total physiology.'[5] And research continues to point toward the critical role of imagery in learning.[6] The tyranny of left brain domination has gone too far. Is it any wonder that most children's artistic impulses start disappearing at age nine, when they have been 'brainwashed' from age six onwards to use only their left brain? The present educational system abandons children who may be naturally visual, imaginative thinkers.

The conduct of our education in astrology has been no different. In the beginning most of us sat before a teacher, passively memorizing the planets, signs, houses and their meanings. Then we passively sat in another class learning how to synthesize those planets, signs, and houses into meaningful interpretation. What other means of learning do we currently have? We have books to read and conferences to attend. Again, most conferences are set up in familiar left brain learning style: one active participant, the lecturer, speaking to a passively compliant group of 25 listeners. And our books are too often a dry parody of the same form. We have been — and still are being — educated only to *think* about astrology. By now the conclusion must be obvious: to teach an astrology of the right brain we must use its language, a language not of words but of images.

Consider this: You are an astrologer, holding a consultation with a client about transiting Neptune. Instead of talking, you show her a picture of San Francisco shrouded in fog to illustrate her upcoming encounter with that planet. Or with a group of students you hand out crayons and have them draw what Mars square Uranus 'feels like', or you lead them blindfolded around the block to give a direct experience of the Neptune square Mercury aspect. Or, to better communicate the essence of Pluto, you work together on a sprawling collage of Pluto images, replete with magicians, world leaders, atomic explosions, and erupting volcanoes. Going even further with a group, you might stimulate the use of the holistic right brain by having members enact their internal images of Mars — with the aid of some energizing dance music, contacting the Mars energy, and expressing it through movement and dance. (The term *astrodrama* has been given to this form of acting out the planetary energies.) The group may further refine the process by exploring how different the Mars energy feels in Scorpio or Taurus or by noticing the different feeling tones between expressions of Mars/Jupiter, Mars/Saturn or a Mars/Uranus conjunction.

Music is perhaps the most time-honored means of communicating to the right brain. Music that elicits the particular energy of each planet can be found. Holst's *The Planets* and Tomita's reinterpretation are classics. The album, *Deep Breakfast*, by Ray Lynch suggests Venus/Jupiter and the song 'Icarus' by various artists conjures up a beautiful Venus. 'Hearing Solar Winds' by David Hykes and the Harmonic Choir profoundly evokes Neptune and Pluto.

Even without these more expressive techniques, you can enhance right brain response by the use of verbal images through skilful employment of metaphors, analogies, and fairy tales. For instance, you might tell a client or a class that Neptune is 'like wearing glasses with the wrong prescription.' Or illustrate a Saturn return as 'a baby chicken breaking out of its shell.' Hypnotist *par excellence*, Milton Erickson, and the NLP (Neurolinguistic Programming) psychotherapists have shown that the proper use of metaphor more than illustrates — it *heals*.[7] To sharpen your skills in this area you might, for example, learn to tell the story 'The Frog Prince' from Grimm's fairy tales to bring to life the transformative nature of Pluto, or you may draw upon Greek and Roman mythology for those stories in which the planetary archetypes themselves are the primary characters.

That ancient tales contain expression of the astrological archetypes is, of course, no accident, for the understanding that both the planetary energies and the gods have profound influences upon humankind (if indeed they are not identical) springs from the same ancient sources. In fact *Astrology Alive!* will make the argument that the 'new' astrology described here is in reality a re-emergence of the very old, from a time in which the archetypal energies were readily available and deeply felt. Chapter One illustrates this point with the Demeter-Persephone story that was for the Greeks the founding myth for 'the Greater Mystery' of Eleusis, a ritual repeated in spectacle, pageantry, and reverence at each consecutive fall equinox for 2000 years! Every year the residents of Athens abandoned the city to walk the 14 mile Sacred Way to Eleusis to partake in this 'sacred theater' and its rites. As we will see later, this myth had extraordinary power within Greek culture and in the unconscious minds of the Greek people.

Our focus need not remain on the Western traditions alone since astrology has flourished in the East for centuries, often integrated with spiritual tradition. You will find evidence of my background in yoga especially in the latter chapers of the book.

*Astrology Alive!* will show the relevance of these myths and rites for a new kind of astrological practice that provides a corrective to the 'left brain bias' of both astrology and culture at large. Myth contains, in story form, the deepest truths of a culture. Today, in the West, we seem to have an impoverished mythology, weakened by a too strict adherence to the Newtonian-Cartesian scientific world view. And we should suspect that astrology, as an 'institution' which participates to some degree in that culture, is in a weakened state as well. We who have an interest in astrology have been carried along with the technological tides of our time, often to our benefit, with new methods of computation and research, but also to our detriment in that we have forgotten that our original encounter with the heavens was immediate, direct and alive. Are we not hungering for a deeper knowledge of ourselves and others? Isn't that precisely what astrology purports to do? Doesn't it put us more deeply in touch with our true nature? All too often, it seems, we have simply gone along with our cultures, just *thinking* about astrology. Shouldn't we begin to *feel* about it as well?

With means such as metaphor, music, myth, spiritual practice, and dramatic and artistic expression, we can move into more *direct* contact with the planetary energies, and in so doing we rediscover the depths of ourselves. Astrology becomes, then, not just a tool for abstraction and intellection, but a way of self-knowledge and a means to vital, primal communion with that which is beyond. And that brings us to the purpose of this book: *Astrology Alive!* is intended to introduce and to teach what has come to be called *experiential astrology*. It is a book for all of us who are bored with traditional approaches, who want to revive our feelings of planetary connection and communion, and who are willing to pursue deeper levels of experience. The book is designed to be of value to anyone learning or teaching astrology, or to anyone from the arts or psychology who is at least conversant with the language of astrology. If our aim is true, the material will be particularly useful for the growing number of individuals who are beginning to combine astrology with other fields such as *Gestalt*, psychosynthesis, mythology, the Arts and spiritual practice to yield new healing forms.

Consider this book as an invitation to a feast, at the broad table of which you will find the kind of fare that both tempts the senses and sticks to the ribs — that is, practical, direct ways for you to work and play at bringing astrology alive. Any such table needs support, of course. The four 'legs' of our own table include three major thinkers and a 'movement.' The first thinker is Dane Rudhyar, whose lifelong effort was to develop a 'humanistic' astrology. The second is Carl Jung, who gifted us with an enormously fruitful journey into the workings of the human mind. Without his concepts of the archetypes, the self, and the personal and collective unconscious, we would scarcely have a way to talk of important matters of consciousness. The third supporting member is Jacob Moreno and his psychodrama which was a direct stimulus for astrodrama, a particularly well developed form of experiential astrology. As chapter two will detail, the fourth source of support is the 'human potential movement' that brought psychology to popular culture in the 1960s.

Astrologer Stephen Arroyo has noted a major stumbling block for both students and practicing astrologers: the lack of guidance on synthesis of the many disparate elements of an astrological inquiry.[8] It is a rare astrology text that succeeds in teaching the blending of chart symbols. However, synthesis yields swiftly to experiential methods that teach by doing, as will be illustrated by techniques gleaned from my own experiences in experiential performance and theater, teaching, counseling, and marathon group therapy sessions.

To summarize: Part I of *Astrology Alive!* will, after a suitable dose of background and theory, concentrate on conveying to you the excitement and promise of experiential astrology and on teaching you the basic skills that will help you learn from experience. Part II is an even more practical and concrete Resource Workbook, with suggested specific exercises, divided for easy reference by planets, signs, and elements. Each workbook section concludes with a list of widely available musical selections that evoke the energy of the particular planet or sign. At the back of the book is an Appendix which offers tips and techniques for working with groups and particular suggestions for facilitating astrodrama.

Especially important is that you let this book stimulate in you a sense of exploration, participation, spontaneity, and just plain fun. Harvey Cox states it well: 'Man's very survival as a species has been placed in grave jeopardy by our repression of the human celebrative and imaginative faculties . . . Man is by his very nature a creature who not only works and thinks but who sings, dances, prays, tells stories, and celebrates. He is *homo festivus*.'[9] I invite you, then, to join the merrymaking. But be reminded that our play may have a serious purpose: Pluto is now transiting through Scorpio, and with the consequent stirrings deep in the psyche people are increasingly in need of ways to bring about emergence, from the depths, of those forces that transform and illuminate. Experiential astrology, as described here, may serve as a tool for that emergence. I invite you to use it wisely, well, and with pleasure.

# 1
# INTRODUCING EXPERIENTIAL ASTROLOGY

One of the truths of our time is this hunger deep in people all over
the planet for coming into relationship with each other. Human
consciousness is crossing a threshold as mighty as the one from the
Middle Ages to the Renaissance. People are hungering and
thirsting after experience that feels true to them on the inside.
                            Marilyn Ferguson, *Aquarian Conspiracy*

*Scene One*: A young man in a red cape swaggers aggressively up to a large, robust woman. She holds her body rigid, arms folded across her chest, and stands her ground. In the background the Mars movement from Holst's *The Planets* blares from a hidden speaker. As if swept into action by the frenzy of the music, the young man tries repeatedly to force his way past his opponent. The more he pushes, the more the woman is unmoved. The 'hotter' he gets, the 'colder' she becomes. Curbing his frustration he changes his tack, trying to seduce her with sweet words. 'Come back when you're grown up!' she commands. As the scene progresses, a look of recognition flashes in the woman's eyes. She suddenly begins to understand the creative impasse she has experienced in her work as an artist during these weeks that Saturn has been squaring her natal Mars.

*Scene Two*: A group of astrology students are fanned out on a broad, newspaper-strewn floor, sensuously expressing, with fingerpaint on posterboard, the energy and character of the planet Jupiter. With sticky blue hands they swirl and spiral through a series of grand, sweeping movements. They are obviously having great fun!

*Scene Three*: Sitting in the center of a circle (her natal chart), a young woman is surrounded by the eager faces of 10 'planets,' positioned as they appeared at the moment she was born. One by one they introduce themselves. Beginning with the first house cusp is her Moon in Cancer. Cuddling at the woman's feet, she coos, 'I'm your Moon in Cancer. I'm shy, quiet. I like to pull back from the world to nourish myself. I love herbal baths, walks with my lover, and hugging my cat.'

Each planet, after completing its introduction, begins interacting with the others according to the aspects in the woman's chart. The Moon enters the circle joined by her Pluto in Scorpio. (The woman's Moon trines Pluto.) Responding to Pluto's influence the Moon moves more sensuously, gracefully, passionately. Then comes a sudden interruption by a belligerent Mars in Aries. (Our subject's Moon squares

Mars.) Taunting the Moon, he roars, 'Don't be such a pushover! You're always giving in because of your insecurity and need to be liked. Who cares if they like you? *I don't care if they don't!*' The young woman's chart unfolds before her eyes, bringing with it the feeling that each combination of aspects produces in her unconscious. By the end of her living horoscope she is deeply affected, entranced by her uniquely personal drama.

*Scene Four*: In a gymnasium theater-in-the-round, surrounded by an expanse of window glass, the full moon is rising in the night sky. On the lawn outside, a procession of 10 'planets,' actors in costume, approach. Though many in the audience know no astrology, each planet, from the Sun out to Pluto, teaches and amuses, and presses each onlooker toward recognition and understanding of the psychic function within.

*Scene Five*: With learning about the four elements as your objective, you and your students have taken an overnight journey into a forest. To commune with Earth, the group sits on the ground, meditates, and imagines the strength of the earth flowing from the ground and into each still body. To experience Air, all climb to the top of a breezy ridge and take in deep, full breaths of the windy air. To encounter Fire you scatter to fetch kindling and firewood and build a roaring campfire. To experience Water you take the path to a hot spring and relax tired muscles as the new moon welcomes you in the East.

images and symbols on the posterboard before her — a 'birth mandala' of her horoscope. She has spent the last two hours in an artistic and reflective process to create this vivid, rich representation of her psyche.

*Scene Seven*: An earnest young man, sitting in the center of his own natal chart, spine erect, deeply meditative, attunes to the planetary psychic energies within. He knows he has an upcoming transit of Saturn opposite his Sun, and he is about to perform a ritual he himself created to help soften and neutralize that imbalance.

Each of the above vignettes is an example of a contemporary approach to astrology that may be new to you: the field of *experiential astrology*. These innovations in an ancient discipline show great promise in adding impact, depth, and meaning to astrology's already extensive repertoire. The chief defining characteristic of experiential astrology is that its methods offer *direct participation* in the vital energies symbolized by the horoscope. By taking the astrological chart off the page and into movement, encounter, art, drama, and dance, we allow not just participation by the intellect but involvement of the senses and emotions as well. While its methods can be studied, experiential astrology is in essence an adventure to be experienced!

My own trail of adventures began in 1979 while teaching a basic astrology class. We were talking about Saturn and its correspondence with old age. Caught up in a desire to get my message across, I stopped talking and just began to walk back and forth in front of the class. Beginning as a blithe young girl with a bounce in my step, I slowly allowed my gait and demeanor to shift toward middle age, a little restrained, more bent over, nursing some new pain in my back. Then, even more wearied by Time, I crept and staggered, until as an old crone I collapsed in a heap on the floor, clearly dead. The effects of this two minute drama were palpable. For myself, in my attempt to communicate a planetary symbol I had actually envisioned my own death and had enacted it, thus having a taste of Saturn's bitter pill. And the discussion with my students that ensued after a hushed silence showed that their encounter with Saturn had been real too.

Several months later, while leafing through a magazine, I spotted a photo of an exploding volcano. There was Pluto — more clear now in my mind's eye than any verbal description could make it. Thus inspired with the recognition that images can teach the astrological principles, I spent that week poring through a stack of old magazines, creating collages of images and photos for each of the 10 planets. I put the 'imageboard' I had created of Mercury in front of a group of new students. With no previous understanding of the planet Mercury, they told *me* what Mercury meant!

With these insights came teaching methods that brought a level of interest, energy, and sharing in my classes that I had noticed only fleetingly in my experience as a teacher and student in the traditional mode. Because my classes encouraged spontaneity and play, the students became more relaxed with each other and found it easier to be themselves. They were more inclined to 'tell their own stories' and share their insights with the others. This created an environment of increased group participation, deeper sharing and intimacy.

Some time later I read an article in *Astrology Now* by Jeff Jawer about astrodrama and the work he was doing in Atlanta.[1] In 'Living the Drama of the Horoscope,' Jeff described his first experiences with the acting out of individual aspects in the horoscope, for both teaching and counseling. He cites J.L. Moreno's work with psychodrama and the work of Dane Rudhyar as influences on his practice. Jeff's article gave me new inspiration and a host of ideas to try. He confirmed my own sense of excitement with the potential of an 'interactive astrology' — an excitement that we shared, then as now, after 10 more years of invention and discovery.

From 1982 to 1984 I convened a series of extended workshops in Chicago in which we enacted the natal charts of at least two group members each week in astrodrama style. One particularly exciting group included two tall, strong, and handsome male students, one dark-featured and the other light, who were also superb dancers. Instead of using their voices to enact their roles (usually the Sun, Mars, or Jupiter) they danced the energy with their bodies! I remember one day while we were warming up in our Mars characters with John McLaughlin's 'Birds of Paradise' playing in the background, these two men exploded in the room, running from opposite sides toward each other in great leaps. They were so Martian the rest of us ducked for cover! Here was another way to enact the planets — *dance them.*

## Planetary Theater

October of 1983 brought an opportunity to test out all these new tools for astrology. In that month the 'New Center of the Moon' conference took place, an extraordinary blend of experiential astrology and public theater that the 200 or so who made it to Santa Fe still fondly remember. The event, organized by Santa Fe astrologer

Tom Brady, was played out against a planetary backdrop of transiting Sun/Mercury/Pluto conjunct in late Libra/early Scorpio sextile Neptune in Sagittarius. Tom assembled a unique cast of characters to create and participate in an outdoor astrological theater open to both conference participants and Santa Fe residents. This 'Theater of Planetary Memory' was constructed in Cathedral Park, a spacious outdoor square next to a magnificent old Spanish church. The center of the theater was an inflatable, black domed planetarium the inside walls of which were studded with a luminescent map of the zodiacal belt and other constellations. Around the central theater dome were ten 'planetary rooms', each creating an experience of a particular planet, complete with lighting, music and images. With the aid of creative video producer Bob Shea, crack lighting technicians, and a crew of carpenters, these rooms came to life. For example, in the red-hued Mars room a Green Beret soldier in full battle dress stood at silent attention, conveying strength and an undertone of menace. Here was Mars incarnate!

Approaching the grounds one passed under a huge flashing sign, 'The Theater of Planetary Memory', and entered a space defined by the 12 neon zodiac signs strung high in the trees overhead. Entering Mercury, first stop on the planetary tour, each visitor gave their birth data which were entered into a computer that calculated his or her chart and transmitted it to a monitor in the starry dome.

Inside, 10 actors dressed in their planetary costumes had less than three minutes to find each visitor's key aspects, to talk about how they might be portrayed, and to scurry into the positions that the planets occupy in the natal chart. Knowing I had experience with astrodrama and experiential work, Tom had invited me to be the theater's director. My job was to mold the 10 planetary actors into an effective astrodrama troupe and to direct the performances in the theater. Only two of the 'actors' had theatrical training or performing experience prior to this weekend.

When the actors were ready, our 'psychopomp,' the clown Wavy Gravy of Woodstock music festival fame, led the expectant subject into the darkened celestial dome and seated him in a tall director's chair in the center. As the lights came up, each visitor was met with the spectacle of his own inner life, dynamically portrayed. Arrayed in full costume, complete with make-up and props, the planetary actors played out the particular planetary struggles and co-operations in the visitor's natal chart. In a bare three minutes the troupe was able to enact a number of brief vignettes, rapidly moving from one natal contact to another. By revealing their inner nature, the troupe both delighted the participants and moved them to tears. Not having anticipated the power of astrodrama, many left with a look of sheer wonder.

If the effect of the encounter was so great for the visitors, you might imagine the impact it had on those who created the astrodrama. In the two nights that the theater operated, we performers must have presented well over 100 enactments of natal charts. Each of us played a planetary energy throughout the 12 signs and in every possible aspectual relationship. We were, by mid-performance, virtually *humming* with our planet's energy, and though time constraints were sometimes stressful we felt exhilarated, not overwhelmed. Long after the theater had closed for the night the energy of the actors seemed still to be bouncing around the dome, and we stayed long after the performance reliving our experiences with an astrology few had encountered before. The impact of our experiment with astrodrama spread throughout the conference as well, and we players, incognito without our costumes, overheard many a conversation praising our efforts. And maybe this and other presentations of experiential astrology are having an even broader effect: we are slowly beginning to see more of our conferences include some form of theater or performance as well as workshops in experiential methods.

The conference weekend was to prove especially important to me for another reason. At some point Tom Brady mentioned, in an offhand way, a titbit of information that was to propel me into an investigation that, to some extent, was to culminate in this book. While researching in the University of New Mexico's library, Tom came across a sampling of early Greek Orphic writings, with a cryptic reference to 'horoscopes being danced.' This notion so captivated my imagination that I began extensive research into the origins of Greek sacred theater and the Graeco-Roman mystery schools. (Oddly, the reference itself has remained a mystery — neither Tom nor I have been able to find the quote.) Ultimately I was to spend a month in Greece at a number of the sacred sites. Though Delphi, Epidauros, and Delos each had its magic, I was most drawn to the sacred theater and to the healing rites and ceremonies of Eleusis.

## Ancient Mysteries

I was in Eleusis at the fall equinox, 1985 — the very day on which, so many centuries before, the annual celebration of the 'Greater Mystery' in honor of the Great Mother was held. I spent long days alone envisioning, meditating upon, and 'feeling into' what we know, and what we must imagine, of those sacred events. From the spectacle of the 14 mile processional walk on the Sacred Way to the ritual dancing at the Kallichoron well, participants in the Mysteries danced in the ceremonies of initiation, and in the *dromena* witnessed the re-enactment of the myth of Demeter and Persephone. I had pored over the books of the experts on Eleusis; now I walked the grounds over and over again hoping my soul might catch a glimpse of the sights and sounds of the holy dances. I meditated in front of Pluto's cave, the Ploutonion, and performed my own private ritual. From the hill above the city I gazed down into the ruined outlines of the sacred precinct, trying with my mind's eye to replace column upon pediment, to lay knowledge upon intuition, until at last I believe I was able to arrive at the truth of the place. Eleusis and its mythologically-rooted healing ritual has long since passed away. Yet, on this day, I was able to imagine that the mythic archetypes were being summoned once more. This is what I saw and heard and felt . . .

*Eleusis, Fall Equinox, Boedromonion 20 (530 BC).*

I dreamed, I danced, as far back as I can remember. For that I needed only to be alone among the small mountain creatures around my native town of Mandra. The flowers and the birds were my audience. The high mountain meadow where I tended my father's sheep was my stage. I was 10 when my mother and father took me southward down the mountain to attend the great festival at Eleusis. I shall never forget it. For the first time I saw my secret joy of dancing shared by others. I remember being barely able to sit in my seat as I watched the dancing in honor of the Corn Goddess. My heart pounded. Though I didn't understand much of the secret meaning of what I saw, my soul was aflame with the magic of the festival.

And tonight, five years later, because of my dream I myself dance for the first time in honor of the Goddess Demeter. 'Demeter' — even her name teaches us: *De* is the 'letter of the vulva,' the delta, the triangle of the female trinity of virgin, mother, and crone. I have worked hard all year to absorb her teachings, to prepare for this moment, instructed by the priestesses who demand that the dancers keep the traditions in precise detail. There are hundreds of dance movements to learn.[2] Errors rob our ritual of its power. The dance is highly structured and carries us in a snakelike winding through the passage of life to death and back to life again.

Yesterday, Iacchos led the long procession from Athens, and I and my sisters, with thousands of other citizens, escorted the sacred statue of our Great Mother to the temple grounds, the place sanctified by the Goddess herself. Throughout we sang the ancient calling song:

Come, arise, from sleep awaking,
Come the fiery torches shal ˙ ˙g,
Morning Star that shinest nightly,
Lo, the mead is blazing brightly,
Age forgets its years and sadness,
Aged knees curvet for gladness,
Lift thy flashing torches o'er us,
Marshall all the blameless train,
Lead, Oh lead the way before us.[3]

Tonight is the sixth night of the festival and the first night of the temple dancing and of the *dromena*, the sacred re-enactment. Now I must go. The dance begins.

I pass, with a hundred other dancers, through the great stone Triumphal Arch, with the inscription I will soon know to be true: 'Only Those Who Dance the Mysteries, Know the Mysteries.'[4] We enter the new eastern courtyard of the temple, built over the ancient court on which others like us have danced for nearly a thousand years. Now outside I can see throngs of people sitting on the sloped eastern terraces around the courtyard, facing the altar to the Goddess in the southwest corner of the square. I feel a gentle breeze from the sea enticing me toward my place at the Kallichoron well, the 'Well of Fair Dances.' I stand in my place. I look at my bare feet. I am both excited and afraid. My mouth is dry. I feel my heart beginning to beat a quicker rhythm. I keep my eyes on my feet, take a deep breath and begin with the others.

Slowly, tenderly, with measured steps we move, establishing a rhythm that lulls perception. We take the time needed to set the pattern, weaving in and out, in and out, of the labyrinth. I pound out the rhythm of the drums with my feet. In and out. In and out. Repeat. Repeat. Repeat. 'There is no part of me that is not part of the Goddess.' Move deeper. Use the ritual knowledge. I take each step with loving attention, not forcing but gently moving beyond my limitations, my weariness, step by step, penetrating to the place of stillness. 'Receive the power of the dance.' Step.

Jephthah's daughter coming to meet her father

Step. Step. My heart beats in rhythm with the drums and my feet. My feet, no longer fettered by fear, dance like the beat of steady rain, sensing they have danced these steps a thousand times before.

There are no longer just a hundred bodies twisting in the dance. Now I can see and feel many more shapes whirling around and around, communing with Her, honoring Her. The shades of my ancestors are dancing with us in the circle.

My feet dart about like fish in tumbling water, my body *is* the rhythm, the circle, the dance. I breathe in time to my movements, in and out, in and out as I spiral deeply into the circle and out again to its edges, each repeat of the sacred pattern entrancing me more. Out of me, like the cycle of nature herself, arises an endless succession of new springs from old winters.

My eyes blur as I close them, then open wide, not knowing what it is I see in the enveloping silvery fog. I come to life in the dream I dreamt last spring, living the vision that brought me to this moment! I am whirling, with torrents of moving lights, lights circling around and around, being drawn into a dark, ancient well. I'm afraid of the dark abyss but cannot stop myself being sucked into the center, being propelled and drawn nearer and nearer its gaping mouth. I reach inside and sense my strength. With the pressure of whirling forces against my legs, I am able to stand at the abyss. No longer afraid of being swept in, my feet stand firm. My eyes follow a stream of moonbeams up into the night sky to see the full moon gracefully reaching her summit. I bathe in her soft light. She flows into me, through me. I feel her gentle but strong soul-arms reach down, embrace and transform me. As she illumines my face and body, a shadow dances with me — hand-in-hand we pause, choose, then plunge into the abyss!

I reach my core, Her within me, the solid stuff of earth within. Steady, Enduring. I merge with the ancient feminine spiritual root, embracing a lineage millions of years old, back to our ancestors who lived the first principle of harmony. I drink of Her strength and am empowered.

I drink of Her healing and am made whole. The steady, eternal breathing of the Great Mother sounds in my ears.

I feel my hair streaming across my eyes as I whirl. I feel the tears drying on my cheeks. The moon above overwhelms me. The Goddess is present. The Goddess is here . . .

I hear a woman's wailing faintly in the distance. The other dancers hear Her too, and as one move toward Her cries at the 'Mirthless Stone' beside the Sacred Way. The dromena itself begins. Demeter, our Earth Mother, has just discovered that her daugher, Persephone, has been kidnapped by Plouton, Lord of the underworld. Consumed with passion, he has carried the young Persephone through the Gates of Hades to become his Queen. Demeter wails in her grief at the loss of her daughter. I realize I am sobbing too. I see an image, permanently etched in memory, pass through my mind — it is the day my father died last winter. I see his last breath, his death shudder. I feel helpless, wanting to seize his life force and restore it to him. I cry. She cries. Thousands cry. I rage with the Goddess in anger, storming up and down, shaking, my body bathed in hot sweat. I journey into the cold darkness, facing my fear, my terror, shuddering and trembling. I sink in a heap, utterly exhausted from enduring the mystic catharsis.

I am jolted! A feeling of ecstasy bubbles up within my spine and a wave moves toward my head. I look up. I look again with my eyes straining at the very edge of the visible. I see there the mist and within it the Vision. I see there the Return. I am jolted again and then transported, lifted to a region of pure light, a place of celestial brilliance, suffused with loving sounds of the holy voices and surrounded by the sacred dancing of the Goddesses. I wander free in this joyful realm in communion with Myself . . . With Her . . . With All That Is, fused to the cosmic rhythm. What I truly saw I cannot tell you. There has been a sacred seal placed upon my lips. I must speak no more.

And countless lips did remain sealed, so that the secrets which were orally transmitted for two thousand years died with the death of the last hierophant. A veil has now descended on Eleusis. The Kallichoron well has gone dry.

What exactly was done at Eleusis to create such powerful effect? We do not know. We do know the rites brought about an experience of the death-rebirth cycle, stimulating a deeper understanding of the esoteric spiritual meaning of this collective human event. Themistios, drawing upon Plutarch, an initiate of the Mysteries, wrote, 'The soul (at the point of death) has the same experience as those who are being initiated into great Mysteries.'[5] And Pindar wrote, 'Happy is he who, having seen these rites goes below the hollow earth; for he knows the end of life, and he knows its God-sent beginning.[6] George Mylonas concludes his book on Eleusis saying that whatever the substance of the Mysteries was, the fact remains that the rites of Eleusis satisfied the most sincere yearnings and the deepest longings of the human heart.[7]

The ritual at Eleusis built to an ecstatic climax in which the accumulated psychic discord and tension was released. Fear turned to joy, and the participant experienced a powerful healing catharsis. The rising action always included intense and repetitive physical activity to produce the proper receptivity. After hours and hours of chanting, singing, dancing, drumming and musical rhythms participants were transported out of everyday awareness and opened to more subtle realms. The dancing was preceded by days of purification, fasting, and very little sleep, during which all walked in awe-inspiring processionals with hundreds of like minded souls. Magnificent ceremonial vestments and holy symbols were displayed, and sacred words and formulas spoken. The impact of the whole experience reached its peak in a magic moment, when the inspired participant had a direct experience of cosmic forces. With participation in this manner, a divine communion was made and the individual was no longer merely an onlooker of the cosmos but a dynamic, active part of it. The individual became co-creator of the cosmic drama.

## Astrology and the Gods

The rites of Eleusis re-enacted the death/rebirth experience which astrologers recognize as the process of the archetype of Pluto in the individual psyche. The astrological archetypes and the myths of the gods and goddesses draw from the same pool. Mythology contains the particular manifestations of the archetypes in their various patterns. Astrology incorporates a basic 10 (and many more) of these essential archetypes into a language for understanding.

It is particularly clear, at least for Western culture, that the same cultural and historical forces that produced the myths of the gods and goddesses drove the forge in which astrology was formed. The gods of the Greeks — Uranus, Chronos, Hades, Poseidon, Hermes and Aphrodite — are the embodiment of the distinctive psychic qualities of the planetary forces that we now call by their Roman names — Uranus,

Saturn, Pluto, Neptune, Mercury, and Venus. Thus Saturn, which can signal death and destruction in the horoscope, is the same power represented by the Greek god Chronos who devoured his children and who, in the guise of Time, may in truth be said to destroy whatever has been brought into existence.

Joining in a ritual event and re-enacting a myth that resonated with a truth beyond cultural bounds gave the Eleusian faithful a peak experience of cosmic communion. If indeed the astrological archetypes arise from the same deep, unconscious realms of the mind as the gods and goddesses, then vivifying the astrological symbol should provide the same kind of communion. If, for example, we learn to actively express our Pluto, bringing it to life consciously, then we no longer deny or repress its power, and we might avoid the usual explosions of emotion or conflict that characterize Pluto. We learn to use our own Pluto in more conscious ways by embodying the symbolic truth of the planet — penetrating into, transforming and assimilating its power.

I do not want to imply that astrologers must spend four days dancing and fasting in order to come to know a planetary archetype, though this level of intensity might be an appropriate experience for some astrologers. I *am* suggesting that, like the ancients, we step beyond the boundaries of observation and thought and use direct experience to understand our own internal planetary forces.

In so doing you pass from seeing the planets as isolated mental images, to actually experiencing the vital rhythms of their interactions which reveal deeper subconscious feelings and previously unexpressed aspects of being. The horoscope, then, is no longer a static, black-and-white, one dimensional assortment of data with inanimate glyphs and signs. It becomes a moving field of planetary action: vibrant, interactive, deeply personal and alive!

# 2
# MODERN ROOTS OF
# EXPERIENTIAL ASTROLOGY

Dem bones, dem bones, dem dry bones . . .        Negro Spiritual

Reader, brace yourself! This is the most 'left-brained' chapter you will encounter in this book, since it includes a foray into the domain of the theoreticians of both astrology and psychology. Some of you may even wish to skip this chapter for now in favor of Chapter Three's description of practical applications. But if you're the type that likes to get right into the heady stuff, read on!

## Dane Rudhyar and Humanistic Astrology

The modern origins of experiential astrology can be traced to the late 1970s when the doctrines of the human potential movement in psychology (and the culture at large) began to find expression in astrology. The work of Dane Rudhyar and the humanistic astrology he developed over a lifetime is fundamental to my approach to the natal chart. His work shifted the focus of astrology from an outdated predictive, event-oriented, and even fatalistic stance to that of a person-oriented one, emphasizing human growth and accomplishment.

*Astrology and the Modern Psyche* is perhaps Rudhyar's clearest explication of the relationship between astrology and the 'depth psychology' that underlies the modern approach. In these pages Rudhyar traces the development of depth psychology to its origins in the evolutionary theories of Charles Darwin.[1] The classical psychologist, following Plato, sees a particular stone, tree, or person as a pale copy of some pre-existent eternal form. For Darwin and those who embraced his ideas, all life, including our own, *evolves* from more primitive beginnings — 'the depths' — and is in a continuing state of creation. Thus, as Rudhyar states, 'The individual "I", instead of being seen as an *a priori*, archetypal Self — as some "pattern of perfection" transcendent to life on earth — begins to be understood as the end result of human living, as a victory to be won, as the result of the slow effort of integration and . . . individuation.'[2] Sigmund Freud was the original master of the probing of the human mind in its instinctual depths, and his work, with that of his followers, undergirds much of the modern view of mind and human life.

Rudhyar's interest in depth psychology began in 1932 with his introduction to the works of Carl G. Jung, an early associate of Freud.[3] For the astrologer this signaled the beginning of a lifelong effort to reformulate 'classical' astrology along the lines of a developing humanistic psychology, an effort that was to culminate in the now widespread 'humanistic astrology' associated with his name. Experiential astrology's debt to Rudhyar is clear; the humanistic orientation provides the *essential theoretical framework* for the experiential use of astrology in becoming whole, healthy, human beings, integrated in body, mind, and soul. But experiential astrology goes beyond Rudhyar's program by further synthesis of elements from humanistic psychology, and from the arts and ancient spiritual tradition, thus yielding a *body of technique* for the purposes of self-actualization and self-realization.

## Contributions of Jungian Psychology

To introduce astrology into a discussion of Jung is no imposition upon the great psychologist. He spoke often and favorably of the astrologer's art. In his many writings Jung emphasized that astrology was a 'map of the psyche' that included the sum total of all ancient psychological knowledge, describing both the innate predisposition of an individual personality as well as providing an accurate way of timing life crises. Because of their relevance to experiential astrology, these Jungian ideas demand attention: the process of individuation, concepts of wholeness and polarity, the model of the psyche with its conscious, personal unconscious and collective unconscious levels, and the theory of *archetypes*. Also, central in Jung's thought is *mythology* as the key for understanding the human mind.

In Jung's view we each begin life in a state of undifferentiated wholeness. As we mature we emerge from the cosmic womb of the unconscious, evolving into increasingly complex structures capable of expressing ourselves in more refined and elaborate ways. This is the process of individuation. First to appear is a fundamental polarity. Jung states, 'The psyche consists of two incongruous halves that should properly make a "whole" together . . . but consciousness and the unconscious do not make a whole when either is suppressed or damaged by the other. If they must contend, let it be a fair fight with equal right on both sides. Both are aspects of life. Let the consciousness defend its reason and its self-protective ways, and let the chaotic life of the unconscious be given a fair chance to have its own way, as much of it as we can stand. This means at once open conflict and open collaboration . . . It is the old play of hammer and anvil: the suffering iron between them will in the end be shaped into an unbreakable whole, the individual.'[4] Thus individuation is the result of the continual integration of consciousness and the unconscious, and human growth proceeds by organizing separate elements into a complex whole.

Astrology, no less than Jung, incorporates ancient notions of wholeness and polarity. The astrological chart itself represents the whole of an individual personality. It is composed of two halves, one that represents the conscious, solar, active, masculine, day side of consciousness, and the other, the unconscious, lunar, passive, feminine, night side. As Jung's discourse often centers upon the interaction of paired opposites, i.e. conscious-unconscious, thinking-feeling, sensation-intuition, Animus-Anima, so does the chart consist of polarities of similar explanatory power — pairs of opposites of signs (Taurus/Scorpio), of houses (second/eighth), and of archetypes (Venus/Mars). And even the most left-brained of astrological consultations has the result of bringing what was unknown into consciousness, thus proceeding towards individuation as Jung describes it. Experiential astrology is intended to extend this result and to promote the 'open conflict and open collaboration' between consciousness and the unconscious to which Jung refers.

In 1909 Jung had an extraordinary dream which crystalized his theory that the psyche is composed of three distinct but interacting systems or levels — a conscious mind and an unconscious one that consists of two parts, the personal and the collective unconscious.[5] The dream led ultimately to the publication of Jung's seminal work, *Symbols of Transformation*. Joseph Campbell summarizes the themes of this great effort:

> . . . the essential realizations . . . were, first, that since the archetypes or norms of myth are common to the human species, they are inherently expressive neither of local social circumstances nor of any individual's singular experience, but of common human needs, instincts, and potentials; second, that in the traditions of any specific folk, local circumstance will have provided the imagery through which the archetypal themes are displayed in the supporting myths of the culture; third, that if the manner of life and thought of an individual so departs from the norms of the species that a pathological state of imbalance ensues, of neurosis or psychosis, dreams and fantasies analogous to fragmented myths will appear; and fourth, that such dreams are best interpreted, not by reference backward to repressed infantile memories (reduction to autobiography), but by comparison outward with the analogous mythic forms (amplification to mythology), so that the disturbed individual may learn to see himself depersonalized in the mirror of the human spirit and discover by analogy the way to his own larger fulfilment.[6]

The publication of this book signaled Jung's break with Freud, in that the therapeutic method was no longer to consist solely in 'reduction to autobiography,' the Freudian method, but would emphasize 'amplification to mythology,' or the connecting of unconscious contents to the broader expressions of underlying reality — the enduring myths of humankind. And it is just this shift that makes Jungian thought so relevant to experiential astrology. Jung's great insight was that the mind has, as in Freud's view, an unconscious level that contains the repressed contents of one's personal history, but also that 'this personal unconscious rests upon a deeper layer, which does not derive from personal experience and is not a personal acquisition but is inborn.' Jung called this layer the *collective* unconscious because 'this part of the unconscious is not individual but universal; in contrast to the personal psyche, it has contents and modes of behavior that are more or less the same everywhere and in all individuals.'[7] Therefore we all have a level of mind which is 'identical in all men and thus constitutes a common psychic substrate of a suprapersonal nature which is present in every one of us.'

Chief among the contents of the collective unconscious are the *archetypes*, the primordial . . . universal images that have existed since the remotest times.'[8] Emphasizing that the archetype predetermines form, not content, Jung offers us the vivid image of the archetype as like 'the axial system of a crystal, which preforms the crystalline structure in the mother liquid although it has not material existence of its own.'[9] He further explains that these archetypes, which are our universal heritage, may emerge in any individual consciousness, strike a responsive chord in companions, and be elaborated into myth, ritual, and cultural belief, as they have throughout our history. They are the source of our shared understandings of the Great Mother, the Hero, the gods themselves, and, not least, the planetary symbols of astrology.

We can speculate that Jung's recognition of the deeper, mythical level which he called the collective unconscious is a rediscovery of the same level that produced the divine communion experienced by the ancients of Eleusis two thousand years ago. Jung, it is apparent, did not devise a concept but rather uncovered a psychic reality. We humans invent concepts as a tool for grasping, categorizing, and taking apart. We can replace concepts, but the archetypal structures of consciousness are like vital organs: there is no rational substitute for them. These archetypes are powerful, invisible forces that shape our behavior and influence emotion and belief. Jung — and this is the essence of his therapeutic method — would have us come to know these forms within ourselves and thus become more whole, more free. The Jungian perspective gives us both the rationale and the means for employing the astrological symbol as archetype. In experiential astrology our aim is to put forth methods of evoking astrological archetypes so as to advance Jung's goal of awareness, wholeness, and freedom.

## Experiential Astrology and the Human Potential Movement

I don't want to leave the impression that experiential astrology was designed by a committee of academics pouring over volumes of Freud, Jung, and Rudhyar. In fact, the most likely contributor has spent more time testing the limits of personal growth than languishing in the library. My own background, which includes almost everyone's growth workshop, pilgrimages to Esalen Institute at Big Sur, California, an extended training program in group leadership skills, and 15 years of the study of Kriya Yoga, is not atypical. These are, of course, the opportunities for growth — psychological, spiritual, and artistic — that arose, especially in the United States, as the 'human potential movement' of the mid-1960s. So, when we turn to creating elements of an 'experiential' astrology, we bring a multitude of theoretical and practical notions whose origins tend to blur. However, some patterns are discernible and will get brief treatment below under the headlines of 'experiencing, enactment, and embodiment,' after a particular debt is acknowledged to Jacob Moreno and his 'psychodrama.'

Astrodrama, a form of experiential astrology that entails the 'acting out of the horoscope' in part owes its inspiration to Jacob Moreno's therapeutic method of psychodrama. Moreno was a Viennese psychiatrist and contemporary of both Freud and Jung; he died in 1974 and thus spans almost the entire era of concern to us, though psychodrama has come into special prominence only since the 1960s. Moreno began in the 1920s as a director of experimental theater. His interest in the therapeutic uses of the form began with a marital quarrel among members of his company, which he brought before an audience, with remarkable results.[10] From that beginning Moreno saw the promise of a healing theater and took steps to bring it into being. In effect Moreno threw out the psychiatrist's couch and substituted an impromptu stage where 'individuals could act out their own and the world's problems in the absolute freedom of improvisation.'[11] As one observer notes, 'Moreno's theories are complex and abstruse, but his method is simple, direct and powerful. A psychodramatic performance involves participants, who enact scenes from one of their lives, using a variety of techniques to heighten emotions, and clarify conflicts; and observers who, though they may not be directly involved, often profit from the experience.'[12] Where in classical drama the aim was to bring about a *catharsis* (that is, a healing emotional release) in the audience, psychodrama invites that experience in the actors, with great effect. Astrodrama, in its lighter, more performance-oriented form may be directed toward the audience, or when used as a means of personal growth may have all the intensity and immediacy of a psychodrama. In either mode of expression astrodrama has what astrologers will recognize as the distinct advantage of being informed by 'the map of the psyche,' the astrological chart.

Rudhyar gives us a humanistic point of view on the natal chart, Jung provides us with a larger theoretical framework within which astrology can creatively operate, and Moreno supports the importance of participation of the individual as the means to return to the central role of protagonist in one's own unfolding life drama. But there are other influences upon experiential astrology. Out of a great complexity of possibilities, three patterns or themes appear to emerge.

The first influential theme of the human potential movement is 'experiencing.' We are experiencing when we are actively, emotionally attuned to ourselves in the moment, particularly in a situation that has opportunities for personal growth. At one extreme experiencing may include profound, emotionally cathartic discharge of feeling. Dispassionate and abstract intellectualizing is the near opposite of experiencing. No less an authority than Carl Rogers, the father of non-directive psychotherapy, thought this factor important enough to (along with his colleagues) develop a scale for its measurement.[13] Even casual observation supports the claim that the usual mode of communication about astrology is abstract and dispassionate, perhaps good for transmitting raw data, but not reflective of experiencing, which facilitates growth. Experiential astrology seeks to remedy that.

A second characteristic of growth-oriented practice may be called 'enacting.' You have seen enacting referred to in its most obvious form in the psychodramatic acting out of life episodes in Moreno's work. But enacting includes, especially in the *Gestalt* therapy devised by Fritz Perls, the acting out and integrating of unconscious and alienated contents of the unconscious mind.[14] In an intense astrodrama it may include these elements as pointed to by particular transits to the chart, but may include the bringing into full emotional expression an archetype such as Venus, the Sun, or Pluto. Enacting makes explicit what is implicit in our unconscious and thus allows us to give it form and feeling and so integrate it into our being.

'Embodiment' is the third factor that influences experiential astrology. Beginning, perhaps, with Wilhelm Reich, another of Freud's early circle, the West began to reassert that in some real sense we *are* bodies, we don't just have them as an unhappy appendage to our minds. Reich's contribution (later elaborated throughout the 1960s and beyond, by followers such as Lowen and Keleman) included the recognition that the body is an energetic system, with characteristic blocks to the free flow of emotion and feeling, and the devising of techniques for removing those blocks. [15] As you will see in chapter three, these techniques can, in the proper hands, be smoothly and powerfully enlisted in an experiential astrology setting. More generally, however, embodiment means that we astrologers can leave the chairs of our consulting rooms and can express the meanings of the astrological archetypes in motion, feeling, dance, and touch — and we'll be the richer for it.

## Spiritual Traditions and Transpersonal Psychology

The Western humanistic tradition never had complete sway over the content of the human potential movement. From the advent of the movement, spiritual leaders and their ancient traditions and techniques (largely from the East) had their place alongside therapists and T-Groups. Astrology has a particular affinity for some elements of this spiritual influx, in part due to some common origins. Just one example: in Kriya Yoga, astrological and yogic precepts have long been intimately intertwined, each illuminating the other. [16] Later in this book you will encounter yogic and ritual aspects of experiential astrology.

The Eastern and Western psychologies named above are combined in a relatively new field termed 'transpersonal psychology.' [17] The writings of proponents such as Ken Wilber, Stanislav Grof, and Jean Houston may be a source of continuing inspiration for our pursuits in experiential astrology. Interestingly, through this avenue the classical psychology whose rejection signaled the beginning of the humanistic agenda (see paragraph three of this chapter) is re-emerging. Grof is explicit about this in particular reference to astrology:

> . . . astrology, a discipline rejected and ridiculed by Newtonian-Cartesian science, can prove to be of unusual value as a source of information about personality development and transformation. It would require a long discussion to explain how and why astrology can function as a remarkable referential system. This possibility seems quite absurd from the point of view of mechanistic science, which treats consciousness as an epiphenomenon of matter. However, for an approach that sees consciousness as a primary element of the universe that is woven into the very fabric of existence, and that *recognizes archetypal structures as something that precedes and determines phenomena in the material world* (my italics), the function of astrology would appear quite logical and comprehensible.

Fortunately, in order to use experiential astrology we don't have to resolve whether classical or humanistic psychology is the right view, especially since philosophers haven't been able to do so in 3000 years. Whether we think that the archetypes arise in a dimension of reality beyond our own (as might Grof or a follower of Plato) or that they are a manifestation of mind as our shared inheritance as human beings (à la Jung), or even that they are ordinary but extremely important ideas that reflect cultural truths, we can enlist them as a tool for self-understanding and growth.

So, we have come full circle in our journey into theory and yet have touched upon only a few of the influences upon experiential astrology. In part this is due to the diffuse origins of our endeavor, but perhaps even more because what we are attempting has been arrived at by actual living experience rather than by study. Each of you who chooses to explore experiential astrology will have a chance to experience it in your own way, to embody its principles, and to enact them in your own life.

# 3
# USING EXPERIENTIAL ASTROLOGY

We are enacting, telling, witnessing the Story of our Souls.
James Hillman, *Revisioning Psychology*

Experiential astrology has been used in four principal ways: as an artistic and expressive form of theater; as a teaching tool for students and practitioners; as a context for therapeutic healing; and, as we'll see in Chapters Four and Ten, for self-study, contemplation, and personal ritual.

## Planetary Theater

In ancient times the portrayal of archetypal planetary energies was integral to public drama. Theater was a sacred, cathartic medium, designed to heal through direct contact with the deepest levels of consciousness. Modern theater, on the other hand, though it may experiment with the evocation of deep symbols from time to time, seeks most often to entertain rather than transform. The astrodrama performance, described below, was one in a series of steps toward recreating the healing theater of the past with astrological symbols as the medium for direct interaction with the unconscious. As you read on, note the healing effects of the form on both audience and actors as well as the ease with which astrodrama communicates astrological information to those who may not know so much as their own Sun sign.

This performance was created to express the astrological influences present at the very moment in which it was enacted. (See diagram opposite.) What is described was the first of two connected performances, one staged on the lunar eclipse (full moon), Taurus/Scorpio in May 1985 for a general audience, and the other on the solar eclipse (new moon) in Scorpio for the NCGR (National Council on Geocosmic Research) Regional Conference in Chicago, November 1985.

The setting is the large converted gymnasium of the Noyes Cultural Arts Center in Evanston, Illinois. Large floor to ceiling windows line two sides of the room and overlook a broad lawn. It is a beautiful, warm, spring night. As dusk turns to dark the glow of flickering candles mirrors the star-studded backdrop. The full moon rises lazily in the night sky. An audience of more than 100, half of whom know

## May 4 1985 Theater

Evanston          Illinois
42N03             87W41
MAY 5 1985        00:30:00 GMT
Tropical  Koch    True Node

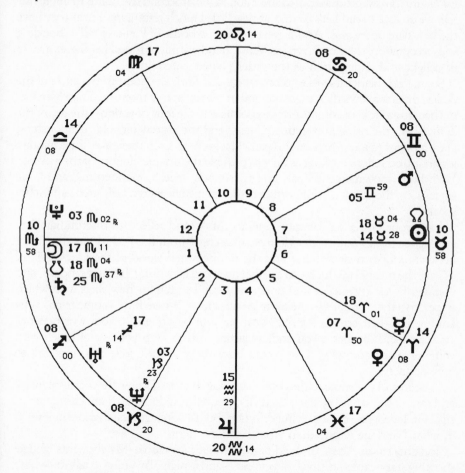

no astrology, settle into their seats to enjoy the performance. Why not join us for the show?

As the lights fade to black, the deep resonant voice of the narrator breaks the silence: 'And God created the sun, the moon, and the planets . . .'

A spotlight catches the brightly costumed 'planets' as one by one they make their entrances. Mars leaps to the stage and thrusts with his sword; Saturn enters with a stately, almost laborious gait. Each planet speaks a three-line 'signature'; 'I am Mercury! I am your power to communicate, the mind behind your brain, the focusing lens through which all others pass. With reason's torch, I search for truth.' Venus enters in a whirl of pink and green chiffon: 'I am Venus! I am all that you love and find dear. I attract through my loving, gentle and harmonious spirit.' When they have entered the theater they spread out, bantering and mingling with the audience. Venus approaches a woman in the back row. 'And what sign is your Venus in?' 'Taurus,' answers the surprised spectator. In a split second she begins to improvise: 'Oh we do love to eat! Let's go to that new little French restaurant. I hear they have the best paté de foi gras. And a great price on a bottle of Pomerol '82!' Chuckling with recognition, the woman grasps Venus' hand warmly. Around her there's a sense of delight and anticipation as the other planets entertain.

Soon, each planet moves to center stage and finds the point in the circle of the Zodiac that represents their exact position in the sky at that moment. Then Mercury, in the natural role of communicator, points out the four directions, the arc of the Zodiac belt, the rising and setting planets, and the aspects (angular relationships) of each planet to any others on this particular evening. Each then takes three minutes for an introduction, evoking as fully as possible the unique identity of their planet. With body movement, feelings, images, sounds, speech, mannerisms, and facial expressions, they paint a living portrait of their planetary energy. Let's listen as Mercury speaks.

'I am your power to communicate, to think, and reflect, to discriminate one experience from another. As Hermes, messenger from the gods, I am the bridge between your conscious mind and the undiscovered world of the Unconscious.'

'I am the means by which you speak. I invented all writing, language, books, and libraries. I seek knowledge and understanding. I search for new ways with which to perceive the world. I ask the ultimate questions: Where have I come from? Why am I here? Where am I going . . . ? I can be your best friend or your worst enemy. As your foe, I can bring you endless distractions to keep you out of touch with your repressed emotions. I keep you busy so you won't *feel*. Emotions are so unreasonable!'

'In Scorpio, I penetrate to the depths, seeking the core. I know the secrets of magic and tantra, but what I've discovered I'll never tell you! In Virgo, I am clear, precise, efficient. I recognize error and imperfection, but I'll admit I'm much more interested in what I've done wrong than what I've done right.'

'Tonight, I'm in Aries. I'm bold and brash and impulsive. My thoughts are like shooting stars, exploding in all directions — and tonight, I'm going to tell you what's on my mind, like it or not!'

When each of the planets has spoken the lights are dimmed, signaling the next phase of the program, a retelling of the myth of Demeter and Persephone. This myth was chosen because it evokes the strong Taurus/Scorpio energies (betrayal and forgiveness) available to us on this evening.

Scene one introduces Hades pacing back and forth in uncontrollable anger, ranting and raving, growling and grimacing at the noisy, wrathful Giants imprisoned in Mt. Etna, above him. Determined to restore quiet to this domain he makes off for the upperworld. Arriving there he spies Persephone in a meadow picking flowers.

Viewing the scene from a hillock, Venus, in a moment of irony, sends Cupid to pierce the unsuspecting Hades with the arrow of love. Thus struck, his anger turns to lust for the innocent young girl. Utterly consumed with passion, he circles her, hissing and licking his jowls in anticipation.

A surging drumbeat echoes the rhythm of Persephone's heart as she spots the lustful Hades circling her. Immune to her screams of terror, the dark god seizes the girl, carrying her off into his underworld cave. When Demeter, the maiden's mother, learns what has happened, she first shrieks in rage then collapses with a convulsive sob, utterly stricken with grief. No one, not even the gods, can console her. And for that all must suffer. As Goddess of the Grains and caretaker of all that lives upon the earth she neglects her duties. The earth withers. What was once green and beautiful turns brown and bare.

Finally, with the aid of Hermes/Mercury and the intervention of the all powerful Zeus/Jupiter, a bitter compromise is struck. Persephone will spend the six months between the equinoxes in the underworld, re-emerging in the spring to restore life on earth. All must reconcile themselves to the new arrangement. The primeval power of Hades and Demeter is played against the innocence of Persephone. The three are bound together against their will by passion and grief. All had both betrayed and endured the betrayal of another.

The final words of the play are spoken by Hermes: 'This is a myth that reveals our purity and innocence, our desires and betrayals. It is a story about our tolerance of the intolerable, acceptance of the unacceptable, and ultimately, forgiveness of the unforgivable. It presents the mystery of man which resides in these contradictions, opposites that forever meet in rhythmic and creative interplay of light and dark. The solution resides in man's courage and ability to enter the threshold, meet the demons, and pass through the flame. Man is the fire and the hearth, the log and the sacrifice . . .' The lights fade to black. The emotional roller coaster of the last 20 minutes ends with a moment of pregnant, reflective silence, filled as several audience members will say later, with stirred up feelings and with their own remembered experiences of betrayal.

But, swiftly, the tone of the performance changes with the commencement of a series of playful, creative improvisations drawn from the charts of audience members. From the back of the room comes a request to see 'Mercury in Gemini, square Uranus in Virgo.' After a moment's consultation, Mercury and Uranus move quickly to center stage. Mercury begins an energetic monolog, blurting out her favorite opinions, books she's going to write, and great questions she's found the answer to. Uranus, drawing near Mercury, seems to radiate a kind of erratic energy to which Mercury must respond. She is unrelenting in her criticism of Mercury's ideas, flooding her with wild options to consider. The improvisation ends with an exhausted Mercury begging for peace and quiet.

A request to see 'the Sun in Aries opposite the Moon in Libra' invites another spontaneous skit. The Sun and Moon take the floor, engaged in a psychic tug of war over marriage plans. The forceful Sun insists they should schedule the wedding as soon as possible, while the evasive Moon shuffles across the floor with a confused expression. She tells us in an aside what she's thinking. 'This guy! He's cute but I did just meet him last week. He looks a little like Brad, but he really acts more like Tom.' The scene ends without resolution, but with much good humored applause from the audience.

As the finale of the evening's production nears, each planet steps forward to offer a symbolic gift to the audience. Mercury gives the seed of positive thought; Saturn gives clay with which to mold a structure for our lives, Mars a sword to inspire courage to cut through what holds us back. The close of the performance bonds the evening's participants, performers and onlookers in a moment of reflection. The very last words of the evening are spoken by Carl Fitzpatrick, as Pluto:

'Nine beautiful gifts. But wasn't there something forgotten? Something you could have had from anyone, but somehow . . .? Anyway, what can you ask from Pluto, when in my realm I gather all that remains after you have accumulated in Taurus all that you value, stamped your mark on it, and called yourself secure. Some of that refuse rots to poison your depths, and to survive you'll have to return to me to dig it out and find the power to heal. As for *real* treasure, you never recognized it. And if I give it to you now you'll only throw it away again.

The eclipse shows the mystery. The Moon is in Scorpio, and you whine and cry because I bring you betrayal and death. But what have you known of trust, or of life? I'll test your shallow innocence in a crucible of suspicion and maybe then you can learn to commit yourself whole and inspire trust. Betrayal? You bring that on yourself! I call on you to be transformed through your deepest passions so you will know the fullness of life. Death, too, you bring on yourself.

The Sun is in Taurus and you dwell in a block of stone, with me as the sculptor hacking away at your prison, and it bleeds when you clutch at the pieces of what you have instead of valuing what you are. You can bring *me* your resentment and bitterness because all you hold precious has been corrupt and stolen. The one gift I'll have for you is the last thing you will ever ask for: your true self!'

Following the performance there's a live band, dancing, drinks, and hors-d'oeuvres. It's been a stimulating, thought-provoking and emotional evening, reflecting all the deeper drama that lies behind the familiar symbols of the full moon eclipse in Taurus/Scorpio.

As co-producer, director, and the planet Mercury, my memory of the event is still vivid. Our troupe of players was able to evoke the aspects of the moment and use them to create an astrological 'happening.' The Mercury sextile Jupiter, trine Uranus allowed us to communicate and teach astrological principles and understandings. The strong Taurus/Scorpio square Jupiter gave us access to a level of consciousness that permitted a healing release; and the Venus sextile and Mars trine to Jupiter ensured the success of the evening celebration and feast. The performance also provided a means to reach not only experienced astrologers, but many who were entirely new to astrology. Rather than touching just one person in the usual one-to-one consulting style, we reached out to more than 100. In this time of Pluto in Scorpio, when people were looking for deep, cathartic experience, we were able to show a glimmer of the psychological potential of astrodrama and experiential astrology.

Those who made this undertaking a reality are of particular interest from an astrological perspective. The co-producers of the theater were Clay Bodine (Saturn conjunct Pluto), Betsey Means (Sun in Scorpio), and myself (Saturn conjunct Pluto.) Of the 10 'planets' four were practicing astrologers, three were actors/actresses and the remainder were therapists/healers. (Five of us had astrology backgrounds. The others had no previous knowledge of astrology.) Of the 10 'planets', four had Sun in Scorpio, two, Moon in Scorpio, two, Scorpio rising, and three, Saturn conjunct Pluto! What struck me as more than coincidence was the strong Scorpio energy within this group that came together for a performance on a Taurus/Scorpio eclipse. That organizing point seemed to attract a group not only interested in deep psychological, emotional experience, but capable of evoking and communicating the powerful energies of the eclipse.

For us in the cast, of course, the experience extended far beyond the evening's performance. We rehearsed twice a week for an intensive eight-week period. Rehearsals included astrology, movement, body awareness, sound, voice, guided imagery, and creative improvisation, in addition to the creation of the play within a play (Demeter and Persephone). We were fortunate also to have available to us the special expertise of two well-known area women, sound therapist Vickie Dodd and dance therapist Jane Siegel. Both did much to help the performers develop their voices and bodies as instruments of expression. Each planet actor spent many hours literally living with their planetary identities: thinking, sensing, feeling, becoming their planets, and finding ways to communicate what they experienced on the inside. Using inner images, creative imagination, guided meditations, voice, sound, movement and body imaging, they explored the connection with the archetype within. Over the weeks of preparation the troupe helped each other develop their planetary roles, refine ideas, write scripts, design and create costumes and make-up.

We also shared our feelings about our roles. Pluto told about how, on his way home from the first rehearsal, he heard a voice within him crying out, 'What are you doing? You haven't acted in anything since eighth grade!' And on another occasion, with tears in her eyes, Neptune shared her struggle to find a way to express her planet: 'I realized a part of me has really been out of touch with anything spiritual. It's been hard to open up and trust that I have it in me.'

The effects of the performance were far greater than we might have imagined. Photographer and friend, David Hartwick, made the following observation: 'My strongest impression of this experience is that it is healing theater. Those receiving the most healing were the actors themselves. Being able to get out there and *be* those things, that's where the real healing was taking place. I've always been a fan of people's theater with an everyman quality to performance. Down the road in this process you should look to getting more people directly involved. That is where the greatest healing may ultimately lie. We all need to get up at some time, and act out what we are.'

David's comments were certainly prophetic in light of the post-performance experiences of the actors (associated astrological keywords have been highlighted in italics). The Sun (Clay Bodine) decided to *expand* the number of classes he would teach and set a goal to double his working/theater space, which he did within six months. The Moon (Ann Trompeter) stopped *vacillating* and decided to commit herself to her career as an actress. Mercury (Barbara Schermer) began to *write* this book. Both Venus actresses (Saren O'Hara and Randi Wolferding) decided to get *pregnant*. Mars (Dennis Brittan) is quickly becoming a recognized Chicago therapist, specializing in psychological aspects of the *battle* against AIDS.

Saturn (Betsey Means) pointed to three related outcomes: new realizations about the way in which she had been *restricting* her life, and a new commitment to overcoming those, her acceptance of a key role in a Chicago play as a burdened woman who eventually goes mad, and her catalytic role in helping 'Uranus' get her new business *organized*. Uranus (Vicki Dodd) finally accepted herself as a *maverick* therapist and opened a New Age networking center, New Voices Networking. Not surprisingly, Neptune (Gina Bader) had the most *vague* of connected experience, though she did say she was recently more inspired. Jupiter (Jim Redmond) noticed no particular Jupiterian elements in his life, but astrologers would note that any effects were likely to be outweighed by the influence of his Saturn return at 26 degrees Scorpio, and transiting Pluto conjunct his Mars at four degrees Scorpio.

Pluto (Carl Fitzpatrick) had the most dramatic experience. Within weeks of his performance he fell from a 40 foot ladder, fracturing his pelvis, crushing his foot, and breaking his right arm. (Transiting Uranus was conjunct his first house Mars in Sagittarius as Pluto made a sextile to Saturn. Carl feels it was the Pluto sextile that helped save his life.) Here is what Carl wrote about his experience: 'Shortly after our November performance which was timed with a solar eclipse in Scorpio, on my birthday, I lived through a serious accident that brought me close to death. It may have seemed to others that Pluto aspects brought me disaster, but in my own heart and mind it was as if my communion with the Pluto archetype prepared me to survive a moment of crisis. Pluto, the healer, gave me inner strength to survive it almost fully whole.[1]

'As we rehearsed I meditated on the meaning of Pluto and the need for transformation in every life, and I became subliminally conscious that a turning point in my own life was approaching. In retrospect, I can focus on the decision I had been putting off for years that, for many reasons, I should give up the work I'd been doing on ladders. It took a speeding car to literally knock the ladder from under me to help me make my decision. It seems laughable to call this experience a disaster. Who would have suspected that I could fall four stories and escape with only a very minor disability. It seems clearer than ever that if accepted with instinctive awareness, Pluto represents a deep liberation of the essential self.'

In sum, our astrodrama was an extraordinary group experience. The impact it had on the performers is clear. The effect on the audience was apparent from the good feelings shown at the dance and celebration that followed. People were obviously affected and moved, and were made more aware of their own deeply personal connection with their cosmic neighbors. Both performers and audience joined together to provide a superb example of a renewed astrology, amplifying and elucidating human experience with a healing touch for all.

# Teaching Astrology by Experience

Nearly everyone educated in the Western tradition experienced a common 'approved' method for assimilating new information. Learning took place in a classroom where a teacher presented ideas verbally while we, as students, sat quietly at our desks recording them. We have been conditioned to think this is the only way we learn.

In your first basic astrology class you probably struggled with what seemed an impenetrable mass of data. There were pages and pages of detailed notes about 34 new concepts. There were the 10 planets, 12 signs, and 12 houses, not to mention the five key aspects. Learning the basics may have impressed you as very much like your experience of third grade, with concepts implanted largely by rote memorization. Only when the 34 symbols were finally memorized did you probably begin to get a sense for how all the data fits together to form a cohesive interpretation.

But with experiential teaching methods we can now learn and teach in ways that communicate to our whole selves simultaneously, rather than just our left brain cognitive side. Not only can we use the 'Air mode' (talking) to teach, we can use Fire (action), Earth (sensations, pragmatic tools), and Water (feelings). With multiple approaches astrology becomes more interactive, making learning easier and synthesis more complete.

## Activities

One of the key concepts we learn in beginning astrology classes is the relationship between the four elements: Fire (Aries, Leo, Sagittarius), Air (Gemini, Libra, Aquarius), Water (Cancer, Scorpio, Pisces), Earth (Taurus, Virgo, Capricorn). Let's see how experiential astrology might approach the elements.

If you're teaching the elements in the traditional way, you might introduce each element with a verbal description and perhaps draw four triangles with their respective elements and signs on a chalk board. This approach appeals to the intellect. To have a more complete experience, why not add an activity for each element that the entire group can participate in.

For the element Fire we might ask the group to stand up, spread out, and stretch. (You'll need some floor space.) Once they've loosened up, try playing some fiery Aries music — active, insistent, aggressive rhythms. Then encourage the group to feel, to *be* the Fire quality, move and burn like a fire. Be direct, definite, emphatic. Ask them to move their arms, legs, torsos, and heads. This process can be used to bring their whole selves into synchronism with the Fire element. When the music is over observe the highly charged energy in the room. Notice the chattering and huffing and puffing to catch a breath. That's Fire! To broaden the learning, get feedback by asking the group what this exercise was like for them. This can lead to a discussion of the Fire element in their charts. A person with a fiery chart will probably have no difficulty in doing this, while a person with a water chart might feel more inhibited.

After a short discussion, move to the element Air. After talking about Air give the group an experience of it. Try creating an imaginary situation. Ask your group to suppose they are having a cocktail party. The guests have just begun to arrive and it's their job to see that they're comfortable. Ask them to be the social butterfly, moving from group to group, interacting with everyone. Then turn on some upbeat, jazzy background music to add to the atmosphere. That's Air! Once everyone has had the chance to interact, again take a moment to ask what this experience was like for them. Do they have much Air in their charts? Was this easier for those with strong Air charts? Who has the most difficulty with this exercise? Does this reveal anything about the elemental components in their charts?

Move on to the element Earth. Since Earth relies on sensing to form impressions, ask the group to sit cross-legged in a circle, close enough to barely touch knees. Have them close their eyes. Then pass around natural objects they can touch, smell, taste, etc, such as a bag of soil, herbs, stones, clay, gems, iron, incense, gold, a leaf or bark. As each person touches, feels, or smells an object, they are using their Earth element. After all of the objects are passed around, ask the group to open their eyes. Were any of the objects distasteful? Pleasant? Unidentifiable? That's Earth!

Finally, work with the element Water. Ask the group to lie down in a comfortable position on the floor of the room. Then turn off the lights and invite them, through guided imagery, to go to a beach. Let them feel the warm sand and water. As the tide rises they float safely atop the water and out to sea. Play ocean sounds softly in the background. Let everyone melt into this. Be silent for five minutes. Then guide them back into the room, slowly making them aware of their environment. When the time is right turn on the lights. What was this like? Almost everyone enjoys this kind of passive, introverted Water experience, especially those strong in Water. The more restless ones may have strong Fire, or Fire transits affecting their charts. Now, let the initial flush of excitement at experiencing the elements open into a further discussion.

Students learning experientially are likely to understand elements more deeply. They will not only have an intellectual understanding of Fire, Air, Earth, and Water, they will also have a kinesthetic experience of the elements and how they feel to their bodies.

## Imageboards

Imageboards for teaching or learning also create a range of new possibilities. These collages of visual images are effective and stimulating tools for teaching basic astrology to beginners, helping intermediate students to learn aspects and hone their interpretation skills, and even jiggle the creative juices of experienced astrologers when preparing client's charts.

For a basic astrology class you might create an imageboard for the planet Venus with sensual images like a baby llama sitting in a field of daisies; a photograph of a freshly dipped, chocolate-glazed hand holding a chocolate covered ice cream cone;

a little girl dressed in her mother's hat, purse and high heels, carrying her doll; a pair of sensuous, wet, women's lips; a dolphin; two lovers; a beach full of sunbathers; a man peacefully fishing in a boat at dusk; and a ballerina dancing. Show students with no knowledge of astrology an imageboard like this and ask them what Venus symbolizes. They'll tell you!

Then put out an imageboard of Uranus. On it might be a graphic silhouette of a man with colorful lightning bolts, spirals, meteor streaks, and stars imposed over him; exploding fireworks; an image of computer circuitry; a hi-tech mechanical arm; a spaceship; punky, hip young men with sunglasses; a photo of Silicon Valley; and a view into deep space. Ask what Uranus represents. Then ask what happens when you blend Venus and Uranus energies together.

When teaching how to integrate aspects, put the boards of Venus and Uranus out together. Again, use the combined images to illustrate how these energies interact in a conjunction, sextile, square, trine, or opposition. What do the boards tell students about the quality of relationships you would seek if you had Venus trine Uranus in your natal chart? What might be a typical sequence of events in a relationship if a client had Venus square Uranus in their natal chart or a transiting Uranus opposite their natal Venus? What kind of a love affair would ensue if their Venus was conjunct their new lover's Uranus?

If you are using imageboards therapeutically have your student or client look at the images of their natal Venus square Uranus. Ask them to spontaneously describe what they're seeing. Can they see a parallel between these images and the way they relate to others in their daily lives? Ask what this energy feels like inside. Can they associate any of these feelings with their current relationship? Can they draw their own image of what this feels like to them? An half hour investment in this process will reveal much more than a mere description of their Venus square Uranus.

To make imageboards get 10 large (at least 12"×14") pieces of cardboard, a stack of magazines, scissors, plastic photo protectors to keep the boards clean and a gluestick. (By using a gluestick or rubber cement you can change your imageboards frequently to keep both you and your students interested, and make it possible to add better images when you run across them.) Make it a practice, when browsing through magazines, to keep an eye out for appropriate planetary images. In time, your imageboards will really begin to evoke the planets they illustrate.

## Experiential Astrology for Healing

Experiential astrology can stir emotions, encourage catharsis, and promote personal growth; in short, it can be used *therapeutically*. On the Saturn station point in Scorpio, January 1985, I was invited by my friend, astrologer Susie Cox, to facilitate a 12 hour marathon astrodrama workshop, for a dozen participants, at Canyon Ranch in Tucson, Arizona. The weekend was chosen for its aspects: Mars/Venus in late Pisces, trine the Saturn station point, with Jupiter/Mercury in Capricorn intervening with two sextiles.

As it turned out, the group was nearly all women (one man), and the elemental

energy of Water was very strong. I began, as I usually do, by taking the 'group pulse.'
To do this we made a table with each group member's Sun, Moon, and Ascendant.
Tallying these three factors into the elements — Fire, Earth, Air, Water, I added
the totals. This gave us a reading on the overall elemental quality of the group and
identified the energies that are most accessible to us. I began the discussion of
modalities with some observations about the group's elemental character — for
example that the lack of Fire energy in the group could create resistance to physically
active techniques and the strong Water element would tend to favor the sort of
exercises that encourage emotional stirring, catharsis, and healing.

During the marathon, we spent 40 to 60 minutes enacting and processing each

## Sandi's Chart

Tulsa            Oklahoma
36N10            95W55
OCT 16 1948      12:30:00 GMT
Tropical Koch    True Node

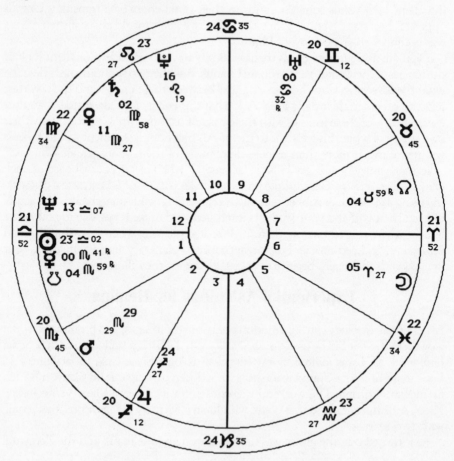

person's chart and drama. Beginning with the chart, we observed and discussed the dynamics briefly. To create the scenario, the 'director' (the person whose chart we were performing) would decide which of the psychic dynamics they wanted to explore. Planets were then chosen and a brainstorming session was begun to decide how best to portray the aspects and interactions.

## Astrodrama Marathon: An Example

When the preparations had been completed, each drama was performed and video-taped. I have documented one of these individual astrodrama sessions below.

Rebecca wanted to work with her fixed T-square between the Moon/Jupiter, Sun/Venus, and Pluto. The drama began with the five planets in their T configuration moving into a circle with Rebecca at the center. The 'sweet', flowing Moon spoke first, then Jupiter lovingly stroked and supported the Moon. They talked about their Aquarian nature and how they knew astrology could help Rebecca see her true nature. Then they were interrupted by a boisterous Pluto. With rising volume and intensity, all the plants were forced to withdraw except the powerful Sun in Scorpio who soon challenged Pluto to a control game, and the wrangling continued. Finally overwhelmed, Rebecca covered her face with her hands and screamed, 'AAAIEEEE!'

After a pause to collect herself, Rebecca sought to gain distance from the action as the T-square continued to intensify. Moving closer to her Mars in Capricorn on the sidelines, she unconsciously aligned herself with the energy that made her feel more stable and in control. But she received only momentary comfort from Mars as he reacted to the opposition to Uranus. Recognizing that Mars couldn't help her now, Rebecca backed completely out of the circle. In the highly charged atmosphere her feelings had reached a peak of intensity. I, as facilitator, intervened shouting 'FREEZE!' Everyone stopped where they were. The uproar ceased abruptly.

Facilitator (Barbara Schermer): 'What are you aware of that's happening inside right now?'

Rebecca: 'My heart's beating a hundred miles a minute!' (Takes a deep breath.) She begins to cry, saying, 'This is too much. I'm overwhelmed.'

F: 'What do you usually do when you're overwhelmed?'

R: 'Cry!'

F: 'The T-square with Pluto is an intimidating part of your psyche. Do you have any way to resolve these feelings?. What other planet can help you?'

R: 'My Mars. It can give me a sense of my own power.'

Looking around the room, she sees her Moon. 'And you, I feel so out of touch with you.'

(Taking the cue, I then positioned Rebecca and her Moon in a seated position across from each other.)

F: 'Tell your Moon why you feel so out of touch with her?'

R: 'You're always off somewhere. You aren't in touch with the people you say

you care about. You're always manipulating people. not really caring for them.'
Moon: 'But I'm close to so many.'
R: 'That' the point. You can't care about everybody. It isn't quality when you care about a lot of people, it's only quantity.'
F: 'Do you hear the different voices talking? And their contradictory points of view? Part of the Pluto psyche is self-centered, seeing only herself, and is suspicious of relating to anyone. It's the part of your psyche that is more self-protective, wanting to control relationships by manipulation. The Moon/Jupiter part of your psyche wants to express feelings freely, giving tender loving care to everybody. One retreats from contact, the other gives too freely. Can you recognize that manipulation might actually get in the way of getting you what you want?'
R: 'How do you resolve it? It seems I haven't done a very good job.'

Suspecting that the root of this conflict might lie in an early childhood trauma of separation (Moon opposite Pluto), I directed Rebecca's attention to her childhood.

F: 'Did you have an abandonment experience with either parent when you were young?'
R: 'Yes. My parents divorced when I was seven. I didn't see my father again until I was 21.'
F: 'Pluto opposite Moon can bring intense early abandonment experiences which have a strong impact on the psyche.'
R: 'That's why its easier to love everyone, instead of just one. I don't risk getting left behind again. In fact, *I'm* the one who leaves first. I just don't trust men!'
F: 'How do you resolve this dilemma?'
Mars spontaneously answers: 'You have Neptune trine your Moon. You have many wonderful people in your life. You can use them to help you.'
F: 'How does Neptune help a hard Pluto square?'
Group: 'Faith . . . Meditation . . . It gives her a strong channel to knowledge . . . With Moon conjunct Jupiter trine Neptune, she has a foundation of strong feelings.'
F: 'That's true, but she has a powerful abandonment experience from early childhood which brings the pain of deep unresolved conflict. We can talk about the spirituality of Neptune, but its not going to do her much good until she effectively deals with the unresolved issue about her father. It has been central to every relationship she's had with men since.'
(F to R): 'The problem that occurs in relationships is created by the contradictory feelings that you have. I would guess that you give men complex and mixed messages. The Scorpio part of you *wants* a strong relationship that is intimate and close. But when you respond to that you get scared, feel vulnerable, shut your heart and back off. It is an attract-repel response.

'One thing that I notice about your chart is that the upcoming transit of Saturn over your Sun will trigger your T-square at the end of the year, and again next year. You can use these events as opportunities to contact the unacknowledged energy, the repressed emotions of the anger and hurt, and you can face, release, and integrate them. By recognizing what you are doing unconsciously, you can work to defuse it. This can counteract the pattern you've been experiencing with men.

'And more than likely the upcoming Saturn influence will force you to dig deeper to get the answers you need. This will probably be difficult for you at times and will take some courage, but you can emerge more emotionally able to deal with the world. You have a real opportunity here.

'You know, Rebecca, you're a powerful woman, though your conscious mind may not know it. And it's important now to recognize that some of that power hasn't been available to you since you were seven years old. With all the upcoming eighth house stimulation, psychotherapy could probably serve as a catalyst now to help you get free. You might even take a risk and get into therapy with a man! Your Mars in the twelfth in Capricorn is another factor which supports your T-square . . . It also represents energy repressed in the unconscious, energy you may not be aware of, but that affects you just the same. I notice that you have a very tight jaw right now.'

R: 'It's *real* tight.'

F: 'OK, we've been stirring you up for 20 minutes now. Do you want to do something with this energy?'

With her agreement we all stood. (It was obvious that not many in this particular group were in touch with deep Pluto energy, but we had all been strongly affected by Rebecca's drama.) To assist in releasing this energy we spent several minutes with the following exercise.

The group spread out, finding their own private space in which they could see no one else. Taking a few deep breaths they focused their attention on their stomach areas (Mars/Pluto chakra). They then began to let out a barely audible growl. As it increased in intensity they slowly moved their growls deeper within. I encouraged them to be as loud as they wanted. They were just to let their sound come from the solar plexus. Then we transformed ourselves into strong, wild animals voicing deep, guttural, primal sounds. After several minutes I asked the group to move out of their private spaces and begin to interact with the other wild creatures.

Singling out Rebecca, and taking over the role of her Pluto, I began to stalk her. She responded as we spontaneously became lions. After circling each other for a few moments, I turned and faced her. Still facilitating, I followed her lead. She growled at me, I growled back with matched intensity. Then I pushed her a little, growling more fiercely. I encouraged and confronted her. Slowly she moved into that scary place where her power was, growling deeper, more fiercely at me until it was clear that she had broken into new territory. The experience ended, we changed back into our human bodies and sat down to process. I asked Rebecca what the exercise was like for her.

R: 'I got far down there. (Long pause.) It's been a very long time.'

One member of the group then told Rebecca that her own father had died when she was 15. (At the time that woman had the Saturn station point opposite her Sun.) Rebecca moved to her side, put her arms around her like a tender mother, and the two of them cried and hugged each other. After a long pause I asked, 'Once the pain of Pluto's unresolved repressed energy is released, *then* what can Neptune do?'

Group members: 'Bring her to a higher perspective and help her to realize how idealistic she's been about men. She wanted an ideal relationship to make up for everything her father didn't give her. And maybe once she's free of the unconscious stuff that's holding her back, she'll fly.'
R: 'I can see I've got some work to do.'

We ended Rebecca's astrodrama with what felt just right. We rocked her, making a cradle with our arms. (This exercise is described in the Workbook section, 'Moon — Rocking.') We encouraged her, in quiet voice, to let go, trust us to hold her, and just release her tensions. We rocked her for a long time, then slowly eased her to the ground. We sat around her silently, savoring the sweet nurturing power of that special moment . . . In all, the experience was not one of emotional *distress*, but emotional *release* and healing.

In these dramas we did more than talk about our charts, we actually experienced them. And although they generated pure, naked emotion, we always took care to reflect upon and process the results. It's the presence of *both* elements that makes these dramas effective. Catharsis was possible because there was a balance between thought and feeling in an atmosphere of trust.

We ended this long, tear-soaked, reflective day, emotionally exhausted yet spiritually exhilarated. Each of us had touched deep, long lost feelings and applied the soothing salve of reflection.

In the emotionally difficult weeks after the drama, Rebecca worked intensely with her psychotherapist. Many unresolved issues were stirred for her, not only her feelings about her father but her mother as well. The drama proved to be the catalyst to helping her confront her unacknowledged anger and hurt, release it, and apply the healing salve of forgiveness and acceptance. I present this particular example because of the lesson it offers to both you and me. The scope and depth of the work demonstrated clearly to me the power and effectiveness of therapeutic astrodrama and reinforced that its methods must be approached cautiously. If you are going to venture deeply into the Plutonian depths of another's psychic life, first make sure that you are qualified to do so, and second, see that your group members have follow-up resources to help with any stirred-up material.

## Astrodrama and Psychotherapy

In my experience astrodrama, in conjunction with the methods of psychotherapy, has demonstrated its healing potential time and time again. It can be used with many therapeutic approaches, Jungian, *Gestalt*, psychosynthesis, etc. Astrology can mesh particularly well with aspects of the neo-Reichian body therapies and Alexander

Lowen's Bioenergetics, particularly when astrologer and therapist work together as a team. My husband, psychotherapist Bob Craft, and I have presented a number of 'Astrology and Psychotherapy' workshops in Chicago for astrologers who want to work more deeply with their charts. We work in much the same way as the Tucson marathon workshop I described above. The difference is that we have the added dimension of Bob's experience and skill as a therapist. Here is an example from a workshop we conducted together.

The group was focused on the chart of a woman who wanted to work with her problem of Saturn/Pluto conjunction in Leo in her seventh house. She had never been married and had a history of running away from commitment when her relationships became intimate. When she was five years old her brother became critically ill with polio, and for her protection she was sent to live with relatives. She remembers almost never seeing her parents. To her, the family disintegrated and she felt abandoned. Now, as an adult, she was becoming aware that the insecurities and doubts surrounding this period of her life contributed to her deep fear of intimate relationships.

Beginning with a brief astrodrama, she responded to her Saturn and Pluto with confusion and frustration. Bob then asked if she would be willing to let him do some body therapy with her. She agreed and followed his instruction to lie down on her back. Because intimacy with a man was a threat for her I sat alongside for reassurance. When she was comfortable with the situation, Bob placed his hand on her sternum and gently began to press, asking that she focus on whatever feelings emerged.

As he continued to press on her heart area, her eyes teared and soon put forth a gushing stream. She first spoke, haltingly through her tears, of feelings of hurt in relation to men in her past. Then she began to mobilize herself against Bob. She grasped his hands trying to push them away. (She had already been told that she could end the exercise at any time by saying 'stop!') He resisted, she pushed harder. She finally pushed him farther away by getting her feet underneath and shoving angrily and defiantly against his chest. With his full weight against her resisting feet, Bob asked her to hold this position for as long as she could and to 'stay with her feelings.'

Her legs began shaking from the strain of resisting, and she quickly appeared to feel overwhelmed with the effort of keeping him away. She began to show evidence of feeling suffocated and started to hyperventilate. Frightened, she cried 'Don't suffocate me. Don't suffocate me. Leave me alone. Go away. I can't breathe.' At this point, as she was to describe it later, she 'broke through' and relived a forgotten and repressed near-drowning experience she had in Lake Michigan when she was four.

In the throes of the experience she struggled with an initial terror. Her fear then turned to another response — she let go of struggling, yielded, and accepted her fate. 'I moved to a place of deep peace and calm. I was amazed to actually see a little minnow in the water in front of me and a floating piece of seaweed, then a shaft of light shining down through the water. Then I felt myself snatched out of the lake by my next-door neighbor, who must have seen me drop out of sight.

We finished this evocative session by discussing how this repressed experience, the feelings of suffocation, and her inability to make a commitment with a man fit together with her Saturn/Pluto conjunction in the seventh. The woman recovered a new and valuable piece of information about why she had felt the way she did about men. Since the workshop the woman has continued to work with Bob. He has used further bodywork, art therapy techniques, and dreamwork to help her integrate her suffocation experience and overcome the problems connected with it.

Experiential astrology and psychotherapy in combination offer an exciting array of techniques and concepts for exploring the psyche. Both have something unique to offer. And, with Pluto now in Scorpio, it would be no surprise to find more people interested in a synthesis of approaches that could lead them to the core of their charts and themselves.

# 4
# DO IT YOURSELF!

When I can't find words to express what I mean, I get up and
dance it.

Zorba (Nikos Kazantzakis)

I hope that what you have read so far has whetted your appetite for some direct
experience of your own. That's what this chapter is designed to do — to get you
started in playing with, and learning from, experiential astrology. The goal is to
help you wake up your right brain with visual artistic (Venus/Sun), active (Mars/Sun)
and reflective (Moon/Mercury) techniques.

## Visual Arts Techniques (Venus/Sun)

Although you'll need paint and other supplies for the activities below, don't think
that you need to be an artist to take part. Each of us has an innate sense of color,
line, and shape, and even though we may not be trained to create works of art,
there is much to learn from the way we arrange things visually. In this section I'll
describe four techniques: imageboards, birth chart mandalas, masks, and healing
images. The first thing you'll want to do is make a resource box of art supplies with
as many different types of media as you can find — magazines to use as a source
for mandala, imageboard, or collage images, scissors, glue, tape, string, construction
paper (white and colors), newsprint, posterboards of different sizes; water colors,
Magic Markers, crayons, pencils, fingerpaints, tempera paints; an assortment of paint
brushes, white, gold, silver, and colored face paints; surgical gauze for maskmaking,
cardboard, glitter, sequins, feathers, pipe cleaners, gold, silver, and colored enamels,
ropes, and paper straws. (Obviously it would be expensive to buy everything at once,
so you may want to add to your art box a little at a time.)

### Using Imageboards to Explore Your Chart

You've been introduced to imageboards in Chapter One; now let's talk about them
in detail. Making personal imageboards of your own planets will give you a new
tool for self-study, contemplation, and ritual. These colorful, symbolic picture displays
can become a visual extension for your chart, giving you a means to arouse thoughts
and feelings and deepen your inner process.

Begin by creating an imageboard for each of the 10 planets in your horoscope. Cut appropriate pictures, words or phrases from magazines, or draw or paint whatever evokes your planets, their signs, and house positions. For a conjunction of two or three planets make an imageboard which blends both energies. I have one imageboard that shows my Sun/Uranus conjunction in the sixth house in Gemini. It's yellow, with a radiant sun, lightning bolts and spiraling galaxies, images of computers, books, words, a television, used plane tickets, weird Aquarian-looking people, an office desk with the word 'Serve' above it, a woman deep in thought, the words, 'Soothe your nervous system', 'Focus your energy', 'Breathe', and 'Learn to be patient.' I use this whenever I need to remind myself of what my Sun/Uranus means to me.

Once you have made your 10 planetary imageboards find an open space and place them around you on the floor in the order they appear in your chart. Sit in the center (Asc/Dsc,IC/MC axis), facing your midheaven. Now, take up each imageboard, moving around the circle from planet to planet. Are there any that you're feeling out of touch with now? Which of them feel less accessible? What planets being activated by transits or progressions are affecting your current life circumstances? What planetary energies give you problems right now? Which ones help out? What effects have you been noticing? . . . or ignoring? How are you feeling about them?

First focus on the planets that are your greatest strength. Use a piece of paper and a crayon or marker to draw what this current strength looks and feels like. Talk with these planets. What do you have to say to each of them? What do they have to say to you? How can they come forward and help you to achieve the balance you're seeking?

Now focus your attention on a current problem and note any planets affecting you in a disruptive way. Take out a piece of paper and draw what the problem looks and feels like. If it's a transit of Saturn conjunct your natal Mercury, put those two imageboards directly in front of you. Imagine that a specific archetypal image is standing behind each imageboard. For example, Mercury might be Hermes the messenger, and Saturn Father Time, Chronos, or a wise old crone.

Try speaking with these images, allowing yourself to give your own inner archetypes a voice. What do you have to say to Saturn? To Mercury? What does Mercury have to say to Saturn? What do they have to say to you? Ask each what he or she can do to help you feel more balanced? How would they affect each other if these two planets were in trine instead? In what ways can you act as if your difficult conjunction were a trine? Re-affirm your control with the planets that are now your strength.

Acknowledge each planet you have interacted with, giving thanks for what they've shown you. Treat them as you would any valued relationship. This may seem like a silly exercise but experience will prove it isn't. It is a good way to establish a more conscious relationship with your inner voices.

The only limits to the power of astrological archetypes are those imposed by the consciousness using them. Each astrological symbol is a living organic entity within you that is bottomless. By entering into this life-enriching symbol and its mystery consciously you are interacting, expanding and deepening your relationship with it. You no longer live out its energy in an unconscious and perhaps compulsive way.

If you're having trouble getting a planet to talk with you, this planetary energy is probably the one you are most suppressing from your awareness. If you feel anger or discomfort toward any of them this too may signal conscious or unconscious suppression. To return to a sense of wholeness, these may be the most crucial ones to learn to relate to.

## Your Horoscope as an Artistic Mandala

The mandala is a universal expression of wholeness that arises from the integration of the human psyche. Natural mandalas appear around us, in snowflakes, the spiraling galaxies, tree rings, and the annual unfolding of the seasons. In their book, *Mandala*, Jose and Miriam Arguelles speak of the earth itself as a living mandala, '. . . a structural matrix through and from which flow a succession of changes, elemental forms, and primal surges, each surpassing the other in an infinite variety of organic structures and impulses, crowned by the supreme attribute of reflective consciousness.'[1]

Since time immemorial the mandala has been depicted as a circle with a centerpoint. The horoscope, a circle with a centerpoint, is your own personal mandala and can be a living and vibrant tool for contemplation. Symbolically, the centerpoint is the point of intersection through which all life flows. By maintaining contact with the center we are helped to keep our psychic equilibrium.

To make your birth mandala you'll need a large posterboard (30"×40"), a pencil, Magic Markers, colored construction paper, magazines, perhaps photos of yourself and of people important to you, and a gluestick. To set the mood you might want to play some soft, meditative music. Then clear your workspace of distractions and place your posterboard in front of you. Now use your pencil to draw a circle two feet in diameter. Divide the circle into 12 equal, wedge-shaped, segments. This gives you the basic form you'll need to make your mandala.

Next, focus your attention on the centerpoint and become aware that this is the focal node through which your life force comes. It is the vital living part of you that moves out in ever widening waves toward the perimeter of the chart. Meditate on this point. Take your time. The more fully you enter into the creative process of the mandala the more deeply you will enter your chart. Imagine yourself spiraling down into this point. What do you see emerging there? A rose, a star, a black hole, a being of light, a yantra, a word? In your mind's eye, see the center of your mandala. Merge with your image, pick up your Magic Marker and create it fully.

Now become aware of the planetary forces on the periphery of your attention. Which planet do you most notice? Focus your attention on it. How does this particular planet relate to the center? How does it relate to the others? What colors, words, phrases, and images come to mind? If your Moon is in Virgo you might begin by coloring the house it sits in green. You might draw a large moon and include a photo of a mother and children, or anything that seems to evoke this planetary energy. When you finish turn your attention to the next one that calls you until you've represented each planet in the horoscope. Don't think too much about what you're doing. Add whatever feels spontaneous and right.

Try drawing a birth mandala each year near or on your birthday. You will concretely observe your psyche unfolding as it changes through time. It will reveal much to you about the feeling, depth, and direction of your inner process from year to year.

## Making Masks to Experience Your Chart

Mask-making can be a fun way to experience your chart in three dimensions. Alone or with a group, masks move you into more intimate contact with the pure planetary archetypes. Mercury in Gemini might wear a fluorescent yellow mask, with pipecleaner antennas. Scattered across the mask's surface are words and phrases: Study. Learn. Write. Teach. Speak. Move. Travel. Do. 'Give me more data.' 'I love to learn.' 'When do we go?' And pictures: of books, libraries, universities, bicyles, planes, trains, telephones. Masks like this create a more open channel between astrological archetypes and the psyche. Using them as a kind of shield of invisibility we can suddenly be free to express ourselves without fear of judgement by others.

To make your planetary mask you'll need these supplies: a handkerchief or barrette to tie back your hair, Vaseline (petroleum jelly), scissors, a bowl of warm water, tissues, towels to protect your clothing, paints, fabric, ribbons, glitter, etc., to decorate your mask, and a roll of plaster gauze (one standard roll will make two masks). Gauze is available at any medical supply store. You'll also need a partner to mold the gauze strips to your face.

First, cut about 20 strips of gauze, two inches wide and about four inches long. You'll also want to cut some smaller strips to work into smaller areas and fill in the gaps. Next, tie back your hair with the handkerchief, and apply the petroleum jelly to your entire face except eyes and nostrils. Be sure to cover your eyebrows well. (You men with beards will want to coat them generously or your beard will end up in the mask instead of on your face.)

Decide what planet mask you're making and turn on some appropriate music. Then lie back with your head on a towel, get comfortable and focus on your breathing. Have your partner cover your eyes, nose,and lips with small damp pieces of tissue. Now you are ready for the first layer of gauze. If you have not done this before, remember to keep your face relaxed and neutral. Focus on the nature of the planet you are creating. Breathe. Have your partner dip the gauze strips into a bowl of water and apply them to your face, making sure to smooth them down with the fingers. They should cover your entire face three times, using the smaller strips to mold around your eyes, mouth, and nose. Place the second layer of gauze perpendicular to the first. Then allow the mask to dry for approximately 10 minutes. (If it's a humid, rainy day, you'll need to allow more time.) When the plaster has set, pull the mask away from your face gently. As soon as it's fully dry you can bring your mask to life with paint and other materials. Variation: If you want your facial expression to be mirrored in your mask (for example, an angry Mars), make the most exaggerated expression you can. You'll need to sustain it until the mask has set, up to 10 minutes, so be prepared. These masks are usually more interesting, but take more effort.

## Creating a Healing Image for Inner Balance

Another visual approach you might try is to create a healing image of your chart. Recently, I had a group of students do this. One woman with the transits of Uranus/Saturn conjunct in Sagittarius opposing her Moon/Mercury (Gemini) square Neptune (Virgo) drew a forest of trees and green earth. Her healing image helped her ground and balance her highly mutable, nervous energy.

A Pisces physician who just completed her first Saturn return, also had transiting Pluto in Scorpio trine her Venus/Mercury in Pisces. She drew the symbols of Pisces and Pluto at the top of her paper, with golden rays pouring down into four fetuses. She said that the one fetus represented her new 30 year cycle, and the other embryos were her patients whom she wanted to touch with her healing Pluto energy.

Another woman in the midst of Pluto in Scorpio opposite Moon in Taurus drew an elaborate green penetrating spiral that represented her moving into her depths, her contact with her feminine whose center became an eye, the 'eye of her soul.'

To make a healing image use the same art supplies you used for your birth mandala. Begin with some soft, meditative music. Then place a piece of posterboard, about two feet square, in front of you. Close your eyes and spend a few minutes focusing on your breathing. When you feel relaxed open your eyes and imagine your chart transposed upon the blank posterboard. Look for a healing image to emerge that represents your chart/life at this moment. When you begin to see it let it flow through your paintbrush or markers onto the posterboard. Keep in touch with its healing, integrating quality as you draw.

# Active Techniques (Mars/Sun)

Experiential astrology not only uses the visual arts (Venus/Sun) to experience the horoscope, but the more active form, astrodrama, too. A central principle underlying the holistic therapies is that all our thoughts and emotions are inextricably interwoven with physical movement. Eastern philosophies have included active practices like yoga, karate, and sacred dance for thousands of years. When it finally began to break with Descarte's dualism, Western thought also affirmed the unity of mind and body. Psychological theorist Wilhelm Reich hypothesized that memories and emotions are stored in the muscles as well as the brain.[2] Biochemist and body therapist, Ida Rolf, found that pressure on particular muscles evoked memories, sensations and emotions.[3] More recent research supporting the idea of a mind-body wholeness has evolved into the field of biofeedback.[4]

If we are to fully realize astrology's potential we need to use our bodies to learn about our psyches, so let's get right to it. Try this. Turn on some lively, pleasant music that is easy to move to. Stand up and slowly begin to move to the music. Dance. Turn. Bend. How does Venus move? *Be* Venus.

Now play more aggressive Martian music. Feel Mars in your body. Respond to it by dancing energetically. Be Mars. Shake yourself up. Get your heart pounding. Get moving! Now turn on some ethereal Neptunian music. Settle into its rhythms, returning to slow, flowing movements. Do you feel how Venus and Neptune are similar? Both are flowing, easy, soft energy. Can you see why astrologers call Neptune the 'higher octave' of Venus?

Now that you've got your body up and moving, take out your natal chart and put it in front of you. Choose one of your planets to express. Is it your Mars in Gemini? Moon in Pisces? Venus in Leo? Go through your music collection and find something that captures the feeling of the planet. (Commonly available music for each planet is listed in the Workbook section after the exercises for each planet or sign.) Play a selection for your Mars in Gemini. How does it aspect the other planets? How would contact with them affect Mars' movement? If there's a trine from Jupiter your movements may become grander, more expansive, more sweeping. Is it squared to your Saturn? That might limit your movement or cause it to be more staccato and jerky.

With a little research you can gather your own collection of planetary music. Then, when you are feeling the frustration of a transiting Saturn conjunct your Mars, you can put on Mars/Saturn music, dance it out, and release the blocked energy. Whenever I feel the effect of the scattered, nervous energy of my Sun/Uranus in Gemini I turn on 'Dynamic Meditation' Music from the Shree Rajneesh ashram.[5] Its insistent, driving rhythms get me moving and shaking my body, discharging the excess mental buildup. I always feel relieved and more centered afterwards. If I am feeling a little blue and 'Saturnized' I'll turn on 'Fanfare for the Common Man' by Aaron Copland and dance with big sweeping movements to counter Saturn with Jupiter.

Try these dance forms for your planets in their signs:

Aries — direct, definite, hard-pounding, forward movement.

Taurus — rooted to one place on the earth and crouched low. Move slowly, methodically, lazily.

Gemini — quick, butterfly movements, lightly touching here, there, everywhere. Use your arms, hands, facial expressions.

Cancer — rhythmic swaying, rocking, curling over into a fetal position, or on the floor feeling like a small child.

Leo — grand, dramatic gestures, regal bearing and movement.

Virgo — meticulous attention to your small movements.

Libra — movements of balance and grace.

Scorpio — hips and pelvis gliding in slow, sensual circles, moving your hands over your body sensuously.

Sagittarius — movements that direct the body upwards, stretching up, climbing higher.

Capricorn — concise, authoritarian, sure, efficient, grounded movement.

Aquarius — 'gathering in' movement which includes others, move as a group.

Pisces — flowing, willowy, tumbleweed movement.

If you love to dance and be physical, turn on some rhythmic, flowing Venusian music and move from planet to planet, dancing out your horoscope! Try this at least once. It will make you more conscious of the different types of energy within you.

# Reflective Techniques

The reflective (Moon/Mercury) techniques constitute another class of experiential method you can use on your own. To get started on these try keeping a transit diary, a dream/transit journal or a reflective/writing journal.

## Transit Diary

Here's what a typical transit journal entry might look like:

(18 March)

> Transiting Mars square Natal Saturn — Thought my boss was going to drive me nuts today! Had a big blow up with him when I gave him the status report on the project. He kept interrupting me to ask for totally unimportant details. The meeting took twice as long as it should have. I was so angry with him I slammed down a glass, badly cutting my finger. God, I felt so out of control and reactive.

Do you know what occurred when Mars last squared your Saturn? Or what happened when Jupiter last opposed your Venus? Are you consciously aware of the movement of the transiting planets in your life, especially those of Mars, Jupiter, and Saturn? If you don't know the answers to these questions, keep a notebook to record your transits and the experiences you have. (This is a fine tool for beginners in astrology.) It will help you to be more conscious of how planetary cycles are operating, and to learn what effects transits produce in your life.

A transit diary will also reveal two important things: which planetary energies manifest in a consistent way in your chart (for me, it's the planet Mars when in contact with my Sun/Uranus — consistently unexpected accidents), and when they are likely to be strongest. With planets that retrograde (all but the Sun and Moon), when will the transit fire most intensely? Is the strongest effect on the first, second, or third pass? For example, watch the forward and retrograde phases of Saturn in aspect to your natal planet closely. When does it manifest most strongly? This is an important key to the pattern of intensity of *all* the retrograde planets.

Keeping a daily diary of all the transits affecting you, you can get to feel Virgoan very quickly, so if you get overwhelmed try this abbreviated version. Buy a thick, lined, spiral bound notebook and divide it into 12 monthly sections labeled for easy reference. Leave the first three to four pages blank for noticed effects of the long-term transits (Uranus, Neptune, Pluto) you experience during the month. Start your diary by spending time once a week reflecting on the outer transits of Pluto, Uranus, and Neptune. In what ways are you noticing their effects in your life? Write down active transits in the left-hand column, allowing a third to a half page of blank space to write in during the month. This way you need only read through the first few pages of every month to see the effects of the slow moving transits.

Then focus on the three more perceivable transits of Saturn, Jupiter, Mars. In the second section of each month keep a daily diary with dates and transit listings on the left-hand side. List the transits in order of strength — all Saturn, Jupiter, and Mars transits that apply. Write down to the right of the listing what you observe occurring in your life that corresponds to the transit.

The transits of the Moon, Mercury, Sun, and Venus last from a few hours to a few days. Sometimes they will be the trigger for the more powerful transits. Keep your eye on them and simply list these transits and experiences below the entries for Saturn, Jupiter, and Mars. If you keep a record of the faster moving plants for four months you will get a feeling for how they operate. The transits of the Moon may last only a few hours. To fine tune your awareness of the Moon, pay attention to the days that the Moon transits your natal planets during a two month period. Keeping a transit diary takes some discipline but you'll find that your efforts definitely pay off. You will learn to more accurately anticipate your upcoming transits, and can prepare yourself more consciously.

## Keeping a Dream/Transit Journal

Last night I had a dream that someone put a dog choker around my neck. I went into a panic as the chain squeezed off my breath. I clawed at my throat desperately trying to get air into my lungs. (Transiting Saturn opposing my Sun/Uranus.)

There is an intimate link between the messages of your dreams and your experiences in daily life. In fact, many events in your conscious world can be foretold by listening to what your dreams tell you. Teachers of the yogic sciences go so far as to say that a symbol that appears in your dream-state will manifest in the conscious waking world within 72 hours.

Because there is a direct link between your conscious experiences and your transits, it stands to reason there is a relationship between your dreams and the transits as well. Keeping a dream journal in conjunction with a transit diary can demonstrate this connection. I've kept a dream/transit journal on and off for 12 years. Many times this practice has given me important information about my inner process that I probably would have missed had I not kept a record.

When you keep a dream/transit diary you will notice two things. First, that active transits do correspond to your dream symbols, and second, that those dream symbols *can* manifest in your waking life.
Here are some examples from my current journal:

When transiting Venus opposed my natal Saturn, I dreamt I was robbed. Three days later, I received a bad check; when Jupiter conjuncted my natal Moon, I dreamt a white female owl landed on my head and made a nest. In retrospect during that month, two supportive new and important women came into my life. With the transiting Moon in my twelfth house I had a dream that I visited a prison where the prisoners were kept confined to a swimming pool. The following weekend on a trip out of town with my husband an enormous thunderstorm hit, flooding many roads. We drove in a maze for over three hours trying to find a way around the flooding. With transiting Mars conjunct my Jupiter at Christmas, I dreamt I was downhill skiing pushing for speed, riding the edge of the fall line down the mountain in perfect control. On Christmas morning, I unexpectedly got new skis and bindings.

Many people say they don't remember their dreams. If you want to remember your dreams you must train your unconscious to do so. Every night before going to sleep plant an auto-suggestive seed, 'I will remember my dreams vividly.' Then just drift off to sleep normally. It may take a week or two but your dreams will start coming through.

As soon as you wake stay focused in your dream state without opening your eyes. Remember as much as you can. Immediately roll to the side of your bed and without distraction record your dream, in present tense if you can, in your dream journal. Don't edit, just spontaneously write. Read it through and write down any first responses you have to its meaning. Underline the key elements in the dream. Is the dream speaking about a specific issue in your life now? Take out your daily ephemeris. Are there any transits during this week that correspond to the dream symbols? Write them beside the dream. Pay particular attention under the planetary station points. By being aware of the symbols in your dreams occurring over a two week period, you will begin to see a parallel between your transits and your experiences in your waking state. You will soon discover that your unconscious is speaking more loudly than you knew.

## Contemplating the Horoscope

'Know thyself' is an essential dictum that has survived the ages and come down to us from the temple inscriptions at Delphi in Greece. The horoscope offers us a method for knowing ourselves that is based on a dynamic blueprint of our conscious and unconscious realms. Through deep study and contemplation of our horoscope we gain self-knowledge.

Self-knowledge is crucial if we are using astrology as a tool to help others, since we can only go as far with others as we have gone ourselves. A good way to accomplish this is to keep a reflective writing journal. With this journal you can contemplate and study aspects of your self/chart, dialog with yourself and record your innermost thoughts and feelings. The page will become a living mirror for seeing yourself more clearly.

In a spiral bound notebook (or other durable diary), write a question, selected from the list below, that has particular interest for you now. Close your eyes and reflect on the question. What feelings, images, words come to mind? Are there any physical sensations you notice? Write or draw your responses. When you have written or drawn your answer, study the indicated planet in your birthchart. What aspects, sign, house position does it have in your natal chart? If this is a question more relevant to how you feel now, study your progressions and transits. Do they correspond to how you are feeling?

Questions for Reflection:
The Sun
    How do I appear to others?
    What facets of myself do I see?
    What is my purpose?
    What aspects of myself am I not consciously using?
    In what ways can I further develop or express my fuller being?
    What was my father like?
    What messages did he give me?
    Did he consider himself successful?
    What were his shortcomings? Strengths?

The Moon
    How do I feel right now?
    How do I nurture myself?
    What does the little child in me feel like now? What are its needs?
    Who/what around me do I turn to when I need support and encouragement?
    What was my mother like?
    What messages did she give me?
    What were her shortcomings? Strengths?
    Did she have a favorite child? Was it me?
    How would she show her feelings?

The Moon/Sun
    What do my inner and outer selves look and feel like now? (Draw what they look like to you.)
    Make two lists. List all your Moon, feminine, yin qualities. Then, list all your Sun, masculine, yang qualities. Is one stronger than the other? (What aspects/sign/house positions do your Moon and Sun have?)

Venus
    What are the things/people I love most?
    What do I love about myself?
    What do I allow myself to indulge in to excess?
    Is there anyone I am envious of? Why?

Mars
    For what am I willing to exert my energy and make an effort?
    What are my favorite physical activities?
    For what cause am I willing to take action?

What makes me angry? What qualities in other people make me angry? What do I do when I get angry?

Jupiter
What are my talents and skills?
What are my positive personality traits?
What have been my most important achievements?
In what areas do I feel confident in my knowledge and expertise?
What are my current potentials?
What areas of my life are smoothly unfolding and offer me promise?
What aspirations do I have for my life in the next five years?
What current beliefs do I have?
What words symbolize my philosophy of life now?
Is there anything now I'm inflated or cocky about?

Saturn
What are my greatest strengths?
What are my particular responsibilities right now?
What attitude do I have toward them?
What are the traits I fear, judge, dislike about myself?
What are the traits I fear, judge, dislike in others?
In what areas of my life do I feel secure and stable?
What am I currently struggling with? Is it from within or without? What does the struggle look like? Name it. Can I see a way to solve my problem? What can I do differently that might make the situation change for the better?

Uranus
Against what ideas/people have I rebelled in my life?
Are there things I like that others consider strange?
What groups am I involved with?
Am I actively involved or on the periphery?

Neptune
What genuinely inspires me?
What areas of my life do I suspect I am not seeing clearly?
Am I holding any illusions now about my life or anyone in it?
To what am I addicted? Does it have repercussions in my life or the lives of others?

Pluto
What are my greatest inner resources?
Are there any problems in my life that I am suppressing or that are crying out to be transformed?
What resources do I have within/without to help me change?
Is there anything/anyone I intensely hate? Why?
Is there anyone in my life I still need to learn to forgive?

What does the transforming healer within me look like?
Is there something I have done for which I still need to learn to forgive myself?

Any one of these approaches will give you a wealth of ways to reflect upon yourself in the mirror of astrology. And most important you will be learning from experience, your best teacher.

# 5
# ASTRODRAMA: PLAYING WITH OTHERS

'In the Heaven in Indra, there is said to be a network of pearls, so arranged, that if you look at one you see all the others reflected in it.'

A Hindu Sutra

It is Allen's turn for the group to act out his chart, astrodrama-style. He wants a better understanding of his fixed T-square of Mercury opposite Uranus Square Neptune. Confused and anxious, he sits in the center of the room, witnessing the struggle between the difficult T-square. His Mercury begins to lecture his Uranus, 'You're always pushing at me.' 'Hurry up! Let's get going! Got to get these 20 things done today.' 'Let me relax. I'm tired of trying to get a million things done. Hurrying up makes me nervous and flustered.' Turning to the Neptune square he complains, 'And you! Always so wishy-washy. You *never* take a stand. Always letting Uranus run over you. He gives you so many options that you just sit there stunned, like you're in some kind of fog! Do something will you!' Then Neptune responds dreamily. 'Oh well, doing's not so important anyway. Dreaming is. I *do* sometimes help you escape. We go off on some nice journeys, don't we? Remember that great idea we had to move to Corpus Christi and open a hotdog stand? Wow! that would've been great, hanging out on the beach.' Uranus interrupts, 'Yeah you're really off in Never-Never Land. No sense of reality. If you had your way, you'd never let us get anything done. You confuse the issue and dilute our action. You're a drag.' Neptune responds, 'And you're abusive. You never see my sensitivity, and sometimes I *do* give you good ideas you know. And you are a know it all, always trying to lord it over me. I just don't know what to do about you any more.'

The energy in the room was intense, scattered, and chaotic, with three strident voices contending in this non-stop tug of war. You could see the frustration in Allen's eyes as he tried to listen to the voices of Mercury, Uranus and Neptune. Spontaneously his Sun in Capricorn in the fourth house (standing behind him), placed his hands on Allen's shoulders and reassured him. 'It doesn't matter how they confuse and frustrate you. You've got *me*, Sun in Capricorn — Strong and Capable. I'll see you through anything your T-square can dish out. We'll deal with them when we need to. When Uranus acts up and scatters your mind, remember to come back to me to ground yourself and get organized before we go off half-cocked. And when Neptune moves in with her dreamy ideas we'll listen to her, let her inspire us, even escape from reality sometimes, but we'll keep tabs on all the grand illusions and confusion she brings. Use me as your balancing force when Uranus or Neptune has your mind going crazy. I'll be there — always.' Within minutes the energies in the room calm down and came into balance, giving Allen the reassurance he can deal effectively with his difficult planetary combination.

## Astrodrama: How To Do It

What you have been observing is astrodrama, a technique within the wider field of experiential astrology which presents the horoscope in dramatic form. Charts literally come alive, giving participants the opportunity to encounter and work with their energies directly. From one person to groups of 25 or more, astrodrama is an exciting and fun way to explore your psychic energies.

When you and a friend get together to talk about charts, try doing improvisational skits. Set up an imaginary set of circumstances for the two of you to interact in. Acting skill is not important. Just take a deep breath and give it a try. Begin by standing up, stretching and getting the Leo in your soul moving! Here are some examples to help you and your friends begin. When you've tried these, create your own scenarios:

Imagine that you and your friend have decided to take a vacation together. One of you is a strong Sagittarius, the other a strong Pisces. What's your process in deciding where to go? Or suppose that you are teenage girlfriends on a trip to New York City for the first time. This is your first shopping day. One of you has a Venus in Virgo, the other in Gemini. Try a polarity of Venus in Aquarius with a Venus in Leo, or Venus in Virgo with Venus in Pisces.

You and your colleague are about to present a paper before a major professional body. He has Mercury in Virgo, you have Mercury in Sagittarius. How are you likely to be preparing five minutes before the presentation? You and your friend are downhill skiing. He has a good Jupiter transit, you a Saturn square. How do you go about choosing which run to take? You and your husband are figuring out your bank statement under Mercury retrograde. You have Mercury in Virgo, he Mercury in Pisces. What happens?

You are about to go into your teacher's office for your final grades. You have transiting Saturn square your Sun. Act this out, then replay the skit with a Jupiter conjunct your Sun. You've just had a 'fender bender' and are getting out of your car to inspect damages. You have Mars in Libra. The guy who hit you has a Mars in Aries, or Virgo, or Pisces. Try each variation.

For some non-verbal improvisation try these: You are a Taurus lion stalking a Gemini gazelle. What happens? You and your friend are puppies, one was born a Taurus, the other a Gemini. You are four-year-old playmates at the beach. One of you has Sun in Leo, the other Sun in Virgo. How do you play together?

Try being Saturn conjunct the Sun, Saturn trine the Moon, Jupiter conjunct the Sun, Jupiter trine the Moon, Mars square the Sun, Mercury conjunct Jupiter,

Mercury conjunct Saturn, Mercury square Neptune, Mercury trine Uranus, Mercury opposite Pluto, Mars conjunct the Moon in Virgo, Mars conjunct Venus, Venus conjunct the Moon in Cancer, Venus conjunct Saturn in Scorpio, Venus conjunct Jupiter in Scorpio, Mars conjunct Jupiter in Sagittarius, Mars in Leo square Saturn in Taurus. Attempt some generational aspects: Saturn conjunct Uranus in Taurus, Saturn conjunct Uranus in Gemini, Saturn conjunct Pluto in Leo, Saturn in Leo sextile Neptune in Libra, Saturn conjunct Neptune in Libra, Saturn in Libra square Uranus in Cancer.

If there are three of you, take turns choosing some aspect in each chart to work on. Let's say your friend has a Moon in Aries square her Mercury in Capricorn that she wants to know more about. Without prior discussion of the aspect divide the roles, the Moon and Mercury, between you. The person whose aspect it is can just observe. Begin by setting the scene in which the two of you will interact. For example, suppose you are a married couple sitting at home. One of you decides it would be fun to go to the movies. How would the Moon in Aries square a Mercury in Capricorn react? Or discuss the aspect beforehand with your Moon in Aries friend, asking her to explain how she experiences this aspect in her life. Then one of you role play the Moon in Aries. The woman whose aspect it is might portray her own Mercury in Capricorn, giving her the opportunity to feel and experience her Mercury. The third friend observes. When you're finished, switch roles, with you playing her Mercury and she her own Moon. Then discuss your experiences. What was each role like for her? Did she learn anything new? Did she see more clearly how these two psychic components oppose each other? What did you feel when playing her Moon? Her Mercury? What did the observer notice about the process? Can you all brainstorm ways in which she might better deal with this square? Have any new insights emerged? If you and your friends have some experience with astrodrama you might want to include houses as well. For example, portray her Moon in Aries in the second house square her Mercury in Capricorn in the eleventh.

If you have a slightly larger group, five or six people, try combinations of aspects, such as T-squares — the Moon in Aries square Mercury in Capricorn with Neptune in Libra making an opposition to the Moon and square to Mercury. What does this psychic pattern feel like? Then to this add the positive effects of the Moon in Aries trine Jupiter/Pluto conjunct in Leo. How does this change the pattern?

Do you have a group of 10 or more? Then try the re-enactment of your whole natal chart! This is when astrology truly comes alive. My first experiences with astrodrama in a group setting occurred in the fall of 1981 at Esalen Institute in Big Sur, California. As a community workshop leader, I taught an astrology class three times weekly for a group of residents who were both students of astrology and frequent participants in *Gestalt* encounter groups. It was a perfect group to work with. They were informed about astrology, knew how to work in a group, and were open to new ideas. From these experiences at Esalen developed the process of enacting the full natal chart.

# The Living Horoscope

The basic form of the 'Living Horoscope' is described below. A more advanced form, using Jung's model of the psyche, particularly his concepts of the personal and collective unconscious, will be described briefly at the end of this chapter.

If you are working with a larger group, you'll probably want to 'warm-up' to each other first. Start with a few ice-breaking exercises (listed in the Workbook). When you feel loose and relaxed, choose planets. Don't worry too much about who should play what energy, just choose and begin. When all of the planets have been assigned, you're ready to improvise some simple aspects. Begin by calling out aspects that group members would like to see. Someone may want to see their Jupiter in Cancer trine Mercury in Scorpio, or their Sun conjunct Uranus in Virgo. When an aspect is called out the two planets should take a moment to compare notes, then use their planetary characters to portray the essence of the aspect. When the group is comfortable with one other you're ready to enact full charts. To do full charts with a group of 10 to 12, try using this basic form below. It is adaptable and yet it provides a simple structure within which to play.

Outline of the Living Horoscope — Basic Form

There are three kinds of roles:

The 'director' is the person whose chart you are enacting. He or she takes the lead in designing the astrodrama.

The 'planets' are, of course, the Sun through Pluto, assigned by the director to group members who have the ability to best portray the particular planetary energy.

The 'facilitator' supports the actions of the director by intervening when necessary to focus the drama. His or her relatively detached perspective allows the participants to stay 'in role' while matters of overall structure and process are attended to. (As you can see, a group size of 12—10 planets plus the facilitator and director — is ideal.) The basic format for a Living Horoscope is as follows:

## 1) Chart analysis

Begin the process by placing the natal chart of the person whose drama you're performing in front of the group. (A blackboard is a handy aid.) The director then leads the group through his or her chart, identifying the key aspects, elemental modalities, etc. If the director is not knowledgeable about astrology, he or she may use the group as a resource to find the aspects and discuss them.

## 2) Assigning Planets

The director then chooses group members to play the planets. She may want a particular person to play her Sun. Or she might want the participants to choose which roles they want to play. Sometimes a group member may feel that they have a special insight into a particular planet in the director's chart, or they may want to experience themselves in a particular role.

## 3) Establishing a Goal

Once the planets have been assigned the next step is to find the focus, or goal for the drama. Concentrating on a particular aspectual pattern or theme in the chart is a good choice. Does the director want to focus on his grand square, his relationship with his lover, his parents? (A beginners' astrodrama group needs a focus for their energy. Without it dramas can flounder. As groups gain experience, they'll find that structure becomes less and less necessary. Groups that are especially attuned to each other can create beautifully meditative and spontaneous work.)

To give an example of how the whole process works, we'll suppose that our

## Director's Chart

| Chicago | Illinois |
|---------|----------|
| 41N52 | 87W39 |
| AUG 13 1984 | 02:30:00 GMT |
| Tropical Koch | True Node |

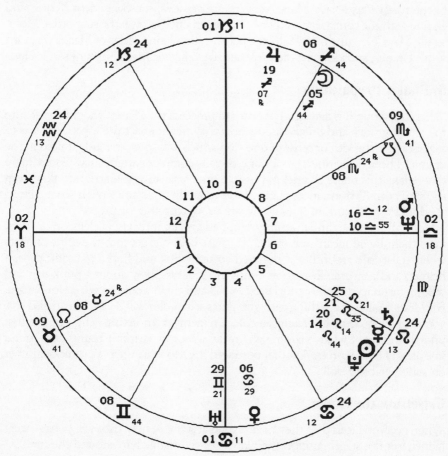

director is a woman who wants to better understand her relationship with men. See Figure 3 for the horoscope of our director, who was born on 12 August 1948.

This woman has never been married, wants a relationship very much, and has a historic pattern of attracting a good relationship followed by an abusive one. (Twice these abusive relationships involved alcoholic men.) The group enacting her chart might want to focus on the relationship aspects and signs of her Sun, Mars, Venus, Saturn, 5th, 7th, and 8th houses, and anything else pertinent to this understanding. How do the participants assess her particular relationship struggle? Where are the points of constructive release?

## 4) Role-playing Order

As the brief discussion proceeds, the Facilitator should begin to devise (and display for all to see) a logical order in which the aspects in this particular chart can be enacted. For example, in this case it seems logical to start with the director's struggle with the powerful and controlling Sun/Mercury/Saturn conjunction, proceeding to the passive/aggressive Mars/Neptune square idealistic/dependent Venus, and ending with the configuration's points of constructive resolve: the supportive Moon sextile Mars/Neptune trine Pluto, the positive stimulating effects of Mercury/Saturn sextile Uranus, and idealizing effects of the trine to Jupiter, Mars/Neptune sextile Pluto.

## 5) Planet Preparation

When the group has agreed what order to proceed, the Planets should divide into the aspect groups and *briefly* discuss how they might enact the aspect. (This is to suggest a sketchy idea or sense of direction which will spontaneously unfold in the drama.) Though beginners groups or especially complex patterns may require more time, make this phase as brief as possible since you want the action to flow from the situation. (Performances planned too carefully in advance often seem stilted.) And add a few extra minutes if you are using costumes or props.

Colorful costumes and ingenious props add an exciting visual element, so if you have them by all means use them. You can't help but get into the spirit of Mars when you rustle around in a cluttered costume box and find a red satin cape, a helmet, and a sword. To portray Venus in Aquarius, how about a punk wig and yellow, star-shaped, glittery sunglasses? A ball and chain would be perfect for Saturn. For Uranus, almost anything with glitz and garish color will do. Props can also give you a starting point in creating a role. I remember an actress who got her first understanding of what Neptune was really about by swirling 'round and 'round in a dress of filmy scarves. Another portrayed the Moon in Virgo as a finicky mother dressing her baby doll.

## 6) Setting the Stage

When everyone feels that they have a general sense of how they will portray their planet, 'set the stage.' Position the planets of the natal chart around the director.

Place the director in the center of her chart facing her midheaven (tenth house cusp). To her left should be all the planets in zodiacal order that are in her twelfth, first, and second houses, behind her back any planets in the third, fourth and fifth houses, to her right all planets in the sixth, seventh, eighth, etc.

## 7) The Drama

a) Introduction of Planets
Now that everyone has taken a place you are ready to begin the action. (You might want to take a minute for the planets to 'center' in their planetary energy.) Starting with the ascendant move from house to house, counterclockwise, letting the planets briefly introduce themselves. 'I am your Mercury in Leo. I am dramatic, think big, and love my ideas. I help you to create and create and create! The others say I'm too egotistic, but it seems to me when I'm having a good time so does everyone else.' Move around the circle giving these brief 10 to 20 second introductions until all 10 have spoken.

b) Role Playing, Interventions
Then let the drama unfold in the agreed sequence. In our example, the Sun/Mercury/Saturn in Leo will come forward first, speak, and interact. When they're finished, the Mars/Neptune in Libra take center stage. And then the Venus in Cancer adds to the action. These are all the aspects which combine to create problems for the director. Then move into the resolution phase of the drama — the Moon sextile Mars/Neptune trine Pluto, Mercury/Saturn sextile Uranus, Mercury/Saturn trine Jupiter, Mars/Neptune sextile Pluto.

When the drama described above was actually performed, it was revealed that this woman idealized men even though she had repressed her feeling that her business executive father was too busy and self-absorbed to give her love. Her longing for a soul mate blinded her to the actual man in front of her. She confused men with her at first overbearing, then dependent and compliant behavior. Her points of constructive resolve showed that she needed to find *a balance* between her desire to rush into relationships (impulsive Fire), and the need to take the time to see through her projections. By satisfying both her dependent Cancer nature and the controlling/demanding Leo with a balanced approach, she could relieve the desperate quality of her desire for a relationship.

In your own astrodramas, as in the one we have described, the order of events may change as the drama unfolds. The 'chemistry' of the planets working together will give the performance a rhythm of its own. If an alternate sequence seems more suitable, feel free to make changes. For example, a planet may spontaneously intervene because he intuitively knows what to do or say. The facilitator or director may want to intervene, perhaps by further drawing out a particular aspect, or the director may want to assume one of the planetary roles. The trick is to have some sense of structure and to allow for the spontaneous 'dancing' of the chart while the drama is moving.

There are many ways to vary the basic routine and make a better astrodrama. If a group is doing your own chart, you might choose to passively observe your planets to learn what insights 10 other minds have to offer you, or you might talk directly with one or more. You might want to assume the role of your Venus in Taurus. What does she feel like? How does your Venus respond to your Uranus square in Leo? After a minute you might want to change roles and play out, for example, your Uranus in Leo. It's up to you, as you gain experience, to arrive at your own best results in an astrodrama. You should also be able to rely on your facilitator to help you make flexible choices. A good facilitator maintains an overview of the drama, monitoring both the director and the planets, and, where helpful, will intervene to direct the action. Facilitators should remember to trust their intuitions while respecting the director's experience. (Interventions for facilitators are covered in the Appendix — Facilitating Groups: Tips, Techniques, and Skill-building.)

## 8) Making Closure

A living horoscope can be an absorbing experience for everyone. Taking time to wind down, separate from the drama, and to find closure is essential. At this point the director is likely to be emotionally stirred, the energy of the chart is 'in the air,' and the individuals playing the planets are engaged. As a group, look for ways to bring the astrodrama to that point of psychological ease that we call closure. How can the group sum up, offer further resolution, and support the director? This may consist of a final strong affirmative speech by a key planet, a spontaneous gathering of the planets around the director with a gentle touch, a moment of silence, or a rousing cheer. Or it could be the gentle 'rocking' of the director in the group's arms, or a soft chanting of her name. Be creative in making sure that closure is not neglected.

## 9) Feedback

Feedback is the reflective stage of the astrodrama, when all can share the observations and understandings that amplify the teachings of experience. At times this can be as enlightening as the drama itself. Still fresh from the performance, participants make comments with such immediacy and directness that they have potent impact. Begin by letting the director share her feelings. What struck her most? What new insights did she learn from her chart? Did any planets hit their portrayal 'right on the head'? Then follow with any insights of interesting experiences the planets may have had: 'My instinct told me you are now having a lot of trouble with my planetary energy but you're not saying so.' Or, 'When I took out after Mercury to confront her, I got the feeling that was something you would never do, but very much want to be able to do. Is that true?' And, 'When we closed with chanting your name, tears came to my eyes. What we did with your chart really touched my heart.'

The facilitator may also make observations about the process itself: 'What I noticed was how dominant Saturn was. As soon as he let up, the chart energy began to move more harmoniously. What do you imagine might happen in your daily life if you let up on your Saturn's need to be in control?' Or, 'The drama felt lethargic and uninspired until Mars responded by gathering up those other planets and activating them to get moving. Do you observe your Mars influence after you've had a period of no action? How does it usually do it?' Another example: 'What struck me most was just how much support you do get from your Moon.' And another: 'That was a powerful piece of work. I suspect that now we're all deeply moved. Does everyone feel this way? Maybe we should take a break from the dramas and deal with what's happening now.'

I suggest that you start out with the basic form of astrodrama that we have described above. Then, as you and your group get more experienced, you might want to try some variations suggested below or invent your own.

## Suggested Variations of the Living Horoscope

### Meditative Astrodrama

If a group has already had some experience with astrodrama they may wish to try working with the meditative form. Here's how it's done. Have the group sit in a circle in the order they appear in the director's natal chart. Ask each planet to examine the director's chart, observing their contacts to the other planets. Reflect on how these contacts affect your planet. Then, if you are facilitating, ask the group to close their eyes and focus their attention on their breathing. As they breathe deeply, ask them to tune into the planet they are portraying, guide them in their imagination through space to where their planet spins in the solar system. What do they notice about their planets as they approach? Ask them to imagine that the lord of their planet has come out to meet them. What does that entity look like? What feelings or vibrations are emanating from the planet lord? Have them sit down facing the lord and note their impressions. What does the planet itself have to say? What might the planet say directly to the director? What might the other planets in aspect say to the lord of your planet? Using this as a focus for meditation, let the group spend 15 minutes to half an hour communing with the planet. Then slowly bring the group back into the room. When they're ready to open their eyes ask them to share what they learned. Insights which come from this kind of deep experience can be eerily perceptive and touch the director in exactly the right place. You might also ask the planets to get up and role play what the lord of the planet said. Or have the group enact the drama as a lord of their own planet.

### Variation — Art Astrodrama

After the group has meditated upon the chart, try an art astrodrama. Have large sheets of construction paper around the chart at the place of each planet. Ask your members to draw what they feel expresses their meditative experience. If there is a conjunction, draw both planets on the same paper. Then ask each planet to move to every other planet they have contact with by aspect in the chart and draw that relationship in some way on that planet's paper. Be sure to have enough art supplies available — Magic Markers, crayons, paints, etc. The first time I tried this art astrodrama the director happened to be an art teacher. She was thrilled with the results and pleased to take her 'astro-art' home with her.

Variation — Non-verbal Astrodrama

This is a fine way to do an astrodrama for a highly verbal, or 'airy' chart. They're always talking about their aspects, so they'll get great value from a totally non-verbal communication. You might even ask them to get up and play an important planet in their chart non-verbally.

## Astrodrama and Jung's Model of the Psyche

My own growing edge with the astrodrama process has been in finding ways to use astrodrama in relation to Jungian psychology. Since the fall of 1988 I have been working with a group in Chicago to further develop these ideas. To describe this fully would take too much space but here's an idea of the basic direction we've taken.

I am now using several different forms, based on Jung's model of the psyche. Instead of working with the circle as simply the natal chart, I'm incorporating Jung's ideas as well. One form divides the chart into three concentric circles, representing the three levels of the psyche — the conscious, personal unconscious, and collective unconscious.

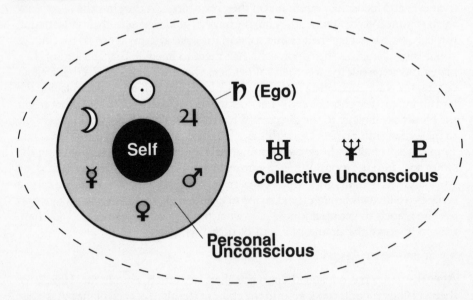

The inner circle represents the center of the Self and all of which we are consciously aware; the second circle stands for the personal unconscious and the planets — the Sun, Moon, Mercury, Venus, Mars, and Jupiter. Saturn represents the ego and acts as a bridge between the second and outer circle. The outer circle whose outer lines remain undefined represents the unlimited collective unconscious and the planetary realm of Uranus, Neptune and Pluto. We can include more of the Jungian archtypes within the collective unconscious — persona, anima, animus, and shadow — by including processes which further define how they manifest in their astrological forms. The possibilities for this new model seem endless, and the Chicago group has had some rich experiences as pioneers of this new territory.

I hope you can see from all that has gone before what the various forms of astrodrama may have to offer you. Spending just one day with your 'Living Horoscope' can inform, stimulate, and even plant the seeds of transformation. A regular investment of time and effort with the same group brings even more reward. As a group member you can activate hidden parts of your psyche, can experience the poignancy of being an intimate part of another's cosmic drama, and can move toward living out your own chart in all its richness and complexity. Why not give it a try?

# 6
# GROWING IN INTUITION

'Rabbit's clever,' said Pooh thoughtfully.
'Yes,' said Piglet, 'Rabbit's clever.'
'And he has Brain.'
'Yes,' said Piglet, 'Rabbit has Brain.'
There was a long silence.
'I suppose,' said Pooh, 'that that's why he never understands anything.'
*Winnie the Pooh.*

If you are an astrologer who tends to rely primarily upon your intellectual understanding, consider the examples of Albert Einstein, Carl Jung, and Friedrich von Kekulé.

Albert Einstein claimed he never thought in words, but in images. In his famous letter to Jacques Hadamard,[1] he describes the important role that images had in his own abstract thinking: 'The words or the language, as they are written or spoken, do not seem to play any role in my mechanism of thought. The psychical entities which seem to serve as elements in thought are certain signs and more or less clear images which can be voluntarily reproduced and combined.' Thus the man who has shown us reality at the edge of space and time arrived there by first *seeing* that reality in his mind.

Carl Jung describes a dream of being in the upper story of a strange house. The rooms were pleasant but he had an urge to look downstairs. Here the furnishings were much older, dating he thought from the Middle Ages. He moved from room to room intent upon exploring the entire house. He found a stone stairway leading into a still lower part of the house. Descending again he found an ancient, beautiful, high vaulted room. Looking carefully at the stone floor he discovered a ring attached to a slab. He pulled at it. The slab gave way, revealing another stairway at the bottom of which was a dark cave cut into the rock. Heavy dust lay on the floor and scattered bones and pottery were everywhere, like the remnants of a primitive civilization. Just before waking, Jung discovered two very old human skulls, half disintegrated. In *Memories, Dreams and Reflections*, Jung credits this dream as the origin of his theory of the structure of the psyche.[2]

Chemist Friedrich von Kekulé sat before the fire, musing about the peculiar qualities

The gathering of the waters

of the substance benzene. Dozing, he had this dream: 'The atoms were gamboling before my eyes. My mental eye could now distinguish larger structures all twining and twisting in snake-like motion. But look! One of the snakes had seized hold of its own tail, and the form whirled mockingly before my eyes. As if by a flash of lightning I awoke.' From this came the invaluable discovery of the structure of the benzene ring.[3]

By having access to their intuitive, imaginative, and symbolic processes, these creative thinkers brought forth discoveries which have had enormous impact upon us all. Most of us experience only intuitive 'flashes' or brief moments of clarity about the deeper nature of reality. If we are strongly anchored in our left brain, the rational, and analytical side, we may have little awareness or acceptance of the process of our right. Likewise, we may be spaced-out and creative, but unable to use the left brain to discriminate between wild fantasy and what might realistically be workable solutions. If we are cut off from either we are not using our full natural ability. To profit from our own deep intuition we need to cultivate this deeper way of knowing and learn to listen to its messages.

The intuitive realm may be likened to a deep underground river within Mother Earth. Its sustenance and nurturing is available to anyone who taps into it. Imagine that your contact with this realm is like a pump. To begin the flow of water you'll need to prime it daily with the use of a technique. When the water is first tapped and brought up from the depths it will be very rusty and full of sludge. But as you keep pumping the water becomes clear, the impressions true.

## Intuition: It Takes Practice

There are many useful techniques for deepening intuition. Below are a few for you to try. As astrologers we also know that there are particular times when we will be more open and have greater access to our intuitive sources. Following the techniques are a list of transits that will help you to identify those times.

As a practicing astrologer there is one daily resource you have available to help you develop intuition, your clients. Try this: before you meet a client for the first time, visualize what they look like. Find a quiet place free from distractions and put their chart in front of you. Reflecting on it, notice anything that represents their physical appearance symbolically — the ascendant (if the time is accurate), the Sun and planets in aspect, any planets near the ascendant. By free association with each of these symbols what body or face type do you imagine?

If Aries is prominent, will their face be forceful? Will their gaze be direct? If Cancer is prominent, will their face or body be fleshy, with a thick neck and gentle eyes? If Libra, will they be tall and graceful, with a refined face and poise?

See if you can imagine what mannerisms this person will have? If they have a strong Mars will they be abrupt in manner and have an aggressive handshake? If Venus is in Pisces on the ascendant will they be sensuously attractive, with a gentle handshake? Or if Scorpio is on the ascendant, will they walk in, sit down, fold their arms across their chest and in so many words say, 'prove this to me'? Being more consciously aware of what a person may look like or how they may initially act will, over time, deepen your image-making, intuitive capacity. Let your imagination go. Get a mental image of this person and compare it with the person you see when you open your door for the appointment. With a little practice you'll find that your impressions are remarkably accurate.

Try simply sitting down and meditating on a chart. Focus your attention on the central point, the 'bindu' marked by the intersection of the ascendant/descendant and MC/IC meridians. Imagine you are penetrating deeper and deeper into this point. While keeping a gentle focus on the center, become aware of the archetype on the periphery that catches your attention. Now move naturally from one image to another, from planet to planet, to sign to house. Notice how an image changes spontaneously and is influenced by the next aspect, sign, or connection you are aware of. Allow the images to come uncensored, unforced, one after the other. Periodically bring your focus back to the central point of the chart. As you continue to deeply experience this free association of symbols you may find that the chart actually begins to move, like a collage of dancing planetary images. More than one of my students have reported this phenomenon when trying this free form association.

## Left Eye Dyad

One of the most elusive skills in astrology is that of chart synthesis and interpretation. Many students tell me that they're afraid to do interpretations, that they don't know enough, or have difficulty comprehending the key themes of a chart. Chart synthesis is elusive because we have not yet developed and effectively integrated both means of perceiving the horoscope.

We know more than we think however. To demonstrate this you will need a minimum of four people. This experience works best in a group of eight to 20. Ask each person to pair up with someone in the group they don't know. Designate one A, the other B. Take a few minutes for the pair to get comfortable with knees touching, either sitting cross legged, or both in chairs. After they've taken a few deep breaths, designate A as the active communicator, and B as the passive, receptive listener. Then instruct them to look gently into each other's *left* eye. (The yogis call this eye the window to the soul.) Have them spend several minutes allowing themselves to look, breathing deeply, slowly penetrating further and further into the eye of their partner. Ask the passive partner to open up, relax, and be as receptive as possible.

Partner A, or the active communicator begins to silently ask, 'Who are you?' Images and feelings will begin to come. As this happens, A shares out loud what she is becoming aware of about the other person. (I see your face surrounded in the color purple and I wonder if this is your favorite color. You have a Greek feeling to you. You are a night owl who does her best work at four in the morning. There is some issue about money bothering you now . . .) A should feel free to say whatever comes up, without monitoring or judging. Partner B, the passive one, listens without giving feedback. After five minutes stop the experience. Partner B then gives feedback to A regarding accuracy.

Now change roles. As become passive and receptive, and Bs communicate their impressions. After five minutes give partner A a chance to give feedback to B. When 20 minutes is over, have each pair share their experiences with the group. Most will be amazed. Many of their spontaneous images and impressions are accurate! We *do* receive a constant flow of information about each other when we tune in.

I've done this exercise with many different groups and the results are always fascinating. In a recent group, one woman was astonished because she saw the subject 'in a university setting on the West Coast — a place with ivy covered walls.' In reality the woman had just come back from delivering her son to one of the East Coast 'Ivy League' schools. Another saw, 'a large low table full of books and a feeling of excitement and joy.' Her partner identified her astrology table, loaded with books, and her newly renewed enthusiasm about astrology, something she hadn't touched in 14 years. Another twosome were particularly tuned into the way each other felt, and shared descriptions of character and behavior which was true for both of them. In one dyad, an individual had a difficult time receiving any information about her partner. When questioned, the partner said she found the exercise uncomfortable and invasive. The woman who shared this then added, 'But then even my best friends say I'm hard to get to know, that I don't let people in easily.' A little further discussion revealed that this woman had six planets in the fixed signs, including a fixed Moon! In this group, as in others that have tried this exercise, nearly every pair felt success with their ability to tune in and perceive relevant intuitive information.

## Send an Object

This is a very simple exercise to employ with a small group. Ask your members to pair up with someone they don't know. Have them designate one as the sender and the other as receiver. Ask the senders to decide on a very simple object to 'send' mentally to their partner, such as the image of a lighted candle, an arrow, or a rose. Then have the couple close their eyes as the sender concentrates on projecting the chosen image from a point between her eyebrows to a point between the eyebrows of her partner. They should do this for five minutes. Then have both open their eyes and ask the receiver to share what she saw.

Here are some results from a recent group: One sender sent a teacup. The receiver didn't receive a teacup but showed her partner an elaborate doodle she had drawn an half hour earlier — it was a teacup! Another sender had immediately decided to send a red rose, until I used it as an example. She then changed her mind and sent a pencil. The receiver clearly saw a red rose.

## Remote Sending

If you have a friend who'd like to collaborate with you, you might make an agreement to practice a remote exercise together. As above, one of you will act as the 'sender,' the other the 'receiver.' For one week arrange a time that both of you are available to spend 15 minutes with this exercise. A few minutes before your daily prearranged time get comfortable, sitting or lying down. Take a few deep breaths, let the noisy inner chatter subside, and focus your attention on your practice. If you are the one who is sending, select a simple yet clearly defined object — an apple, a blue champagne glass, or a yellow chair — and send the same object all week. If you have experience with sending and receiving you may want to send a different object every day. See this object in your mind's eye as clearly as you can. Concentrate solely on your object, imagining it moving through the ether straight into the mind of your friend. Remember this formula: Intensity × Duration = Force. The Intensity of your effort times the Duration = the Force your effort will have.

As the 'receiver,' simply minimize distractions and relax, allowing your mind to be a receiving station. Let your imagination move naturally and see if a definite image comes to your attention. If an image is fuzzy, pay close attention and see if it becomes clear to you. After 10 minutes, write down every impression you felt was strong. Practice this together for one week and then compare notes. After one week switch roles — the sender becomes the receiver and vice versa. Here are some results of a group of students that did this twice during the week. One sent a white candle shining against a blue carpet. The other received a white light that turned to blue. Another sent a chalice of water. While sending he realized he was being distracted by the tick of his clock. So he pretended the chalice was dripping water one drop at a time. The receiver heard the rhythmic beating of a drum. She also got confused and sent instead of received the second night. She brought into class what she had sent. It was a water goblet!

You may discover you are far more adept at sending or that you are better at receiving. When I first did this, it was clearly easier for me to receive impressions than send them. I practiced more on concentrating and sending images and now feel equally able to do both. In effect, this is an exercise of one person's left brain sending to the other person's right brain. As you improve your ability to both send and receive you are developing greater brain hemisphere integration.

## Dream Control

Another important dimension in opening the intuitive channel is dream state awareness. If you can use techniques which strongly connect your dream and waking states, you will naturally begin to experience a flowing access to intuitive information. Of course, these techniques are most observably effective when practiced over time. Two techniques may help get you started.

The purpose of this technique is to begin to soften the division between the sleep and waking states of consciousness — the feminine, night side of existence and the masculine day side. As you gain experience with the methods you will notice that those boundaries begin to dissolve, and the content of the two states will be more available to each other.

Begin by making the transitions between sleep and waking as gradual as possible. Arrange to go to bed early. (For some this may mean changing some habitual patterns like falling into bed exhausted, or waking up with a startling alarm clock or early rising children.) If you are able to alter these patterns even temporarily you will get great rewards. Take a warm bath before going to sleep. Once in bed, shake your mind free of daily distractions, begin to breathe deeply, focusing on your breath. Be aware of any images you see before losing your consciousness. Each night try to extend your awareness as you slowly fall asleep. As you practice you push your awareness and control further and further into the dream realm. Upon waking try to consciously remember more of your dreams. Keep a dream journal beside your bed and record your dreams as soon as you become conscious. Go as directly as possible from the dream to your journal and write uncensored. By working to be more aware at both ends of your dream cycle, you will begin to extend your consciousness into the dream state.

## Looking at Your Hands

The last method is one given to Carlos Casteneda by the Yaqui Indian shaman, Don Juan. In *Journey to Ixtlan*, Carlos relates a story in which Don Juan begins to teach him how to *see*. After explaining that seeing involved a concise and pragmatic control over the general situation of the dream, Don Juan simply tells Carlos, 'Tonight in your dreams you must look at your hands.' Carlos asks Don Juan for pointers. 'There are not any pointers. Every one of us is different. What you call pointers would only be what I myself did when I was learning. It would be simpler for you just to start looking at your hands.'[4] I've followed Don Juan's instructions and with patience have had good results. Your success with any of these techniques will depend upon a disciplined effort. The more you can master any one of these, the more deeply you can gain conscious control and increase the flow of intuitive information.

# Intuition and transits

As astrologers we know there are specific times which are more conducive to accomplishing particular results. There are times we are personally more open and available to the intuitive within, and these are the times to take advantage of. Any good Moon aspects — especially the progressed Moon in the fourth, eighth, and twelfth houses and in good aspect to a natal planet — are classic in their enhancement of intuition. A good progressed Moon aspect will function from four weeks preceding to two weeks past the exact aspect, with the week before the exact transit having the greatest intensity for good results.

There are other transits which also allow you to be more receptive and open. On a long term basis, transits of Neptune trine to your natal Moon (increased sensitivity/imagination), Neptune trine natal Mercury (feelings and intellect work as a team and innate psychic abilities come forward), or Neptune trine natal Mars (concentrated effort brings results) are good. Pluto trine Moon (deep activation of the workings of the unconscious) is particularly effective if Pluto and the Moon are in Water signs. With Pluto now in Scorpio those individuals with Moon in mid-to-late degrees of Cancer or Pisces will find the next few years a golden opportunity to develop and tap into the deepest currents of intuitive wisdom. Pluto trine Mercury (single minded pursuit of the depths) is also potent, and again especially in Water signs.

To a lesser extent, Jupiter trine Uranus can be effective (sudden insights, the ability to break restrictive patterns and experience the new). On a twice yearly basis, for approximately a five day period, transiting Mercury trines your natal Neptune, Mercury trines Pluto, and Mercury trines your natal Moon and twice every two years, Mars trines your Neptune for 10 day period. You might want to work with psychic techniques during the two week period that the new moon trines your natal

Neptune, Moon, or Mercury. If a full moon, particularly in Water signs, trines your natal Neptune, Moon, or Mercury, take advantage of the one week prior to the exact full moon.

On a monthly basis, the transiting Moon trines your natal Neptune twice and transits your fourth, eighth, and twelfth houses for several days each month. If you are planning to schedule a class devoted to learning and practicing intuitive techniques, do them under any of the above transits.

If there are times conducive to developing your intuition there are also times to exercise caution in opening up the psychic floodgates. I would be particularly cautious with transiting Pluto square your natal Moon (dredging up of internal refuse, difficult psychic energies to control, possibly irrational intuitions of impending disaster) and watch as well Neptune square Moon (hunches may mislead you badly), or Neptune square Mercury (imaginary fears, fantasies, phobias). Watch the rare transits of Neptune square your Pluto (repressed compulsive fantasies, obsessions), Neptune square Uranus (new levels revealed abruptly, upsetting revelations), and more commonly Saturn square Neptune (uncertainty, fear states, negative state of mind).

With difficult Neptune transits, stay away from intentionally opening the intuitive realms. Speaking from a yogic point of view, the aura is already fuzzy, weakened and prone to being breeched by external forces. In other words, your energy is very prone to suck up everything around it like a dry sponge. The ego is possibly in a weakened state to combat negative influences. As permeable as the aura is at this time, there is greater vulnerability to strange, obsessive experiences. By all means watch drug and alcohol use during these times, especially the use of psychedelics, to force open new states of consciousness. There may be unintentional consequences.

Opening to the intuitive realm can be immensely enriching, and bring greater wholeness to life. As our culture begins to honor the feminine intuitive it will put an end to the doubt that robs our intuition of its power and will allow it its proper place in guiding our lives.

# 7
# HEALING WITH THE POWER OF IMAGES

What to others a trifle appears
Fills me with smiles or tears
For double the vision my eyes do see
And a double vision is always with me
With my inward Eye 'tis an old Man grey
With my outward a thistle across my way.

William Blake.

Imagery has been used in healing since the first shamans appeared in early tribal societies. Their ritual work had direct effect on their patients by inducing altered states of consciousness conducive to self-healing. Indeed, the entire history of Western medicine is rich with examples of image used as a healing tool. (In early medical training schools, the gift of imagination was more highly regarded than either surgery or pharmacy. Aristotle, Galen, and Hippocrates, fathers of Western medicine, used imagery for both diagnosis and therapy.[1]) A priestess of the dream incubation temples of Asclepius prescribed successful remedies for patients by listening to their dreams. Hundreds of these healing temples were established, based on the premise that vision and dreams contained seeds of knowledge about emotional, psychic and physical health. The ancient use of imagery in healing is now being rediscovered in medicine, psychotherapy and the arts. Similarly, imagery has emerged in astrology as a powerful medium for healing and teaching.

## Using Images With Clients

While holding a consultation with a female client last week, I noticed that a distinctive image kept arising in my mind during the course of the session. There were two figures in the image: one was a waifish, vulnerable-looking girl of about four; the other was a fearsome, half clad male warrior. Neither figure seemed to pay attention to the existence of the other. When I described the two individuals to my client, she saw that they precisely represented two aspects of her character that she had never before quite recognized. In retrospect it was easy to see that the images were prefigured in the chart. Her Moon in Pisces and Cancer rising were constantly threatened by four planets in Aries — Sun, Uranus, Mars, and Mercury in the tenth house. With this information, I suggested she try to find ways for the two images to communicate with each other. How might the young girl within feel more confident and empowered in the presence of the warrior? How could the warrior within acknowledge the existence of this shy little one, learn to be patient, gentle, and nurturing toward her? I also suggested that, in the next six months, she drew these figures in a series of images aimed at understanding their nature and relationship. The results are not yet in, but I expect this client to learn a great deal from the experiment.

Recently I held a consultation with a male client who had transiting Pluto in Scorpio conjunct his Sun/Mercury, and transiting Uranus in Sagittarius opposite his Saturn in Gemini, trine Jupiter in Leo. We discussed his current problem: an acknowledged love-hate relationship with his father, for whom he also worked, now manifesting as an intense tug-of-war (the Saturn-Uranus opposition) over the client's innovative ideas — ideas that his father freely ignored. The younger man struggled with this 'no win' situation, while at the same time understanding his father from a more philosophical perspective (Uranus trine Jupiter). The story, and a glance at the client's chart, called up for me the image of a porpoise swimming in a strong and turbulent current, while above a lightning storm crackled in the air. The client and I talked at length about this symbol of his inner state. On reflection he recognized that as a porpoise (Scorpio), he was in his natural element (Water) and was able to swim easily through the currents. Even though the lightning could upset him and stimulate some unpredictable 'adrenal rushes', he could dive and surface at will and would therefore prevail. He left my office much relieved.

Some of you who have examined your thought processes while working with clients will recognize that images like this have come to you, too. But you may not have yet taken the more difficult step of realizing how valuable they can be when shared with the client. When I first began consulting in 1974 and became aware of images, I refused to share them, writing them off as a distraction. The first time I took a chance and did share, both my client and I were amazed at the richness of meaning that emerged and I've made full use of these pictures in my mind ever since.

Coming to accept the use of images in my consultation had a curious affect on me. Until then I had been strongly oriented toward my rational left brain (Sun/Uranus conjunct in Gemini) and took no note of visual images. Astrology, for me, was the usual: read, think, talk, talk, talk, with only the occasional spontaneous image for spice. By 1979 I had become increasingly uneasy about my work, feeling that my approach to it had become dry, uninspired, and mechanical. Astrology was no longer fulfilling, and this was especially painful since I had so enthusiastically devoted myself to it a few years before. Now I was bored and disillusioned.

Struggling to find a reason for my apathy and frustration, I stopped doing charts for a year. Turning to other interests I entered the Facilitator Training Program of the Oasis Centre in Chicago. Learning skills in group process, encounter, *Gestalt*, and psychodrama, I spent a year in intense interaction with 12 other seekers, not in my role as an astrologer but just as a human being. I never once asked for anyone's birth date! My experience was of incalculable value. I became aware of deep feelings, sensitivities and capacities. I was able to experience and regenerate the feminine, intuitive, imaginative side of myself that, before, I hardly knew existed. And I learned much about the power of experience and of the image as opposed to the word.

As young children we are natural visual thinkers in touch with the imaginative, symbolic realms. But those abilities are soon suppressed. Albert Einstein, an admitted visual thinker, failed a primary grade. Obviously his 'failure' had more to do with the expectations of his teachers than his own inability. Speaking of right brain processes, the source of visual thinking, one writer states:

> Because we operate in such a sequential-seeming world and because the logical thought of the left hemisphere is so honored in our culture, we gradually damp out, devalue, and disregard the input of our right hemisphere. It's not that we stop using it altogether; it just becomes less and less available to us because of established patterns. [2]

Astrologers need to remember the role of the image in stimulating the right brain and should take note that at least one brain researcher has identified the right brain with some aspects of the unconscious mind described by depth psychologists. [3] A well-chosen image strengthens our work with clients. You will find it especially useful in conveying the meaning of the outer planets.

## Images For a Saturn Return

Suppose you have a client who is about to experience his Saturn return. How would you explain this process to him? You might say that it is a time of trial and major restructuring, confinement and the falling away of old patterns and relationships. But how much more descriptive would it be to begin with the metaphor of a baby chick in its shell. You say to your client, 'As the chick gets bigger, it begins to push against its shell. What once represented security is becoming confining. What was once his snug little envelope of safety is becoming a prison. As he pushes out and strains against the confinement, he breaks more free. Finally, he pecks with his little beak through the shell and begins to be aware of the space beyond his world, the greater world. He struggles through the shell, creating more and more space, until finally he merges into a whole new life.' You remind your client that, just like the baby chick's struggle with his shell, the process of transformation in our own lives is exhausting, and that after such an effort he or she will need to relax, catch a breath, and survey the surroundings before moving on. Your client can't fail to understand such a vivid image.

To further the process, pursue the client's feelings about the experience as expressed in the image. Write those feelings down on a piece of construction paper and elicit responses. Which one is most problematic now? What resources can be mobilized? What can be done to change the situation? You might even get an agreement that the client will take certain actions to improve the situation. Together you can arrive at a deeper understanding of what needs to be done.

Another image for a client with a Saturn return might be the tearing away of an old foundation and the pouring of a new one. Stress the importance of dismantling old, outworn assumptions so that your consultee can build a stronger foundation for use in the next 30 years. Just as a new foundation is still soft and malleable, so are the new patterns he is establishing. I keep a 25 pound bag of potter's clay in my office closet. Sometimes, when I'm describing this transformation, I'll hand a client a ball of soft clay which offers a palpable symbol of this stage of life. By physically handling the clay, the client has a compelling sense of the opportunity that this time of uncertainty holds.

I'll suggest a final illustration for the Saturn return. Visualize a great machine with whirring, grinding gears. The return, especially if Saturn retrogrades and repeats its pass again, places the one who has it between the cogs, caught between two giant forces, not yet free of the one wheel and faced with going through the crunch to board the other — no longer able to fit into the old life, but not yet equipped for the new. They are sure to feel 'stuck in the works' until the transition is complete.

## Images for Saturn

If someone comes to you who has a Saturn station point influencing the chart, try likening it to leaving a hot iron on a pair of good pants. Or, use the familiar kitchen metaphor to describe a retrograde transiting Saturn as the feeling of being on the back burner. As the transit goes direct and moves toward an aspect, it makes you feel like you're being put on the bigger and hotter front burner. You might also suggest that Saturn aspects may feel like the experience of rowing a boat to shore when the tide is coming out. The closer you get to shore, the more difficult it gets to row. Your oars begin to get stuck in the wet sand bottom, making it difficult to move forward. Eventually the boat gets stuck in the sand and you need to find another way to solve your problem. Getting out of your situation and trying a new approach may be what's needed.

A metaphor that I particularly like for a Saturn transit is the dual nature of the carbon element. Under usual circumstances we know it as a chunk of coal. But where it has lain under enormous pressure for thousands and thousands of years it becomes a fine diamond, harder and more valued than any other gem material. Buddhism uses this metaphor to describe the 'adamantine diamond self' arrived at after lifetimes of spiritual advancement.

An anecdote may be thought of as an image or metaphor extended, or as a short story in its shortest form. For an impatient fiery client with Saturn you might want to relate an anecdote that gives the message of patience. Tell the story of the little boy who is given a seed to plant. He goes out, digs a hole in the earth, plants it, waters it, and sits down to watch it grow. After a day with no results he goes out that night and digs up the seed. Angry and frustrated, he complains that the seed is dead and that all his effort has come to naught. It takes his wise old grandfather to explain that growth must happen in its own time. If a young child is undergoing a difficult Saturn transit, you might even make the story actual by giving a seed to plant and nurture. The child will soon learn that patience brings reward.

To be the complete astrologer build up your own catalog of appropriate stories. Pay particular attention to your own experiences under transits. Parables and traditional tales can be revealing, but there's nothing like the immediacy of a personal account. When you have a client with a similar transit, use a personal experience to explain it. This is healing, for it creates a sense of shared experience. Clients will be encouraged that someone else understands what they are now feeling, and so might have useful advice.

## Images for Uranus

Uranus evokes a very different set of images. The most obvious is the lightning bolt coming out of the blue and striking with a searing jolt. Invariably, when a client has a Uranus transit, I'll draw a series of lightning bolts surrounding a head. (Assuming we all have a number of visual thinkers coming to us as clients, you'll find it extremely useful to have a sheet of construction paper beside the chart as you do the session. Use it to 'doodle' while making a specific point, drawing the person's attention to the visual imagery of their experience. For visual thinkers this doodle may have more impact than words.)

The image of Jack and the Beanstalk is good for anyone struggling with restrictive, habitual Saturn patterns in the face of the restless urgency of Uranus transits. Jack was offered a handful of magic seeds of unknown worth for his valuable cow. By accepting the bean seeds he took a risk, moved into the unknown, and in the end received the hen who laid golden eggs. This tale can help you convey the possible rewards of taking a risk to someone who is clearly clinging to an outmoded pattern like staying in an unfulfilling job, or living too long with parents out of fear of the unfamiliar. The power of Uranus can be harnessed to create healthy new alternatives.

My favorite anecdote for Uranus is a true story. Several years ago the Ringling Brothers, Barnum and Bailey Circus came to Chicago. Channel Twenty, a local TV station, did an interview with the circus's animal trainer. The trainer arrived at the station on a Sunday afternoon for the interview accompanied by his trained bear on a leash! Well, Channel Twenty's studio is in the heart of downtown Chicago on top of a well-known office building. The trainer and the bear got into the elevator and rode up to the top floor. As the trainer was getting off the elevator, the bear got startled and reared back, breaking his leash just as the elevator doors closed! The bear, by himself, was automatically brought back down in the elevator to the lobby where people were waiting. Want to know what a Uranus transit feels like? Those who were waiting when the doors opened can tell you! And any client who hears this story will get the point.

Recall with your client what it was like to be a kid in a Hallowe'en fun house, both the chills and the thrills. You don't want to go down the hallway because you know you'll be surprised. If you only knew when, you wouldn't be so scared. Is it around this corner? No, now maybe this one. No, now, Eeeekk! Your heart pounds. Your palms sweat. Now, *that's* Uranus. Or take your client, in imagination, for a ride on a super-duper roller-coaster for the first time. They don't know where to expect the dips, quick turns, and loops. The whole first ride is like a Uranus transit. If they still haven't got the point, end your flight of fancy with a fireworks display. You never know where to look next. You wait in anticipation, and are thrilled with spectacular colorful explosions. The creativity and breakthroughs possible with Uranus transits can be as spectacular.

## Images of Neptune

The planet Neptune brings a very different kind of image to mind. When under the influence of Neptune, we never seem to quite know what's going on. It's fuzzy and confusing, like scuba diving in a murky sea. Getting excited only makes things worse, fogging your mask with panicky breath. You must feel your way along, keeping your attention on what is just before you, so as not to get lost in the craggy caves. You might continue this analogy with your client by stressing the need to keep his or her focus close at hand. Stick with day to day planning for achievable successes rather than thrashing about blindly, and taking the chance of staying lost at sea.

Try this for your consultations. Neptune is like a walk in the country as evening is approaching. As you walk on the path and climb a rise there is no mist. Your vision is clear. When the path dips down you sink into a misty fog. Descending, the fog is thicker. You have little awareness of the countryside around you. Sometimes you look down and can't see your feet let alone the path. This is what it feels like when the Neptune transit is at its peak. Then, by moving slowly, step by step, you ascend to rise above the fog into the starry night.

You might compare Neptune to wearing a pair of glasses with the wrong prescription. It's difficult to adjust your perspective and make sense of the blurry images in front of you. Or liken it to being in a corridor of many mirrors. I remember a time when I went into a woman's rest room. There were mirrors on all sides. I pushed here and there to no avail. Then I began to move my hands up and down along the cracks where the mirrors came together. First I was amused, then embarassed, disoriented and a bit panicked. Finally, another woman came out of the hidden door. I hadn't anticipated experiencing all those emotional changes just to use the bathroom.

When we drive a car down the highway and want to change lanes we look into our rear-view mirror, then check the side mirror. But we also lean forward slightly to check if anyone's driving in our blind spot. Share with your clients that Neptune is like the blind spot. To proceed safely we must always make the assumption we have one, and check it before deciding to move.

Neptune is like going to a film in a theater. We enter into a fantasy world for two hours, swept away by the march of images taking place before our eyes. We know this is fantasy but while we're in it we are so entranced that it is our reality for the moment. The comparison of a movie to a Neptune experience may help your client to perhaps pay closer attention to the balance between reality and illusion.

## Images of Pluto

Pluto, being the most long term, profound, and cathartic of planetary influences, evokes strong imagery. Clients with Pluto transits find deep identification with these images and can use them to help themselves cope with, understand, and transmute these complex and deep processes.

I keep two Pluto images close at hand in my consulting room. One is a photo of an erupting volcano from a range of 100 feet. Red molten lava spewing from the cone fills nearly the entire frame. What many clients don't initially notice is that in the lower right corner a man is standing near the rim in an asbestos suit, with goggles and hat, and with his arms flung high above his head. I have never seen the Pluto experience so accurately or poignantly captured. When clients are able to see the whole picture they spontaneously point to the man and say, 'That's me! That's exactly how I feel right now!' This realization leads easily into other feelings they are experiencing. I remind them that the source of the explosion is deep beneath the surface, several miles down. The lava has probably been suppressed for years, causing the volcano to build up explosive force. As we pursue the roots of this suppression we often locate painful experiences in early childhood.

To follow up with the same client, I might then show a second picture of a volcano, this one taken from a more distant viewpoint. The exploding center has quieted down. It is spewing slightly, still an open wound, but much less destructively. The lava is flowing out in wide slow circles, burning and transforming the earth below. We'll then continue our analogy with a discussion of the kind of change that takes place within weeks of the big explosion. The earth, revitalized by the rich lava and ash, springs to life in abundance. I may tell my client about a friend who lived near Mt. St. Helens both before and after it erupted. Afterwards, his garden produced the biggest, fastest growing, and most delicious tasting fruits and vegetables he'd ever had! The explosion brought the soil back to vibrant life.

Another favorite story tells of a man who lived in a dilapidated one room cottage. He scratched out a living by raising vegetables on the surrounding land. One day a stranger (perhaps Pluto incarnate) passed his humble dwelling. 'You are not living in a one room shack at all, but in a rich and prosperous castle,' the stranger proclaimed. Naturally, the man shook his head in disbelief. Anyone with eyes can see this is the house of a poor man. But slowly, with the stranger's guidance and much hard work, the man began to discover that there were parts of his house that he had forgotten. First he found one hidden room, then another, and another, until a huge beautiful home revealed itself. The man became the owner of a one thousand room palace, the same dwelling that he had mistaken for a hut.

The transforming power of Pluto is also taught in the trite but still useful metaphor of the caterpillar who turns into a butterfly. From the dark, enclosing cocoon, the ugly worm begins his metamorphosis, transforming into a beautiful winged creature. Clients won't fail to get the message that an individual can completely change form, transmuting dark and ugly memories, emotions, and circumstances into a life of great beauty and value.

Another useful image portrays the unconscious mind as a lightless and neglected basement. When you open the door and peer down the creaky stairs, it is dark, full of spider webs, creepy crawly things, and God forbid, *worse*! The horror of horrors lives down there! You certainly don't want to go down, but you know you must.

So you go. On the way down you may meet spiders, and get cobwebs in your hair. But, as you get your bearings and adjust your vision to the dark, you find that it's not as scary as you thought. Maybe you have to wrestle with a demon, but as you keep strengthening yourself, cleaning up the unspeakable, you come to see that the fear was hiding something — something of great value. All this time there has been a hidden treasure chest in your unexplored basement.

Describe the Pluto process as that of a lumpy carpet. The lumpy carpet metaphor is good for Libra types who are good at focusing on their ideal, while stuffing the more difficult realizations under the carpet and ignoring them. It represents all you have brushed aside, ignored and not honestly dealt with. For Libra types this is especially true of their pattern of relating. When a Pluto transit comes along, they realize they have a lumpy carpet. For the living room to be really clean they must lift up the carpet and sweep up the hidden dust.

You might use this conventional image: Pluto is the phoenix rising out of the ashes of destruction. Here you might distinguish between the four classic Plutonian symbols — the Scorpion, the Eagle, the Phoenix, and the Dove. Or describe Pluto as a two part drama — death and rebirth. Most of us are so focused on what is leaving our life, what is painful and is dying, that we can't see further. Pluto does have an Act II, the phase of rebirthing. So, remind clients how important it is not to judge their experience until they have seen the full two act drama.

I can share one image of Pluto with special conviction — that a harsh Pluto transit is like being out in a hurricane, with only two choices: allow yourself to be blown away by the great forces around you, or learn to stand against the storm. The example is special for me because it resonates with a personal experience I sometimes share with clients. In 1982 my father died quickly from cancer of the throat. During the five days it took him to die I went through every conceivable human emotion — fear, frustration, elation, confusion, deep calm, devouring rage, sadness, joy, and wonder. When I reflect on those painful days I remember that it felt precisely like an emotional hurricane. The intensity of the experience was exacerbated by the disintegration of two other important male relationships in my life on the same night my father died — one with a teacher and the other with a lover. (Transiting Saturn/Pluto in Libra in the ninth house, square my progressed Sun in the seventh.) Leading up to that night, I had also isolated myself to the extent that I had just barely enough emotional support to sustain me. Every time I felt deep pain that seemed beyond bearing, someone would come along and give me just the lift I needed to help me stand up again. This went on for weeks. It was wrenching, but in the process I learned to psychically survive. And as difficult and painful as those months were, in time I came to see the hidden treasure. It took an intensive psychic blow to expose it.

Like me, you have stories to tell, replete with images that shine through the lens of your own experience. Man is the only creature that tells stories. But men and women are the only creatures that paint pictures too and thus the communicable image defines us as human as much as does the word. Share your stories. Share your images, and your humanity.

# 8
# BALANCING YOUR DIFFICULT TRANSITS

Superstitious awe of astrology makes one an automaton, slavishly
dependent on mechanical guidance. The wise man defeats his
planets — which is to say, his past — by transferring his allegiance
from the creation to the Creator.

Swami Sri Yukteswar

Light-dark, hot-cold, active-passive, *yin-yang*, good-evil, all are examples of the
fundamental pairing of opposites into which all experience can be divided. In Hindu
thought, the Sanskrit term *Dvanda* refers to this reality, and includes the notion
that the universe itself comes into being through this division. These ideas had great
influence on Carl Jung's developing theories of mind: 'Just as all energy proceeds
from opposition, so the psyche too possesses its inner polarity, this being the
indispensable prerequisite for its aliveness . . . That an ego was possible at all appears
to spring from the fact that all opposites seek to achieve a state of balance.'[1] As
for the significance of this fact, Jung simply states: 'Nothing so promotes the growth
of consciousness as this inner confrontation of opposites.'[2] Though their sources
and methods might be quite different, both Jung and various Eastern spiritual
disciplines intend to resolve the tensions between opposites and promote a balanced
unity of consciousness.

Astrologers know that a principal source of imbalance is the endless permutation
of planets and signs described by the astrological chart. Responding to these we
can feel out of control, overwhelmed, at a loss as to how to deal with the instability
they introduce. Because our squares and oppositions — and some conjunctions
— symbolize what we have not yet mastered and integrated, they are the aspects
that will cause us the most imbalance when stimulated by a progression or transit.
For the average individual the most noticeable psychic triggers are squares, oppositions,
and conjunctions of Mars, Saturn, and Jupiter. The most profound and long term
are the transits of Uranus, Neptune, and Pluto.

This chapter will focus on practical ways to help you, or a friend or client, through
these particularly difficult learning periods. Many of the methods arise from a common
sense application of principles derived from the astrological symbolism itself; others
draw upon a particular branch of Eastern knowledge, Kriya Yoga, that includes

astrological concepts in its formulation. *All* have met the test of my own personal experience. They work!

# Kriya Yoga and Astrology

It is of course impossible to convey the depth and richness of a tradition like Kriya Yoga in a brief chapter. Evidence for yoga as a system of spiritual training extends as far back as 2000 BC.[3] 'Classical' yoga, enshrined in Patanjali's *Yoga Sutras*, is the most common form, though from 1000 BC at least 80 types are known.[4] In the narrow sense, Kriya Yoga is a system of breathing techniques that allow 'the Breath to be stilled and thereby dissolve the mind, intellect and ego in order to achieve the egoless state of pure Consciousness.'[5] More broadly, Kriya Yoga is a spiritual path that may include philosophical teachings and additional yogic practices. As Paramahansa Yogananda, who, as a disciple of Lahiri Mahasay, brought Kriya to the West, notes: 'Kriya is an ancient science. Lahiri Mahasay received it from his great guru, Babaji, who rediscovered and clarified the technique after it had been lost in the Dark Ages.'[6] The yogic techniques described below originate in Kriya Yoga as transmitted through the lineage from Yogananda to Shellyji to Goswami Kriyananda of Chicago, to many students, including myself. (*Note: For more about Kriya Yoga read Paramahansa Yogananda's *Autobiography of a Yogi* and Swami Satyeswarananda's *Lahiri Mahasay: The Father of Kriya Yoga*).

According to Yogananda, 'The *Kriya Yogi* mentally directs his life energy to revolve, upward and downward, around the six spinal centers . . . which correspond to the astral signs of the zodiac, the symbolic Cosmic Man.'[7] And, further: 'The astral system of a human being, with six (12 by polarity) inner constellations revolving around the sun of the omniscient spiritual eye is interrelated with the physical sun and the 12 zodiacal signs.'[8] These spinal centers are the *chakras*, literally 'wheel' in Sanskrit, conceived of as vortexes of energy or as force fields composed of different wavelengths, vibrational rates, or colors which, when stimulated, produce various states of consciousness.

Kriya Yoga identifies the chakras with zodiacal and planetary energies; the pattern of their arrangement corresponds to the natal chart, and they are seer *to* be affected by the planetary transits. Below is a diagram of the chakras with correlated planets and signs. Note that the planets are arrayed from the base of the spine (Saturn chakra) to the Moon and Sun centers in the head and that the lower chakras share locations, Uranus with Saturn, Neptune with Jupiter, and Pluto with Mars. (The latter is of course a revision of the ancient system — both astrology and Kriya continue to grow!) The zodiacal signs correspond to this placement by appearing in order around the spine. Keep this 'model' in mind as you consider the yogic balancing techniques below.

Distilled from my 12 years of study of Kriya Yoga (errors of interpretation are my own), these are the three basic methods of balancing astrological influences as they manifest in the chakras:

1.  We may seek to *counterbalance* them by endeavoring to activate the energies

## Kriya Yoga Chakra System

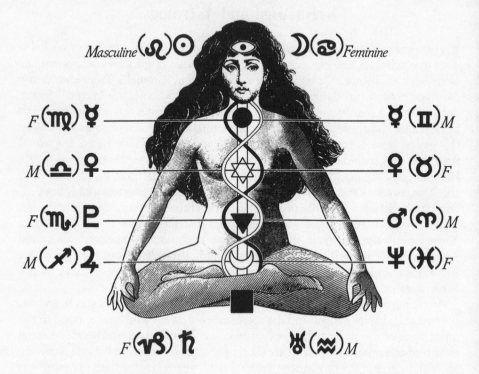

of a higher (or otherwise appropriate) chakra, directly or through use of ritual, thus counteracting the effects of lower chakra activity.

2.  We may elect to *experience* the influences. The experiencing may be largely conscious, identifying with a higher chakra and from this perspecitve *accepting* the problem as part of life — or the experiencing may reach into the unconscious mind, *intensifying* the energies of the chakra and leading to emotional release and understanding.

3.  We may choose to *transmute* the problem by using spiritual techniques to bring about fundamental change, activating the entire chakra system in a holistic solution.

## Balancing: The Techniques

Since transits of the outer planets are especially difficult and long-lasting, much of the rest of this chapter will teach techniques for their mastery. Direct counterbalancing procedures are most accessible and will be abundantly given. Counterbalancing that makes use of *ritual* follows in Chapter Nine. Experiencing methods get so much attention in Chapters Three to Five that they need only brief treatment.here. Although the transmuting techniques are in some ways the most interesting, I will often have to refer to them only tangentially, since like Yogananda, 'because of certain ancient yogic injunctions, I may not give a full explanation in a book intended for the general public.'[9]

## Counterbalancing Saturn with Jupiter

Let's begin with Saturn. Saturn in a difficult aspect tends to stimulate a state of consciousness that constricts and squeezes, creating limits to our movement and growth. This is the 'I can't' state of consciousness that sees the worst, most negative and doubtful aspects of life. Because Saturn invokes a repressive energy it can spawn a chronic state of inactivity, lethargy, and depression. In general, to counterbalance Saturn, move one chakra above to Jupiter. Live and act from the Jupiter state of being. Give yourself a gift of the Jupiter energies. Acknowledge the *good* in your life. What is harmonious, giving you reason for confidence, and satisfaction? What are your blessings? Look in the mirror and affirm the good in you, in your life.

Use the affirmation, 'Every day, in every way, I am growing better and better' as a mantra. (It worked for Anton Mesmer and his followers in the nineteenth century — why not for us now?) Write it on paper and tape it to your bathroom mirror. See it. Say it. Say it again and again during the day. Realign the mind.

Look around you to find the sources of Jupiter energy at hand. Use them. Spend time with optimistic and supportive friends. Stay away from any chronically negative ones. You don't need someone else's troubles right now. Ask yourself who around you makes you feel good? If a series of Saturn transits are approaching, start early to strengthen relationships with friends. They can help you through more difficult, lonely times.

With Saturn you may at times feel doubtful or lacking in confidence. If these feelings drag on, search your collection for Jupiterian music and play it loud until you remember how it feels to be fully self-assured. My own favorite for bringing about this mood shift is a set of rousing trumpet fanfares. Sometimes I'll plug in my 'Walkman' and soak up those brassy melodies while striding about the house or through the neighborhood. Saturn begs for a dose of Jupiterian humor. Stop taking yourself and your problem so seriously. Tell a joke. Read a funny book. Go take a humor workshop. Got out to (or rent) a hilarious movie — *Blazing Saddles*, *Radio Days*, or *Outragous Fortune* can tickle your funnybone and help you laugh those (Saturn) blues away.

Saturn cries 'Me! Me! Me!' Under its influence you are self-absorbed, even egocentric. You dwell on your problems, your failures, your disappointments: '*Mea culpa, mea maxima culpa*'. Under Jupiter you would have found it easy to be expansive, attentive to others, generous; but now is when you need it. Dispel Saturn's isolation by consciously and intentionally turning outward to do a good turn for someone else. Make an effort to serve. By extending outside yourself, you can break the intense 'Me' focus.

As promised, here is a yogic technique for counterbalancing Saturn: the 'Om

Nama Shivaya' mantra. (Pronunciation: 'O' is long, 'a' is as in 'Father', 'i' is short.) *Shiva* symbolizes the divine principle of Death that dissolves and destroys all the imbalances and negativities within. The mantra can be translated as 'Oh, auspicious Lord, to you I bow'. It is chanted repeatedly in a bubbly, brisk, joyful manner, with alternate repetitions ending with first an upward lilt, then a downward inflection. Give this mantra a try. If the several thousand year history of the chant, as well as my own experience, is any guide you will feel lifted from the Saturnian depths by its use.

## Counterbalancing Saturn With Mars

The Saturn state of consciousness is no stranger in this day of the sedentary lifestyle. At times we all have felt depressed, uninspired, and heavy. But haven't you noticed how different you feel when you've managed to lug yourself out the front door for a run or a go at roller skating? You return feeling energized, having increased your circulation and metabolism, and you're not nearly so weighed down. You feel better because you have literally broken your chronic 'woe is me' stream of consciousness and moved into Mars, mobilizing that chakra and its attendant state of being. Saturn nails you to the floor; Mars prizes you loose and pushes you out the door. So: Move! Act! Exercise! Get *physical* and Saturn will retreat. Or use the Martian energy in less direct ways: eat hot spicy foods like Indian curries, Italian and Mexican pepper dishes, Japanese wasabi mustard, hot Thai or Szechuan Chinese foods. They stimulate your system and, in terms of our yogic model, move energy from the base of your spine up to the solar plexus.

Use Mars to elicit an awareness of your courage, rather than the fear that Saturn stimulates. Music, this time Martian in tone, is a help. Who can feel fearful while dancing to Wagner's 'Ride of the Valkyries'? Just listening helps, but movement magnifies the effect.

Saturn yields to Mars, but also to Venus and beyond. But I'll leave the specifics of those approaches to your own inventiveness. Also, remember that counterbalancing may be accomplished by the use of ritual. These methods deserve special attention and are covered in Chapter Nine.

## Experiencing and Transmuting Saturn

As I have said above, experiencing, in the context of this chapter, may be largely conscious, or relatively unconscious in its focus. The first instance involves a shift of *perspective* from a lower chakra to a higher one so that the ego may act accordingly. Note, for example, Mahatma Gandhi's state of mind and his actions when, early in his struggle for racial justice, he was bodily thrown from a South African train, far from Pretoria. 'I did not know where my luggage was, nor did I dare to inquire of anybody, lest I might be insulted and assaulted once again. Sleep was out of the question. Doubt took possession of my mind. Late at night, I came to the conclusion that to run back to India would be cowardly. I must accomplish what I had undertaken. I must reach Pretoria without minding insults and even assaults. Pretoria was my goal.'[10] This 'enobling' of the problem one faces by viewing it in light of the higher good constitutes conscious experiencing. For Gandhi, this kind of test of character and self-respect would become common and thus led him to the principle of 'satyagraha . . . the force born of Truth and non-violence.'[11]

When Saturn bears down upon us we may get some relief by realizing (some might say rationalizing) that without its endless challenge there would be no incentive to character or accomplishment. So, in the midst of your next struggle, try the path of noble acceptance. Allow yourself to experience Saturn and pause to reflect upon the gift it bestows.

Both counterbalancing and experiencing as described so far rely upon the ego's exercise of will to change either the environment or one's conscious response to it. When instead we yield fully to the experience of the moment, amplifying its intensity and allowing feelings and unconscious elements to emerge, we enter a new level of experiencing. At one extreme this way of operating gives us no more than a good cry followed by acceptance; at the other, the change is so profound as to approach the 'transmuting' spiritual techniques. Here is a personal example of experiencing Saturn: When my dad was sick with what was to be his final illness, I took a few hours away from the hospital to go out with a girlfriend. We wanted to see a movie, and as we were passing a theater a parking place opened up right in front. I pulled in thinking, 'This must be fate.' The film turned out to be 'Sophie's Choice,' laden with a full portion of Saturn's death and despair. My friend and I both cried throughout the film. But coming out of the theater afterwards I felt so much relief. I had moved into the pain that I had been avoiding, had spent a few miserable hours being in its grasp, and had cried it out. If you do this, be sure to bring along a good friend!

You have already encountered experiencing techniques in earlier chapters, so they won't be repeated. Refer back, especially to Chapters Three, Four, and Five, as well as to the Workbook section on Saturn/Capricorn. Saturn aspects may provoke you to seek out a guide for experiencing in depth, especially when we bear in mind that Saturn may stimulate unresolved issues with our father or other past authority figures. Psychotherapy or an intensive group experience may be in order. But such drastic measures are not always required. Other ways to manage Saturn while experiencing it are just to 'burn it off' by working extra hard, or by using its evocation of structure to provoke you to get things in order. There is much that can be accomplished under a difficult Saturn, though you won't find it easy or fast work. Be patient and keep on striving. The reward will come later.

## Counterbalancing Uranus with Saturn

Saturn brings order, Uranus dwells in chaos. Saturn enjoys structure, Uranus delights in formlessness. Saturn is the patron of constraint, control, and oppression. Uranus is the high priest of impulse, unpredictability, and therefore the possibility of freedom. Polar opposites, these two are inextricably linked, and they are so represented in the chakra model at the base level. When in balance in the human soul they are like a harmonious chord that underlies the melodic flow of life. When out of balance on the one side they impose the morbid tones of the funeral dirge, and on the other, a mad cacophony. Applying each to the other, we can achieve that harmony. Let's first concentrate on counterbalancing Uranus with Saturn.

When under the influence of a Uranus transit, make a conscious effort to introduce Saturn's self control. Take your time when considering a radical action. Impulsive decisions can tear apart life structures so proceed carefully, methodically. Don't ignore the old saw: Count to 10 — or 10,000 — before making a rash move. And stay grounded. Use any of the grounding techniques suggested below for countering Neptune. By 'earthing' yourself you will anchor more of the erratic, frenetic, scattered energy, giving yourself more control and peace of mind. Also make this a time to create order around you. Spring or not, consider spring cleaning your home. Reorganize your office or work space. As you see order in your outer world it helps you to restore order in your inner one.

Without Uranus there is no impulse to change. Without Saturn change leads to disintegration rather than growth. With too much Saturn, too long applied, change can be explosive. The balanced use of Saturn with Uranus implies *planning*. Look ahead to your Uranus transits and plan how to incorporate their influence before they hit. Methodically compile a list of what has begun to feel restrictive. These are the areas in which to establish goals for change in structure and routine, bringing in fresh action and direction. Your Uranian friends won't be a help in this process. Prefer instead your more Saturnian, calming and responsible friends rather than the frenetic, unpredictable ones who will only distract you from your task. Plan now, party later.

## Counterbalancing Uranus: Other Ways

Planning for Uranus may also include laying out a plan for counterbalancing by evoking the other chakras or by experiencing or transmuting approaches. For example, to prevent the build up of the pressure, choose, before the main thrust of the transit, to activate Mars by beginning an exercise program. But guard against extremes since Uranus can backfire and cause injury through accident.

In another manifestation of its character, Uranus can cause feelings of alienation. Because the inner level has a lightning storm going on, unanticipated and disconcerting feelings and quick changes of mood can separate us from those whose lives seem to be going on as usual. The antidote? Place yourself in the consciousness of the Jupiter chakra. Join a group, workshop, or networking organization that is oriented toward self-help, growth and change in order to give yourself more regular contact with others. Or put out a call to friends and family you've lost touch with.

Some ideas are especially compatible with Uranus. Use the auspices of the Mercury chakra to pursue activities with Uranian content. Learn specific new techniques and skills, for instance, computer programming. Or tackle a complex astrology idea now. Investigate systems new to you such as Harmonic or Uranian astrology.

## Experiencing and Transmuting Uranus

There is a place, of course, for allowing Uranus to spring forth in full measure in one's life and actions. Here's a bit of strange but useful advice which can be attributed, I think, to singer Willie Nelson: 'You've gotta get crazy to be sane.' Chaotic dancing (arms and legs akimbo, with no apparent plan or pattern) to oddly rhythmed or discordant music (some jazz and rock, most punk and New Wave) is an outlet for that hyped up Uranian feeling. A 'chaotic meditation' has been taught by Rajneesh and his followers; music for this practice, which may be one component in a transmuting approach, is available. ('Music of Shree Rajneesh Ashram', Lucern Valley, California, Geetam Rajneesh Sannyas Ashram, 1979.) If you are involved in a spiritual program which includes meditation as a tool for personal transformation, you may already have noticed that meditation during a Uranus transit can be disrupted, but persistence brings reward.

## Counterbalancing Neptune

Saturn makes reality known and certain. Uranus strips away the comforting illusion of predictability. Neptune calls reality itself into question, offering the disturbing suggestion that reality itself is an illusion. Neptune has a major impact at the level of perception. Under an unfavorable Neptune clarity is banished, and we are left with a kind of 'fuzzy discernment' that makes it nearly impossible to distinguish what is relevant from what is merely fascinating. To be sure, Neptune leads us on, but too often into dark pathways and blind alleys. Like Jupiter, with whom it is paired in the chakra system, Neptune expands consciousness, but whereas in Jupiter the expansion leads to integration into a larger whole, in Neptune the expansion is without boundaries and ends in dissolution.

We would not want to do without Neptune's gift of lofty dreams and ideals, but to keep the dream from becoming a delusion we must keep our footing in ordinary reality. Let Mercury advise. Think: Is this idea realistic? Or am I kidding myself? Am I seeing the truth, or am I seduced by a grand illusion? With Neptune about, don't rely on just your own counsel. Reason out matters with a clear thinking friend. Your major decisions at this time are particularly vulnerable to confusion. Postpone them if possible, or make short term contracts rather than long ones, and build in an escape clause. That way, when clarity returns, you still have options.

Neptune in difficult aspect to Venus or Mars can be particularly troublesome for your love life, since you are prone to overidealization, seeing a soul mate in any rascal who comes along. Let any new relationship that comes into your life now prove itself before you rent the hall and order the flowers. Assume there is something you are not seeing.

With Neptune, planning ahead is especially difficult. It is as if you are driving along on a dark, lonely road, the way ahead hidden by dense fog. To get through you must keep your eyes fixed on that white line and follow it home. To counter Neptune you must attend to matters close at hand. Focus on keeping your day to day routines. Take one day at a time. Set little goals you can accomplish and feel good about, thus using Saturn to best advantage.

Note that the Lotus Position of the meditator in our chakra diagram places her on a firm base, solidly connected to the earth. Contact with the earth, grounding, is especially important for counterbalancing the effects of Neptune. Here is a list of simple ways to get grounded:

1. Stand and walk barefoot on the earth.
2. Take a shower (especially good after working with someone else's disturbed psychic energy).
3. Eat grounding foods — particularly red meats and grains.
4. Stay away from all drugs and spacey, confused people.
5. While standing barefoot on the earth, imagine that you are a tree trunk with roots deep in the earth. Imagine the roots expanding in thick, strong shoots deeper and deeper. Allow whatever makes you confused and unfocused to enter the roots, flowing down deep to where it is absorbed by the earth.
6. Spend time with your earthy friends.
7. If you have outdoor space, planting and caring for a garden is an excellent ongoing means for grounding. If you live in the city, tend to the plants in your apartment.
8. Take regular breaks and go away to the country. Contemplate the earth — look at it, walk on it, lie on it.

## Experiencing and Transmuting Neptune

If you've attended to practical matters and set aside time for Neptune, just floating along with its dreamy meanderings can be a delight. I remember a Neptunian day when my husband and I sat from dawn to deep starry night just watching a day go by in a high mountain meadow. Daydreams had equal footing with the natural beauty around us and yielded a 'Rocky Mountain high' to remember. When you know a Neptune effect is coming, look for ways to experience its positive qualities. Revive your neglected practice of meditation. Make a special effort to recover dreams. Allow yourself to escape in a positive sense through inspirational reading — Lama Govinda's documentation of his trip to Tibet, The Way of the White Clouds,[12] or Peter Matthiessen's The Snow Leopard,[13] or John G. Neihardt's Black Elk Speaks[14] would be good choices.

Issues that arise in the deeply afflicted Neptune aspects may yield only to transmuting approaches. I am never surprised to find alcoholism or drug abuse, gambling, food abuse, or relationship addiction in charts with hard Neptune aspects. 'Don't do drugs' is good advice, but an injunction is seldom enough to even faze an addiction, once begun. For alcoholism and other addictions, only one approach has brought recovery to millions: Alcoholics Anonymous and its affiliated 'Twelve Step' program. This must be so because AA is a complete spiritual program, aimed not at alleviating symptoms but at transmuting the energy that provides the impulse to indulge, transforming the life of the sufferer at physical, mental, emotional, and spiritual levels. Eastern spiritual systems are not a substitute for AA — if that is what you need, then by all means go there — but they do offer various means of self-transformation that offer freedom from attachment, compulsion, and suffering. In Kriya Yoga, for example, there are meditations that carry the breath from chakra to chakra, integrating their energies and discharging the burden of karma. Their goal is complete liberation and absolute knowledge beyond the reach of any Neptunian illusion.

## Counterbalancing Pluto

Form, dispersion, chaos, re-formation: all substance, all energy, all being, cycle in the endless chain of Death and Rebirth. And the hand of Pluto guides every turn of the wheel. Every ego is born and will die, only to be born again, even within the boundaries of a single lifetime. Drawing on countless experiences with patients, pioneer in LSD psychotherapy Stanislav Grof describes the quintessential Pluto experience:

> Paradoxically, while only a small step from an experience of phenomenal liberation, the individual has a feeling of impending catastrophe of enormous proportions. This frequently results in a desperate and determined struggle to stop the process . . . the transition . . . involves a sense of annihilation on all levels — physical destruction, emotional disaster, intellectual and philosophical defeat, ultimate moral failure, and absolute damnation of transcendental proportions. This experience of ego death seems to entail an instant merciless destruction of all previous reference points in the life of the individual.[15]

Mercifully, every Pluto transit does not plunge us into these depths — but the potential is always there. Even at lesser intensity, Pluto stirs deep emotion. It uncovers all you have hidden, secreted away in your unconscious, and demands that you come to terms with your inner nature. Pluto is worthy of respect, even fear, but remember that like Kali, the Hindu goddess of destruction, Pluto destroys only to recreate. Essential to managing the difficult Pluto aspect is that you acknowledge your need for fundamental change, thus counterbalancing techniques are not the ultimate answer, but since in Pluto's grasp we are likely to petition for any form of relief I should at least offer what has proved of some use.

The Saturnian grounding techniques offered above for Neptune seem to help drain away Pluto's excess energy. Try them. Since our physiological system is stirred and heated to excess with Pluto, also try to enlist Saturn by eating cooling foods. Stay away from heavy meats and spices that stimulate the Mars/Pluto chakra. And consider fasting; settling your digestive system may bring some relief from the turmoil.

When Pluto visits we are seldom easy company for others. Our feelings are so deep and so intense that we have much trouble conveying them, and we are as likely to lash out as to plead for understanding. So, just when we are most in need of support, we seem least likely to get it. This is the time to draw upon that source of love within. Stimulate your Venus chakra. By intensely focusing on love, gentleness, and compassion for yourself and others you can rob Pluto of some of its force. Love yourself. Find ways to be good to yourself and give yourself pleasure. Eat a favorite dish; if there's a hot tub around, lounge in it. If you are lonely, get on the phone to those you love and tell them that you care — love is the gift that always returns to the giver. Honor your need for warmth and touch — wrap up in a blanket or your old fur coat and sit by the fire, or get a weekly massage from someone with a loving nature.

Self-love often requires forgiveness of yourself and others. Yoga offers a 'Forgiveness Mantra' that I have often used to lighten Pluto's load: 'Hai Ram, Jai Ram, Jai, Jai Ram.' (Hai as in 'hay', Jai as in 'sky'; the 'a' in Ram is like 'Father'.) When Gandhi was assassinated these were the last words he spoke. In essence he was saying, 'I forgive this act.' For your own self-forgiveness or to forgive others, chant the mantra in a steady monotone, allowing the sound to entrance you. Continue the chant for an hour or more if needed; your feelings will guide the decision. On especially intense days, you may silently continue the chant throughout the day, continuously releasing anger and frustration and opening up to the peace and love of Venus. I've found no better tool for counterbalancing Pluto.

## Experiencing and Transmuting Pluto

Pluto penetrates into every level of mind, shifting and breaking up calcified layers of consciousness. Thus Pluto aspects signal optimum times for efforts at self-transformation. You will benefit especially from metaphysical study or spiritual practice such as Yoga, tantra, self-hypnosis, meditation, past-life regression, and from psychological work such as Jungian dream analysis, psychodrama, Reichian release bodywork or Bioenergetics, rolfing or other mind-body therapy. With a qualified guide you might try this simple but powerful method.

Sit comfortably; turn your attention inward. Begin to breathe deeply and with each breath repeat to yourself, 'I'm afraid' (or 'angry', if this is a better match for your mood). As you continue to breathe and repeat the phrase you are likely to notice the emergence of feelings, perhaps associated with images or memories from the past. Don't censor these but allow them to come to some expression: curl into a ball, strike a pillow, or cry. Fair warning! Don't try this on your own unless you are very sure of your ability to tolerate strong feeling.

Methods that give an external form to the emerging Pluto archetype may also be of use. You may, for example, wish to make a mask of your 'dark side.' Try to find a way to represent each of your inner demons on the mask, then place it on your altar with flowers and candles and meditate upon it. (See chapter nine for a more complete description of such a ritual.) Honor the power of the dark side within you. It will be interesting to discover how you perceive the mask and respond to its symbolism. For some, just seeing the inner life in concrete form helps to bring a sense of control. Pluto can then become more personal and less threatening.

When Pluto fires in your chart your desires push you strongly and you are likely to overwhelm yourself with far too much activity. This suggests three solutions: Simplify. Simplify. Simplify. Let the back-to-basics influence of Saturn lead you to a more manageable course of action. Set aside some of the complicated issues and focus only on the most pressing ones. Keep your attention on the task at hand and you will engender more accomplishment and less struggle. If you find that you can't even recall the benefits of simplicity, take a lesson from Winnie the Pooh.[16] Once when a particularly nasty Pluto transit had me in a spin, my husband bought me the complete set of books about the charming Teddy Bear. Affectionately, Bob inscribed the books as 'Something to complete your eduction.' And that they did! Pooh counters the comic complications of his life with Rabbit and Tigger, Kanga and Roo, with such simplicity and wonder that I could not help but see how to apply that to my own life as well. Take an afternoon off from your next Plutonian episode, and read *Winnie the Pooh*. You too can learn to be a 'Bear of little Brain.'

# 9
# CREATING PERSONAL RITUAL
# WITH YOUR HOROSCOPE

> The greatest need of man is to fulfill the patterns of his being
> symbolically. If he does not, disaster follows.
> Shellyji, direct disciple of Yogananda, Kriya Yoga lineage

Among native Americans, the Skidi band of the Pawnee Indians were most attuned
to the movements and meanings of the heavenly bodies.[1] In 1904 Pawnee Chief
Letakots-Lesa made this statement:

> In the beginning of all things, wisdom and knowledge were with the animals; for
> Tirawa, the One Above, did not speak directly to man. He sent certain animals to
> tell men that he showed himself through the beasts, and that from them, and from
> the stars and the sun and the moon, men should learn . . . When a man sought
> to know how he should live, he went into solitude and cried until in vision some
> animal brought wisdom to him. It was Tirawa, in truth who sent his message through
> the animal.[2]

The vision seeker's actions in going off alone and engaging in a series of steps to
attain a goal, in this case wisdom, constitute a ritual. And since it is a personal,
individual pursuit and ultimately calls upon the heavens for inspiration, the Pawnee
practice is close in spirit to the *personal astrological rituals* talked about in this chapter.
You have a choice to make regarding how you want to understand the goals and
effects of these rituals. For some the transformations involved are *psychological*, as
they were for Jung (though no less profound for that); for others *magical*, involving
real forces beyond nature.

Throughout Western history ritual and astrology were intimately connected. The
Babylonians had an intricate system of ritualized worship of the planetary deities.[3]
Much later, the rites of the oriental mystery religions were replete with astrological
symbolism[4] and, largely through texts like the *Corpus Hermeticum*, the blend of
astrology and magic was passed on to regain new vigor during the Renaissance.[5]
One particular flowering of astrological magic was in Renaissance developments
of the classical 'art of memory.' As long ago as Metrodorus (first century BC), the
elaborate memory schemes that functioned as an aid to rhetoric were based upon
astrological symbolism.[6] In the Renaissance, memory systems became increasingly

magical in theme with the construction in 1532 of Giulio Camillo's 'memory theater.'[7] This remarkable structure, never fully realized, held paintings and sculpted figures reflective of occult philosophy and designed to evoke the entire span of creation.

This line of development, the magical art of memory, culminated in Giordano Bruno's efforts in the 1580s to bring all of astrologically symbolized occult wisdom into one great system. As Frances Yates relates: 'the images of decans of the zodiac, the images of the planets, the images of the moon-stations would form and reform in ever-changing combinations, in connection with the images of the houses. Did he intend there would be formed in the memory using these ever-changing combinations of astral images some kind of alchemy of the imagination, a philosopher's stone in the psyche through which every possible arrangement of objects in the lower world — plants, animals, stones — would be perceived and remembered?'[8] (Note: for more information about the remarkable Renaissance memory art based on the Zodiac, read Frances Yates, *The Art of Memory*.)

Alchemy and astrology were 'allied arts' in the Renaissance era. Forerunners to modern chemistry, alchemists were involved in an effort to change lead into gold. In reality their practices were much more directed toward an inner spiritual process in which the dense and grosser states of consciousness were transformed into the higher, more subtle and sublime spiritual states. The alchemists were pursuing what is in essence 'the art of changing consciousness at will'. Note that from the yogic standpoint described in Chapter Eight, turning 'lead into gold' means transmuting Saturn (lead) energy into pure solar (gold) consciousness. This principle guides the astrological rituals suggested below.

Ritual magic, alchemy, and astrology rests on one principle: that man is the microcosm of the universe at large. Thus, to Bruno, 'man is the "great miracle" . . .' whose mind 'is divine, of like nature with the star governors of the universe.'[9] Commonly expressed as 'As above, So below', and endorsed by most astrologers, this statement reflects the understanding that behind all external phenomena lies a totality — one interconnected, interdependent whole which is sensitive and responsive to the movement of its parts. We recognize that the world is a symbol whose ordering is meaningful only as it represents a deeper, more profound aspect of our consciousness. The visual universe is, to some extent at least, a projection of the human psyche that is perceiving it. We can know the forces within and they can be called forth.

## Creating Your Own Rituals

For the astrologer the cosmos is related to the individual through the vehicle of the horoscope. Ritual magic for the astrologer requires the cultivation of that natural relationship, with recognition that the horoscope provides a symbol structure that gives information *from* the cosmos, but also allows action *upon* that larger world. Personal astrological rituals may point in either direction, toward transformation of the inner life through use of astrological symbols or toward bringing about some result in the outer world with guidance from the horoscope. These rituals require sincerity, careful preparation, focused concentration upon the proper acts and symbols, and the choice of the astrologically auspicious moment. My own experience has confirmed that, properly used, they can 'make things happen.' What I share here is drawn from my yoga training, from further study of magic and astrology, and especially from what I have found to be effective in my own life.

The principal purpose of ritual in connection with the astrological chart is to strengthen the effects of positive transits or to soften, neutralize, or eradicate the influences of difficult ones. For example, use ritual during a transit of Saturn trine your Moon to strengthen the Moon qualities — enhancing ties with your family, mother, women friends, or to amplify and support the feminine within yourself. Or use ritual to soften, neutralize, or eradicate less favorable aspects; for instance, to counteract a difficult Mars focus on Venus, or to contend with a trying Saturn transit direct your attention to Jupiter.

First identify likely times during the year that rituals will have best effect. I make it a practice each New Year's Eve to sit down with my chart and ephemeris to search for likely ritual periods. Caution: if Pluto, Uranus, and Neptune together are making hard transits to your horoscope, or particularly if the ruler of the eighth and ninth houses are afflicted by transit, postpone your exploration. These are energies that might give even a master magician difficulties. Assuming you're clear of those hard outer transits, look for times when the progressed Moon is transiting your fourth, eighth, twelfth houses, in good relationship to other planets; when transiting Jupiter is trine Uranus with good aspects to the eighth and ninth house rulers, or, generally when you have good transits of Saturn and Jupiter to your natal chart.

Be alert for times when several good aspects are active at once, such as transiting Jupiter conjunct Mars in Taurus, and transiting Saturn/Uranus in Capricorn trine Mars, the combination of which would be a good time to do a ritual concerning Mars and Mars issues in your life. Write down the dates for each transit. Begin to narrow your choices by checking the position of the new/full moon cycle around those dates. Is the new or full moon in good aspect to your planets, especially the planet that is the object of your ritual? Good daily Moon transits to these positions will further define the best time. With a little interpolation of the moon's daily movement you can determine the exact time your ritual will have its strongest effect.

In yogic tradition the most propitious seasons for ritual are spring and summer when the correct 'Tattvic tides' (in Hindu systems, the forces that make our universe) are believed to be flowing.[10] Lunar cycles are also important, with the waxing moon generally more favorable. Eclipses are most unpredictable in effects, sometimes supporting, sometimes interfering with intentions.

The new moon is auspicious for mental healing when in an Air sign, for practical, physical matters when in Earth signs, for emotional healing in Water signs, and for spiritual, philosophic intent when in Fire. Another way to express this is that there are four different kinds of magic — Fire, Air, Earth and Water magic. You may want to take account of this fact in your rituals, considering the prevalence of each element in your natal chart. If you have predominant Earth you might be more attuned to doing more earthy, practical rituals, or if you lack Fire you might do more Fire rituals to compensate, and bring Fire more consciously into your life.

In getting started, first try strengthening the effect of a positive transit, and then as you get experience focus on a difficult transit that also has a positive transit countering it, for example, if you have a Jupiter conjuncting your natal Moon, or if you have the transiting Saturn opposed your Sun while Jupiter makes a sextile.

## Personal Ritual Illustrated

Consider this. You are looking through your ephemeris and have noticed the new moon in August. At that time you have transiting Saturn (in Sagittarius) in the twelfth opposing your Sun (in Gemini) in the sixth, while Jupiter (Aries) in the third is making a sextile to it. The new moon in Leo makes a trine to both the transiting Saturn and Jupiter, as well as making a sextile to your Sun. This exact new moon is a good ritual time for the purpose of concentrating upon the Jupiter sextile, to call forth its forces to balance and help neutralize the strong Saturn opposition. Your aim is to link the Jupiter within you to that of the cosmic Jupiter, setting up a 'current' you can draw upon. The current needs a suitable conductor through which to flow. An effective conductor is the ritual, when it is complete in every detail. Now that you know your intention and the time and place, you'll want to create and plan your ritual.

The psychological benefits of ritual arise from the fact that everything involved in it has been carefully chosen and includes objects and actions that have rich associations for you with the symbolic meanings of the ceremony. Form, sound, smell, and color are brought together to engage and appeal to the subconscious. So one chooses carefully the appropriate image, color, incense, perfume, herbs, chants, talismans, cabalistic symbols, candle, or music. By 'carefully,' I mean, for example, that there are what we might call active and passive incenses. You cannot make an atmosphere for Jupiter by using an incense that evokes Saturn or a ritual for Fire by using an incense that is for Water. To know what incense or other ritual element is appropriate to use, you may wish to consult a Table of Planetary Correspondences in any good occult text.

Once you know what associations you want to gather for your ritual, begin to plan the actions you will carry out in the ritual, allowing each step to flow smoothly into the next so that you can progressively deepen your concentration and meditative state. Keep your ritual as simple as you can — it can be as spare as lighting a blue candle and chanting a Jupiter mantra. It is not the elaborate ritual that ensures success, but the strength of your concentration and the correctness of your attitude.

With these preliminaries completed, you are ready to commence the ritual proper (though tradition dictates that the ritual actually begins the moment that the intention to perform it is born). Begin to define the time and space as sacred. Disconnect phones and let others know not to disturb you. Bathe and dress in some way that complements your purpose, and prepare the surface. First, clear away furniture to give you a large free area. Orient yourself to the position of the earth (use a compass if necessary) by locating the four cardinal points and marking them on the floor with an appropriate symbol: in the East, and the symbolic point of Aries, place an appropriate symbol of fire (a candle is the obvious choice); at the point of Capricon, the MC, place a symbol of the earth (a rock or pot of soil); in the West at the point of Libra, you might place a bird feather, and at the point of Cancer, a bowl of consecrated water.

Next lay out a circle around the four cardinal positions with a heavy cotton string, marking the boundaries of your relationship to the earth's position and your sacred circle. Now orient yourself to where your planets appear by *house position* in your personal horoscope. In other words, if you have your natal Sun in Taurus in your tenth, imagine it at the MC of this circle. Or your Venus in Gemini is in your seventh, see your Venus near the West, and descending point. For this particular example, in which you are doing a Jupiter ritual, set up an altar at the location of your transiting Jupiter (in this case, in your third house) on the outer perimeter. The altar will allow a focus for your attention. Assemble upon it all the associative symbols you are using.

One hour before the exact new moon you begin your ritual. Here is what you might do:

First sit in the center of your horoscope facing your MC, become aware of the four directions, and acknowledge the presence of each element. Then turn and face your third house, the position in your horoscope of the transiting Jupiter in Aries and your Jupiter altar.

You have covered your Jupiter altar with a blue satin cloth and have placed upon it the items you associate with Jupiter — a photograph of the Greek god Zeus, a blue candle, sandalwood incense, an amethyst, a scrap of tin, your Jupiter imageboard complete with a soaring eagle, mountains, wide open spaces, a Sagittarian arrow, an advertisement for a trekking trip to Nepal, a big happy roly poly person, people smiling, people happy, a yogi in meditative bliss, the written words, 'abundance', 'confidence', 'ease', and 'flow'.

At the center of the altar is a mask, painted blue with gold and silver moons and stars upon it. This is the mask you made months ago to help you embody the Jupiter force within. You have used it periodically to penetrate more deeply into the meaning and force of Jupiter.

You begin your ritual by resting your gaze upon every object of your altar, all symbols of Jupiter. Reflecting on their symbolic nature you say a thankful prayer for the blessings they signify. You write down the names of people and things in your life that you count as your blessings. You turn on joyful music by Beethoven, first swaying to and fro, then rising to dance within the circle of your horoscope, turning in full, sweeping movements. You focus on stretching out the tightness in your body you have noticed since Saturn has opposed your Sun. Invigorate yourself with the feeling of Jupiter.

Sit down facing your Jupiter altar to move into the deepest part of the ritual. You light your blue candle and the sandalwood incense and refocus your attention. It is through intense concentration and imagery that the contact is made with the archetype. You concentrate by closing your eyes and seeing the image of Zeus in front of you. The image of Zeus may be harder for you to imagine in your mind's eye. If you have difficulty, concentrate on a simpler image — that of the symbol of Jupiter, colored a deep blue and emblazoned upon your Sun center (the point between your eyebrows). With your eyes closed trace the blue lines over and over again. Now include your breath in your awareness. With every inhalation you take in the healing, soothing, cool blue of Jupiter into your lungs. With every breath you move more deeply into Jupiter's realm. You use your receptivity to reach out and absorb the positive aspect of the archetype. You draw in its strength. You keep using your mind like a laser to etch the symbol of Jupiter into your consciousness. And now as you near the exact moment of the new moon in Leo, you are using the integrative power of this moment — calling upon your Jupiter to help you to feel abundance in the face of scarcity, to feel confidence in the midst of self-doubt, to feel a flow of ease in the face of struggle, resistance, and obstacles. You ask that Jupiter merge into you, through you, and counter the forces of the Saturn opposition.

Your ritual is over. Its effectiveness can be in part measured by how you feel now. Do you feel flooded with feelings of well being, joy, peace? Is the feeling still there after an hour, a day, a week? Remembering that ideas seeded near the new moon often come to fruition at the next full moon, note the tone and character of events in the next two weeks. Sometimes the effect of your ritual may seem to have no results. Experience will teach you that all ritual works, though it may not work immediately or in the way you might have imagined.

## Choosing a Ritual Time: An Example

If you still have some question about how to choose a ritual time, here is one more example for you to study. This is the chart of one of my clients who has been actively using ritual. (See diagram overleaf.)

Sandi is a career woman, divorced, and living on her own. Her goal for 1988 was 'to be happily married by the end of the year.' What is immediately apparent in Sandi's chart are the transits of Pluto and Neptune in positive aspect to her natal Venus. Her feeling of wanting to be married came on during the first pass of Pluto sextile her Venus.

At this writing in early 1988, there are two rather obvious two week time periods for a ritual concerning Venus/Sun/Jupiter issues: from the new moon on April 16, 1988, to the full moon May 1 and from the new moon on October 10, 1988, to the full moon October 25. Let's look at Sandi's transits at those times: the new moon in late Aries conjuncts her seventh house opposite her first house Sun in Libra and trines her natal Jupiter; the full moon conjuncts transiting Pluto sextile her Venus; Pluto (retrograde) sextiles Venus; transiting Jupiter trines her Venus on April 28; transiting Venus trines her Neptune on the 17th and her Sun on the full moon, and within orb of the opposition to her Natal Jupiter that same day.

In the October moon cycle these are Sandi's transits (the moon cycle here is exactly opposite the April cycle described above). Here the new moon in Libra conjuncts her ascendant and Sun sextile Jupiter, sextile Pluto in Leo; Pluto makes the last pass to sextile Venus exact on the 8th; Jupiter (retrograde) sextiles Moon on the

## Rebecca's Chart

Oklahoma City   Oklahoma
35N30          97W30
NOV 16 1950    16:40:00 GMT
Tropical  Koch    True Node

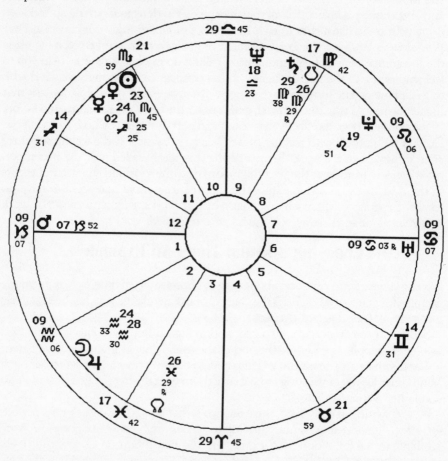

14th; Venus conjuncts Venus on the 13th; her birthday is the 16th. Any of these specific times during the two week period would offer opportunities to work with empowering Venus. I'll leave it to you to find the times in the two week period that the transiting Moon stimulates her Venus/Sun or Jupiter. These too would be good times for ritual.

For a Venus ritual, these symbols are common: colors green or pink, rose quartz, jade, emerald, copper, pink or green candles, robe, and altar cloth, red sandalwood, rose perfume, pink roses, Venus imageboard, and as images perhaps Aphrodite or the Tarot card, Venus. You might wish to pause and reflect on how you would construct a ritual given Sandi's intention and astrological chart.

## Postcript: Sandi and the Results of Ritual

Sandi began regular practice at a Venus ritual in early 1988. In April of that year she was shocked to find out that she was pregnant. An agonizing period of appraisal followed. She and the man with whom she conceived were not suited to marriage or parenthood, and to have the child out of wedlock seemed, finally, to be out of the question. Sandi made the difficult decision to end the pregnancy. Beyond the grief of the event, Sandi came to a new realization: for the first time in her life she had truly put her own needs before others. Thus she came to a new appreciation of her worth, and a deep sense of self-love.

In May of 1988, a man with whom Sandi had been working approached her, at last revealing that he had been in love with her since January! Now, four months later, he and Sandi are very much in love and have talked of marriage. Sandi speaks with wonder about the deep emotional and spiritual connection between them.

Are these the results of ritual? No one can say for sure. You be your own judge.

# Final Note

The mind, magic, the universe without and within — all are vast and beyond our ultimate comprehension. Personal astrological ritual can open a small window upon these realms. Clearly we should not undertake to do so without due care. My suggestion to you is that you enter into ritual slowly at first to get the feel of your internal landscape. Be aware and do only what *feels right*. If a practice or technique disturbs rather than soothes or enlightens, drop it and try something else. The most important function of an astrological ritual is the creation of meaning. If what you do makes meaning, it cannot fail to be positive.

# BOOK II

# RESOURCE WORKBOOK

# RESOURCE WORKBOOK

## Introduction

Succinctly, astrology answers these questions:

'WHO am I?' — The planets — The energies, powers and psychic force fields within.

'HOW am I?' — The signs — The way in which these energies process and express themselves.

'WHERE do these energies manifest?' — The houses — The arenas of life in which these energies will occur.

'WHEN do these energies manifest?' — The transits and progressions — The time period in which to expect a specific type of mental, emotional, physical or spiritual experience.

This Workbook contains a number of exercises and designed experiences that teach you these astrological principles by experience. There are many books available which cover the astrological basics. Any good book which teaches planets, signs, houses and aspects can be used to augment the material contained in this Workbook. For most exercises, you should already have some knowledge of the 39 basic symbols — 10 planets, 12 signs and houses, and five primary aspects.

These exercises/experiences are drawn from many sources. Most I have used in experiential astrology groups and workshops. Others are borrowed from facilitators whose work I respect. Some are widely known and used within the human potential movement.

Most group exercises will work with a minimum of four participants, though 10 to 12 people is the ideal group size. If a group is not large enough it may lack stimulus. Too large a group may be hard to monitor and its energies too scattered.

Whether you do these exercises alone, informally with two or three friends, in a regular group, or in a therapy session, repeating them often will continue to deepen your astrological knowledge and understanding.

The Workbook is divided into 14 sections: The Elements, Ice-breaking and Warm-ups followed by experiences that capture the spirit of the 10 planets/12 signs. Each planetary section gives a short introduction to the planet, a key representative experience, other exercises and variations, popular films that create the mood of the planet's nature, a planetary walk and meditation, and a list of music, both contemporary and classical that evokes that planet's energy.

Incorporating music with experiential astrology adds an important dimension to our experience of the archetypes. Pythagoras taught how certain chords or melodies produced definite responses within the listener. Certain pieces of music stimulate feelings of courage, melancholy, exaltation, or a calming sense of peace. The English composer Gustav Holst, himself a student of astrology, recognized a certain feeling connected to each planet.[1] He captured the planet's meanings in *The Planets*, a symphonic suite in seven movements: 'Mars the Bringer of War', 'Venus the Bringer of Peace', 'Mercury the Winged Messenger', 'Jupiter the Bringer of Jollity', 'Saturn the Bringer of Old Age', 'Uranus the Magician', and 'Neptune the Mystic'.

The music I have suggested will evoke your feeling for the planet. This music can be simply listened to, used with guided imagery, or with more active forms of experiential astrology.

The final section of the Workbook, 'Pluto/Scorpio', ends with a story by a master storyteller, Marcie Telander from Boulder, Colorado. She breathes life into our understanding of Pluto's process, encouraging us to discover our own heroine, through her original interpretation of the story of Tamlaine.

# Elements

It is an ancient conviction that the four elements are the basic building blocks of nature and creation. The endless recombination of the elements of Earth (sensing), Air (thinking), Water (feeling) and Fire (intuiting) literally define the qualities of matter, and symbolically compose our souls. We all have varying degrees of these four elements within and typically are more in touch with one or two than the others. We are all susceptible to an imbalance of the elemental natures within. Let's look at each element and exercises for their balancing.

## Fire

Fire has been revered as the 'life-giver' ever since its appearance on earth when our ancestors captured its divine essence through friction and flints. The presence of Fire greatly increased our ability to survive, providing us with warmth and protection. Fire inspires us. It provides us with a perception of the spiritual quality of life — giving us the experience of transcendence. It symbolizes ideals, passion, spirit, pure energy, inspiration, purification, the color red, and as Cardinal Fire, Aries, the energy of springtime and the spring equinox.

Those with too much Fire tend to 'burn the candle at both ends' which can lead them to exhaustion. Those with excess Fire must learn to relax and breathe. Literally take time to breathe, deeply, slowly, and fully for 10 minutes every day.

Before you go charging off in your enthusiasm, stop and think — 'Is what I'm about to do realistic? Have I prepared a base from which to operate? Do I have a specific plan to bring this about?' Use your Earth function to help ground your idea. Get practical. Organize your idea. Build it and then put it out into the world.

Those lacking in the element Fire can be lethargic, uninspired, lacking initiative or awareness of the spiritual realm. Frequently being in the presence of Fire can help to bring more fire to the personality. One might meditate on the flame of a single candle. Or gaze into a roaring camp-fire in the mountains. Or reflect on the difference between controlled fire in a firepla :, and the consequences of Fire (enthusiasm) out of control in a forest fire.

Physical action is another way to stimulate Fire in our systems. When you find yourself lethargic and psychologically low (Saturn), get out and exercise. Use Fire (Mars) to break the state of depression (Saturn).

In traditional magic Fire is used as the power to purify. If you want to be free of a thought, habit, individual, problem or psychological block, use a symbol of that problem and create your own personal ritual to free yourself of it.

Decide what it is you want to be free of. Next focus intensely on the problem as you write it down or draw a picture of it. Concentrate on the problem. When you have 'empowered' your mind and the symbol with your energy, throw the paper into the fire. Fire will consume the symbol and in so doing symbolically consume the power it had over you.

## Air

Without air most of us could not exist for two minutes. Because air is invisible we are not much aware of it. Only when it blows our hair or tingles our faces do we seem to notice. Yet Air and the power of breath (prana) is the essence of our existence and it is in key relationship to our thoughts and feelings. It provides us with our ability to think and discriminate between the sensory data we are exposed to and allows us to order our experience in a manner we can comprehend. It symbolizes ideas, logic, breath, relationship, sociability, the color yellow, and as Cardinal Air, Libra and the autumn equinox.

The yogis have known that breath is the key instrument toward perceiving and achieving higher states of awareness. In each breath is 'prana,' the primal life force which interacts upon mind and body to make us aware of the more subtle spiritual nature of our existence. We all know, when our thinking or feeling runs rampant, a simple pause and a deep breath can return balance.

Those with too much Air may be overly analytical and are so habitually caught up in thoughts that they are often unaware of their feelings and emotions. Those with too little Air may feel awkward in social situations or lack confidence in their thinking and communicating skills.

The way we breathe is directly related to our thoughts and feelings. To demonstrate this here is a simple yet highly effective yogic nerve purification technique. Through breathing air in a particular way you will notice it calms and brings into balance your thinking/feeling function.

This technique is known as Alternate Breathing. First sit in a comfortable upright position with unrestricted clothing. With the left hand join together your thumb and index finger in a circle. This is known as the Shiva mudra, the 'wisdom' gesture. Rest the left hand on your knee. Place your right thumb over the right nostril and the ring finger and little finger over the left nostril. The middle and index fingers are cupped in the palm of the right hand. Empty your lungs completely. Then, closing the left (lunar) nostril, inhale slowly and steadily through the right (solar) nostril. When the lungs are filled, without any retention of air, close the right nostril and exhale slowly and steadily through the left. Keep the right (solar) closed and inhale slowly and steadily through the left (lunar). Without retaining the air, close off the left nostril, and exhale steadily through the right nostril. This completes one round. It is important to balance the inhale with the exhale breath in one continuous flow of air. Begin by breathing seven rounds each day. When alternate breathing is done for periods of even a few minutes a day, you will notice a feeling of peace and gentle 'intoxication' which results in your calmed thoughts and more balanced emotions. It is traditionally practiced at both the vernal and autumnal equinoxes, for it can deeply attune you to the harmonious balance of the cosmic solar and lunar forces at that time.

## Earth

Earth is the element we know best, since it is our physical home. We know the element Earth through our sensory function. By seeing, tasting, smelling, touching and hearing, we make order out of random stimuli and determine the 'reality' of concrete form. It represents not only our physical earth but anything stable, solid, and dependable, the color green and, as Cardinal Earth, Capricorn and the winter solstice.

Those lacking in Earth will have a more difficult time relating to the physical. Some may appear spacey, impractical, with their 'head in the air and feet off the ground.' Those with an emphasis on Earth may be too earthbound, unaware of or resistant to more subtle states, heavily focused on material success, possessions, and 'the good life.' To experience the element Earth and the function of the senses here are several exercises you might try.

For a group to experience Earth have participants sit in a circle with their eyes closed. Give each person a bag of fresh soil. Lead them in a sensory awareness exercise — feeling and smelling the soil, sensing it on their arms, faces, feet. You might expand this exercise by passing around various bags of herbs with different smells, textures, etc. (Sage, rosemary, basil, bay-leaf, fennel would be good selections.) The group should focus as fully as possible on their senses. If people focus on their breath they will become more aware of the senses. Afterwards ask the group what the experience was like for them. What sensations did they most like? Dislike?

There are many 'grounding' exercises — a number of which are drawn from yoga, psychology, and bodywork — for those needing to get more in touch with Earth. You may want to refer back to chapter eight for a list of ways to ground yourself, particularly when contending with a Neptune transit. Making an earth bed is one method not mentioned there. If you don't feel well or can't shake off a painful emotion, find a spot where the earth is bare, uncluttered with leaves or plants. Sit or lie down on the soil. Mentally, see your illness or difficult emotion sink into the earth. Feel the problem or pain running down into the earth beneath you. Sense the rhythm of the earth. Tune your body to its subtle healing energy, allowing its cool, deep, solid energy to rise from the ground through you. If you are bedridden or cannot do this, have a dish of fresh soil next to you so you can at least feel the Earth.

## Water

Water is a vital necessity in our lives, second only to our dependence on air. Water sustains, nurtures, and brings forth life. It is the element which delivers us into this world. Water is the most frequent symbol of unconscious depths — the deep river of feminine, nurturing, healing sources flowing within the earth and the emotional life within ourselves. Just as we cannot see into depths of a pool, so we cannot see into deeper areas of our unconscious. Many times we can only draw indirect conclusions. (The great gods and goddesses with knowledge of the future are all Water divinities: Proteus, Nereus, Thetis.) Water is symbolic of the psyche, emotions, fluidity, change, absorption, germination, the color blue, and as Cardinal Water, Cancer and the summer solstice.

We are often drawn to water, the ocean or lake, when we are having problems. When a client has a strong, well-aspected Neptune I suggest frequent visits to lakes and oceans. Most of them already know the comforting feelings they experience near water.

Water exercises call for reflecting and turning inward. You might dim the lights and lie down comfortably. Turn on an 'environmental' tape — sounds of ocean waves, a trickling brook, or a thunderstorm. Reflect on the difference of water free-flowing and uncontained versus water in a drinking glass. Or the immensity of water in the ocean versus stagnant water of an isolated pond.

One of the most ancient ways of reflecting is water gazing. A still pond, running stream, roaring ocean, puddle, fountain in the park, or swimming pool are all places where this can be done. Find a comfortable spot to sit. Loosen tight clothing and gently relax your mind. With eyelids relaxed but not quite closed, gaze into the water. Allow all your thoughts to vanish. Sit quietly and wait to observe feelings, or pictures painting themselves in your mind. With practice this begins to open up the channels to the intuitive forces within.

If you have a problem which needs solving, or an answer to a particular question, relax and gently gaze into the water. This is not a mental exercise, rather a psychic one. Formulate the question in your mind. Then simply relax and let an image in response to your question take shape. Don't force it. Wait and let it unfold.

To experience Water, run a bath to the point where water covers all but your face to allow for continued and comfortable breathing. As you are submerged, quiet your thoughts and focus on the rhythm of your breath. Observe how the water moves against your body with the rhythm of your breath.

If you live near a major city try experiencing an hour in a 'float tank', the sensory deprivation experience developed by John Lilly. In the dark and floating in saline water, you feel as if you have returned to the womb. At first you experience your mind's interference (thinking/Air mode) with its barrage of endless thoughts. The more your thinking turns off, the more aware you become of your feelings. For some it is difficult to surrender this much. Others emerge refreshed and relaxed mentally and emotionally.

## Living Aspects

Here is a tool I've found useful in teaching aspects; it simply and clearly demonstrates the nature of the planets' relationships to one other. Draw an imaginary circle on the floor. With the help of a volunteer begin by explaining a conjunction. Demonstrate this by having your volunteer stand next to you. Using that person as 0 degrees, move two paces away on the circle and demonstrate the sextile relationship, 60 degrees. (Each step represents one sign, or 30 degrees.) Both walk toward the center of the circle, having the group notice your new harmonious 'soft' relationship. What happens when you move one more step and both of you walk to the center? Discuss what happens when two forces meet at a right angle, a square position of 90 degrees. Notice the obstructive relationship. Next move to the trine position, 120 degrees, walk to the center and talk about this flowing conducive contact. Then move to the opposition, 180 degrees, directly opposite each other. Walk into the center, join hands, and demonstrate the opposition in a tug of war. Continue walking around the circle demonstrating the closing trine, square, and sextile, back to your starting point of 0 degrees.

## Ice-Breaking/Warm-Ups

The first 10 minutes of any encounter, whether one-to-one or in a group, are the most critical for they set the tone. In working with groups, fun and stimulating opening exercises are a must. These 'warm-ups' are designed to bring about initial contact between individuals, break down inhibitions and shyness, and help overcome initial tensions and hesitancy. To help you choose which ones to use consider the size of the group and whether the participants already know each other.

### Stretching and Movement

Stretching is an easy, gentle way to begin and immediately incorporates the idea of using the body as a vehicle for experience and a tool for understanding. Have the group spread out in the room and stretch and loosen areas of their bodies that seem particularly tense or sore. Ask them to focus on their bodies, and to stretch and move in ways their bodies tell them to. Tell them to exaggerate their stretches. Encourage awareness of their forgotten parts — forehead, tongue, cheeks, fingertips, palms, feet, toes.

Another version is to use a classical Hatha yoga relaxation technique focusing attention and relaxing the head, neck, shoulders, and the rest of the body down to the feet. Do not lie down unless this is a closing exercise. You want the group to begin to wake up, not go to sleep.

Once the group has stretched, turn on some lively dance music and ask them to slowly start moving to its rhythms. As the music continues, gently encourage them to increase the use of their whole body and the whole room. Observing the group's level of enthusiasm, participation, and resistance will help you gauge the pace of the increased movement. Ask them to find a partner to dance with. After a while, ask the pairs to try to dance as a team, following and leading each other's movements. Ask them to change partners, make groups of three dancers, try to dance as mirror images, etc. You can continue adding numbers of people until you have a whole group dance circle.

If there is some group resistance, go slowly with this exercise. The group's willingness or hesitancy will let you know if you need to spend more time in a 'warming up' phase. Be prepared to follow this with other warm-ups if you need to, gently leading the group to a state of feeling more relaxed, open, and at ease with one another. Sometimes you will have a group that is very willing to move, dance and interact with each other. I've been in groups who have gotten so 'into it' we ended with all of us straining to catch our breath, literally bathed in sweat! If a group responds like this from the beginning, it's going to be a highly interactive, stimulating experience for everyone!

## Contact Dancing

Once the individuals in a group have become familiar with each other, you might try having them first pair up and dance with one part of their body touching and in contact with the partner at all times. Experiment with staying in contact with your heads, little fingers, shoulders, backs, hips, feet, etc. If this is a new group, this may not feel appropriate because it is more intimate. If the group members know each other, especially if some are friends, this might be a very good exercise to choose.

## Be an Object!

This is great fun. Have each person think of an inanimate, but moveable object they can mime in front of the group. How about being a folding chair, a balloon that air is rushing out of, a percolating coffee machine, a flushing toilet, a lamp being turned on and off, an exercise wheel for hamsters? Once everyone has thought of an object, take turns non-verbally miming the action of the object for the group. (Sounds of the action are encouraged!)

## Group Animals

This is a natural extension of any physical group activity. Have the group act out what it feels like to be a barrel of monkeys, herd of hippos, gaggle of geese, school of dolphins, pile of puppies, etc. Or have them each choose their own animal and try to relate as they would on Noah's ark.

## Group Band

Put out a variety of percussion instruments. Have each person choose an instrument and one at a time begin to rattle, shake, etc. Before you know it, you've got a complete percussion orchestra. You could also create an all kazoo band, perhaps with kazoo soloists. (If you don't remember kazoos, they are simple metal 'flutes' with a wax paper disc across the air hole. When you speak, sing, or hum into them they make a sound. Kazoos work well because you don't need any musical background to play them.)

## Paper Bag Band

This is an exercise I got from the clown Wavy Gravy at the Santa Fe New Center of the Moon astrology conference in 1983 — it's particularly good for the child in all of us. Have the group sit in a circle and pass out paper bags, large enough to get over your head! Now ask everyone to put the bag over their head and experiment with making sounds in them. You'll find yourself laughing at how silly you feel, how silly the group must all look like with bags over their heads, etc. Try now to communicate via sounds to each other. See if you can identify particular members by their sounds. Next facilitate the group to see if they can create a paper bag band together. This exercise is humbling and becomes hilarious!

## Group Tangle

Begin with the group standing in a circle. Then ask everyone to hold the hands of two different people who are not standing next to them. Now, as a group, try to untangle yourselves without letting go of your hands. You'll need to contort yourselves into some strange positions to get the group undone and back to its original position. (As a facilitator, you might notice who has good observational suggestions during this process; does anyone try to take control, insist they are right, etc? How well does the group co-operate together?)

## String Partners

Cut half as many pieces of string as there are participants, all the same length and color. Hold the bundle of strings in your hand with the ends protruding so that no one can see which end is attached to which. Each participant takes an end, and gets 'strung' to another. Each set of strung partners sits down for a fixed period of time, getting to know each other. Possible topics might be: What is my most prominent aspect? What aspect gives me the most trouble? What aspects do I have the hardest time understanding? What is my current best or most difficult transit? How do I experience my Moon?

# Introductions

Participants in the group introduce themselves by writing their names and drawing pictures of themselves on pieces of paper. When finished, tape the pictures up on a wall. One at a time take turns introducing yourselves by talking about your picture. This may be too intimidating to a group unfamiliar with each other but it works well with a group where some members know others.

Make a collage of yourself using magazine pictures and/or words which express you. Members can then share their collages, commenting on what items they chose. A variation with a group somewhat familiar with each other would be to put the collages up anonymously, and the group tries to match up each picture to its artist.

For another fun ice-breaker, have members introduce themselves silently by miming qualities they most observe about themselves. Or have group participants draw pictures of themselves in which they try to characterize themselves by distinctive identifying features — a Gemini who draws himself carrying a ton of books, a Cancer surrounded by her cats, a Pisces sleeping because she loves to dream, a time-conscious Virgo businessman looking at his watch, etc. Show the drawings to the group one by one. As the group studies each drawing one at a time, make observations and share spontaneous intuitive insights about each drawing. Ask the group; 'What kinds of hobbies might this person like? What kind of vacation would they most enjoy? Tell a story about the person in the picture.

Here's a simple exercise. Pair up and get to know each other for five minutes. Then introduce your new partner to the group.

# Group Story

The group sits in a circle and creates a story. One person starts by setting the story in time and place. Then the person in the next chair continues the story, and so on until everyone has contributed.

# Group Imaging

The group lies on the floor, preferably carpeted, with heads together in a circle. One begins by saying aloud a word which expresses an experience or names an object which elicits a definite response or memory — a puppy licking your face, getting cotton candy stuck on your nose, your first kiss, the first time you rode a bike by yourself, skiing down Ajax mountain, warm fuzzy slippers, hot fudge sundaes, etc. Sharing these memories brings a group closer together.

# Group Jigsaw Puzzle

Buy a puzzle that the whole group can work on putting together. Choose a size which should take the group about 20 minutes to finish. Observe how the group co-operates.

## Advertisement Story

The group chooses an advertisement in a magazine with a number of adjectives in it. Take these adjectives and use them to create a story.

## First Impression

Each participant draws a piece of paper with the name of a fellow group member on it. Write three initial impressions you have received of that person after their name. Collect them, mix them up, and as a group read each one aloud. Talk about the qualities listed. Does everyone agree with them? Disagree? A variation would be for the person being described to try to guess the identity of the writer. (This will not work well if the group has not interacted before to establish some mutual trust.)

## Trust

This is one of the fastest means to get a group in rapport with each other if it is preceded by several other less threatening exercises. It gives a good evaluation of group resistance and builds the essential element of any group process: trust.

This can be done with a minimum of eight people. Form a circle, alternating the physically strongest members. One at a time, stand in the middle of the circle with the group evenly spaced around you. Take off your shoes and socks as well as all jewelry. Now take some time to turn your attention within and get 'centered', closing your eyes and taking a few deep breaths. Fold your arms crosswise on your chest. (For women, this will protect your breasts.) After you've gotten centered, take a deep breath and fall back into the arms of the group, keeping your feet planted in the middle.

The group slowly begins to pass you around the circle, allowing you an experience of trusting others, as well as physical contact. It's important that the group begins slowly. Once everyone has gauged the strength of the group and the person seems relaxed, passing them more quickly or with a change of direction can be fun for the person. If the person begins to feel scared, slow down or stop. Some will like to be moved around faster, others are more unsure. Let the group respond sensitively to each individual.

As a facilitator you might want to pay particular attention to the bare feet of the person in the center. Each member's ability or difficulty with this exercise will be mirrored in the behaviour and body. The feet can be most telling. Do they strain their toes to try to control their movements while being passed around? Do they appear comfortably relaxed? Are they too relaxed, suggesting they might be too trusting or not have enough 'boundaries?' (You may find this with people with strong Neptune in their charts.) By the time everyone who *wants* to has their turn you will have a good idea who has trust issues, which you may expect to find in their charts either natally or by transit.

If the individual is willing and trusts in your skills, it can give you a clear direction in which to work with them later. By all means don't expect everyone to take a turn. Do notice who doesn't. Or who waits until last, or who hesitates — they may need extra attention later. Also notice who takes great care in passing the person or who seems particularly alert, involved. This will give you initial information about the level of trust or resistance in the group as a whole. Following with a feedback session is helpful. Or use this exercise as a warm-up before beginning to work with the charts of individual group members.

## Red-Handed

Here's an exercise with Scorpio overtones from *The New Games* book. It's called 'How Sneaky Can You Be?!' Everyone forms a circle and one person, chosen as It, stands in the middle. While It closes his eyes, the other players pass a small object, such as a stone or marble, from person to person. (The sneakiest way to pass the object is to hold it in one fist, palm down, and drop it into the palm up hand of the next person.) It signals before opening his eyes. Who among all these innocent looking people has the object? If It detects a suspicious look, they'll tap the suspect on the shoulder. If that person is empty-handed It continues moving around the circle. Meanwhile the group passes the object around under It's nose. (Fake decoys by people who don't have the object are an integral part of the game.) If you have the object and It catches you, you are the new It.

## People Roll

This is an outdoor lawn game. Get everyone lying on their stomachs, side by side. Make sure you're packed really close together. Now have the person on the end of the line roll over onto her neighbor and keep rolling down the road of bodies. When she gets to the end of the line, she lies on her stomach and the next person at the other end starts rolling. When the game gathers momentum, this human body line moves quickly and with much glee!

## Hug Tag

This variation of classical tag can be played by any tag rules, only this time a player is safe only when he's hugging another player. After playing awhile, make the game more communal. Rule that only *three* people hugging are safe.

# THE PLANETS AND SIGNS

## The Sun and Leo

The Sun symbolizes the active, energizing principle. It is the 'Spotlight' or true source of light through which planetary energies are synthesized and integrated — what Jung calls, the 'Self.' It represents the urge in each of us to express our total self-identity, and to grow into that which we potentially are.

The Sun/Leo is linked to consciousness, light, day, fatherhood, and will. It is the principle which is expressed in mythology as the Hero. The journey of the Hero is expressed through the symbols and associated images of the natal chart.

Individuals with strong Sun/Leo energy in their horoscope (by sign, aspect, house) can be vibrant, dramatic, and vital. If afflicted the Sun/Leo personality may demand center stage and the constant admiration of others. Those with little Sun/Leo energy may be hesitant to take a risk or to express themselves to others.

The following exercises may bring to the surface contradictory feelings for someone who has a strong extroverted-introverted theme, such as Leo/Gemini/Aries planets on the top half of their chart, and Virgo/Scorpio rising with planets below.

## The Sun — An Experience of Self (the Hero's Journey)

The myth of the hero can deeply teach us about the principle and process of the solar energy within our psyches. The journey can be done in either active or passive ways. As a more active experience, re-create the drama by asking the group to choose and enact the various roles in the hero's journey. (You might be the narrator of the basic story while they embellish and improvise.) Or perhaps each individual can act out for themselves the hero role as the story is told. Or try the hero's journey in a somewhat less active form, perhaps relating the story as a guided imagery exercise, and allowing an opportunity for the group to draw at various stages of the story. (Have newsprint and crayons, Magic Markers, etc. beside each person.)

Proceed as follows. Ask the group to lie down and get comfortable. Turn down the lights. Have the members focus on their breathing, guiding them to breathe more deeply, more slowly. Once the group has reached a state of deep relaxation, begin to tell the hero's story. As you will see, there are several key stages in the journey

The vision of the Empyrean

of the hero. Stop at each stage and ask each individual to draw the feelings and images they are experiencing. How does the hero's journey relate to their current life? (This process will open up much to share and talk about when the experience is over.)

## The Story of the Hero's Journey

To more fully understand the myth of the hero, read, for example, Joseph Campbell's *The Hero With a Thousand Faces*. Here's a bare outline of the themes of the story.

The hero had two yearnings — first, to discover the details of his birth so that then he may learn his True Purpose, and second, to find his Beloved (his other half) so he could be whole. These two urges were the call to his adventure. This call brings 'the awakening of the self' which lifts the curtain on a mystery, a moment of spiritual passage in which the old life is outgrown and shed. No longer content with the old ideals, values or emotional patterns, the hero is urged across the first threshold. With his destiny to guide him, he enters a zone of power which has a guardian of the threshold. The threshold stands for the limits of the hero's present life, both what holds him back and what helps contain him. Beyond is darkness and the unknown. (The regions of the unknown contain all the projections of his unconscious.)

The passage of the magical threshold does not come through conquering the guardian, but in the hero's being swallowed into the unknown and appearing to have died. Once passing the threshold, the hero moves into a lucid landscape where he must survive a series test and trials. The hero is usually aided by helpers whom he met before his entrance, or he becomes slowly aware that there is a benevolent power supporting him. The hero's ordeal represents the beginning of a long path of initiatory conquests, with moments of heightened insight. Dragons must be slain again and again and survival is constantly threatened, yet there were also victories to be had.

Just past his fearsome trials (once his obstacles and demons have been overcome), the hero meets the Beloved, his mistress, bride, mother, sister. She is the promise of perfection, the bliss of comfort and nourishment — the archetypal 'Good Mother.' The image of the Beloved is not simply benign, for it also contains the 'Bad Mother,' and the unattainable, absent mother, the hampering, forbidding mother, the desired but forbidden mother and the clinging, suffocating mother.

At this stage of the journey, the hero gains assurance from the helpful female by whose magic he is protected in a further trial to come: the ego-shattering initiations with father. Father is the one by whom the young are passed on into the larger world. Just as the mother represented both good and bad so now does father, but with the added element of rivalry.

After meeting his trials from both the female and male aspects, the hero is finally granted a boon. Though his obstacles were many, he has triumphed and is revealed to be a Superior Man. And he has come to a realization of his original yearnings. As he crossed threshold after threshold, conquering his dragons, he pushed past his limiting horizons onto a wider plain, steadily increasing his consciousness and his spiritual awareness until he finally breaks the sphere of the cosmos and arrives at a realization transcending all experiences of form.

When the hero's quest has been accomplished, he has yet one more stage of the journey to complete; he must return to his people and community, to humanity. And he must bring them the Gift, the results of his blessing by god and goddess — the healing and restorative Elixir. Herein lies the central problem of the hero's return. How can he communicate even the mere shadow of what he has found? How can he convey the secrets of the Dark, the Unknown, the Unconscious? How is he to translate the revelation which shatters the pairs of opposites, or communicate to people who insist on the reality of the senses alone?

What is the final outcome of the hero's miraculous passage and return? He, or indeed she, for only by convention does the story have a masculine protagonist, is now the whole Self, having found that the voyage to the Unknown does not destroy, but enlightens. Thus the myth of the hero lets us experience, directly, the principle of the Sun within us.

## What's Good About You?

In a group, pair off and sit facing each other. One person begins as questioner, the other will respond. The questioner asks, 'What's good about you?' The person answering gives himself a compliment. The questioner is silent except to nod his head in agreement. The questioner asks again, 'And what else is good about you?' The process continues until the person answering is out of compliments for himself. Switch roles. Then ask these questions. Was this hard or easy for you? Were you easily able to find compliments to give yourself? Do you have your Sun or Leo in challenging aspect, or difficult transits currently to them?

## Memorize a Poem

Memorize a favorite poem, joke, or funny story. Take turns getting up in front of the group and delivering your memorized piece. Pay attention to how you feel as it comes closer to your turn. Are you very nervous, embarrassed, confident, at ease, anxious, anticipating? Find a word that most describes your prominent feeling before your turn. After your 'performance' find a word which most suits your feeling then. Were you relieved, stimulated, energized, etc? Now go back and see if you can capture a feeling while you were delivering your piece. Compare these three words. Do they reveal a typical process you undergo when you express yourself to others or when you are the center of attention? Does this experience relate to the aspects to your Sun or Leo in your chart? Group discussion.

## Name Chant

Our name is strongly tied to our image of self and quality of expression. An extremely powerful experience is to do a name chant. With a group, let each individual take turns sitting in the center of the circle. (In reality the group is making the symbol of the Sun, with the person the group is focused on having become the central 'bindu point.') Close your eyes and take a few deep breaths. Now slowly the group begins to chant the first name of the person in the middle. Spontaneously let your voices roll and crescendo. Listening to your name, hearing it resonate in the circle around you, in you, sounds very ethereal, almost as if angels were calling. It is a moving experience. (Use this as a closure for an individual's astrodrama or try this in particularly soft and loving tones for someone with a Sun/Saturn transit.)

## Tell About a Leo Experience

Tell the group about a Leo experience you have had (lead in a play, presentation at work, TV appearance, leading a group or class, etc.). How did you feel about being the focus of attention? What kind of feedback did you get? How did you evaluate your experience?

## Telling Stories

Tell the group about a funny incident from your past.

Tell about a humbling experience from your past. (This may be good for the Leo, 'I'm Mr Wonderful' character in some of us.)

Take turns reading or telling a fairy-tale or story to the group.

Get up and talk about yourself for three minutes.

Whichever variation you choose, afterwards evaluate this experience. Was this easy for you to do? Did you feel more comfortable with a 'script' in front of you or when you were spontaneous? Was there a rush of adrenalin at any time? Does this typify how you generally are in front of groups?

## Affirmation

Write down, 'Every day in every way I am growing in vitality, self-awareness, and light'. Tape it to your bathroom mirror so every morning you see and repeat this affirmation. This will be helpful when the solar energy is being influenced adversely by the outer planets.

## Warm Fuzzies

This Transactional Analysis exercise begins by forming a circle with the group and sitting down. One person begins with a small, preferably furry, object in their hands. (This could be a small stuffed animal or sponge ball.) That person looks around the group and finds someone they want to give a compliment to. Say the person's name, throw the 'warm fuzzy' to that person and give them a compliment, as sincere and whole-heartedly as possible. (Saying their name will help your compliment have more impact.) That person tries to really feel the compliment, then in turn finds someone they want to give a compliment to. Continue playing until everyone has received two or three compliments from the group. Another version of this is to give hugs in place of throwing the 'warm fuzzy'.

How easy was it to give a compliment? Was it easier to receive one? Did you feel discounted or ignored by any group member? How did that feel?

Another variation of Warm Fuzzies is to form a circle and take turns standing in the center. Either the group can give compliments directed to the one in the center, or that person can give himself three or four compliments. Be as proud, as Leonian as possible!

Those with too little solar/Leo energy may have more difficulty or discomfort with this exercise. If this happens you might give this individual a task to do. Have them *notice* when someone gives them a special compliment. Have them write the compliments down in a special notebook. This may help them become more aware of getting compliments and their responses to them which perhaps may lead to a deeper understanding as to why they respond to compliments in the way they do. This could be a very good suggestion to someone with challenging natal Sun/Saturn aspects.

## King or Queen

In the group, take turns at role playing being the king or queen. (All of us Pluto in Leos should have no problem with this.) Everyone else be their subjects. Hold court. Hear and decide on cases brought before you by your subjects. Afterwards, did you like being king/queen? Did you think you were fair to your subjects? Were you arbitrary? Dominating? A kind ruler?

## Sunbathe

When having difficult solar transits, particularly from Saturn, spend time lying in the sun. Imagine the health and vitality of the sun is pouring into and through your body and psyche. Let the Sun heal you, revitalize you.

## Birthday Ritual

Because each year your birthday is the time the sun returns to its birthplace, it is an important cycle. Have a solar return chart calculated to know the exact time the sun returns to its natal position. Take the day off and spend the day focused on reviewing/evaluating the last year, especially appreciating what you have accomplished or feel good about. Spend the day expressing yourself, drawing, writing, or doing exactly what you want to do. As the time approaches of your exact solar return, put your chart on an altar and meditate on your Sun sign, how you exalt in expressing yourself, what positive contacts does your sun have to the other planets. Breathe as your Sun, bringing in new life, new vitality, new hope. Or use any meditational technique which focuses particularly on the sun center, the *ajna chakra* or point between your eyebrows. Or focus attention on your breath, remembering you are approaching the time of your first breath. Breathe as if each breath is your first. Or light a single candle, symbol of your Sun, and meditate/reflect on it. Use the name chant and softly repeat the sound of your own name.

A nice ritual to do for a birthday friend is for a group to get together and do the name chant or take turns saying what it is you love about your birthday friend. Or light a single candle in front of them and all meditate on that person and their life, sending them prosperity, happiness, and peace for the new year. Maybe close your ritual with the birthday person moving around the circle and lighting a candle held by each group member as a symbol of their light joining and touching yours.

A moving experience for a large conference-size group is for one candle to be lit symbolizing the collective spirit, inspiration, aspirations of the theme of the conference and for the flame to be passed one candle to the next until everyone holds a lighted candle.

## Sun/Leo Films

Go to, or rent a movie with a Sun/Leo theme. For example: *It's a Wonderful Life, The Color Purple, Zorba The Greek, Breaking Away.*

## Sun/Leo Planet Walk

Visualize yourself as a royal person — the king or queen of the world. Concentrate upon expanding your chest. Inflate your whole body. Imagine that it's grand and something beautiful to behold. Now, confidently extend your normal walking stride, carrying yourself in a noble posture. Adjusting your walk will help you to touch the solar/Leo part of your psyche.

## Sun Meditation — The Ball of Light

Close your eyes. Take some deep full breaths, exhaling any tensions, scattered thoughts or energy. Now, *slowly* bring your awareness to the point between your eyebrows — called the Sun center, ajna chakra, or Third Eye. In the body, this point represents the Sun in your chart. It is the light through which all others are expressed. Focus your awareness on a pencil point of light between your eyebrows. Now slowly intensify this light. Let it become a little larger, a little more intense. Put your full conscious awareness on this light of your existence. Let it become even larger and more intense. Let it become a ball of light, filling your head with light like a giant lightbulb. Now let that light slowly begin to expand out, permeating your throat, chest, arms, hips, butt, legs, feet. Let your whole body become a ball of light, radiant in the fullness of who you are.

## Group Ball of Light Meditation

In a group circle visualize a ball of light within your head. Now focus the energy of your ball of light into the center of the circle. Merge and blend with the light of those around you, keeping your focus in the center of the circle. Intensify the ball of light. Now expand it to permeate the bodies of everyone, envisioning it expanding to behind your backs. Slowly expand the light out to touch all of your loved ones. Distance does not matter. Take a moment to visualize your loved ones in the ball of light. Take a moment to feel this. Now pull back the ball of light which has touched all your loved ones, and imagine it once again behind your backs. Intensify the light. Now move it back into the center of the circle. Move it back into your head. Allow the light to gently fade to the pencil point of light. Allow yourself some moments of quiet reflection and reorientation back to the room.

## Suggested Music

'Brass in Pocket' *The Pretenders* (The Pretenders), 'Hot Fun in the Summertime' *Sly and the Family Stone Greatest Hits* (Sly and the Family Stone), 'Good Day Sunshine' *Revolver* (The Beatles), 'Here Comes the Sun' *Abbey Road* (The Beatles), *William Tell Overture* (Rossini), *Firebird Suite* (Stravinsky), *Superman* soundtrack, 'Symphonies for the King's Bed Chamber' *The Baroque Trumpet* (Lully), 'Fanfares for the Royal Tournament' *The Baroque Trumpet* (Lully), 'Soldier'a Air' *The Baroque Trumpet* (Lully), *The Messiah* (Handel).

# The Moon and Cancer

The Niagara above the falls

The Moon symbolizes the passive, receptive, nurturing, feminine faculty of the psyche, the retention of impressions or emotionally charged events of the past that creates our conditioned emotional behavior and patterns. The Moon/Cancer links us to the tides, motherhood, childbirth, the family, intuition, images, and fluid conditions, as well as to our cultural and societal archetype of the feminine. This femininity is now re-emerging, after a period of hiatus, with many being drawn to better understand and integrate it both in their own daily experience and our culture as a whole.

Individuals with strong Moon/Cancer energy can be nurturing and caring. If afflicted one may be too easily influenced, vacillate, or indulge in emotional drama. Those with little Moon/Cancer energy may have difficulty knowing their feelings and tend to be emotionally cool. Those with highly polarized charts, such as Sun/Moon oppositions, may experience contradictory feelings, especially at full moons and eclipses.

The current profusion of women's books offers some enlightenment on the aspect of the feminine within our psyche and its emerging role in our culture. To begin to better understand the feminine try reading some of the excellent books available, especially *The Return of the Goddess* [1] by Edward C. Whitmont, *Descent to the Goddess* [2] by Sylvia Brinton Perera, *She* [3] by Robert A. Johnson and *Women's Mysteries* [4] by Ester Harding.

Because the Moon has to do with the process of reflection, most of the exercises described in Chapter Four, 'Do it Yourself', will be appropriate as Moon exercises. As the Moon symbolizes the unconscious, instinctive realm, dreamwork is also an appropriate technique to understand the Moon more fully. Creative visualizations and guided imagery give added knowledge of the Moon's function. *Creative Visualization*, by Shakti Gawain speaks simply about this process and offers useful instruction. [5]

Here's a tip. Plan an experience to contact your Moon as close to the full moon as possible. The results will have more impact. The best times to reflect and do inner searching are when the Moon is in Water signs, conjunct your fourth house, or transiting through the Water houses, the fourth, eighth, or twelfth houses. For extended research wait until the progressed Moon is in a Water sign, or transiting the Water houses. The best times to do some emotional healing of your childhood or relationship with mom is when the Moon is in water, by transit or for an extended time by progression.

Another excellent experience for the Moon is in Jean Houston's book, *The Possible Human*. [6] In it she describes a two-and-a-half to three-and-a-half hour sequence called 'Exercises in Evolutionary Memory.' It allows us to re-experience the evolutionary unfolding of life on the planet from being a fish, to reptile, and on to a modern human and an 'extended human.' Having done this exercise in one of Jean's workshops, I can attest that this experience stimulates a deep bodily knowing as our brain and body respond to these ways of being, antecedent to our human evolution. Refer to Houston's book for another interesting Moon experience: 'Recalling the Child.' [7]

## Moon Experience — Moon Grotto

Adapted from Diane Marieschild's *Motherwit* book, here is a fine experience for a group of women to partake in on a full moon.

Relax, deepen your concentration, and enfold yourself in protection. Imagine yourself moving deeply, winding through long passageways and labyrinths, winding down and down until you come to a body of dark water on which there is a boat tied. Climb into the boat. Now float further through more passageways, going deeper, deeper. Feel the gentle rocking of the boat and the soothing sound of the water lapping onto its sides. Float until you come to a large grotto. Your boat comes to rest on its shore. Looking up you see this space is lighted by the moon and the moonlight is pouring down from a slender threadlike opening far above you. You know this place is sacred.

Here in this sacred place of magic you meet Sophia, the giver of wisdom. She appears here on every full moon and shares her knowledge with the women who find their way to this place. She is appearing now. Pause for five to 10 minutes. Now leave the grotto, winding back to the point you started. Remember what you have experienced and carry that knowledge with you. Become aware of your surroundings slowly, feeling refreshed and relaxed.

## The Moon and Nurturing

It's healing to take a break from the world to experience a nurturing moment. Several women friends and I meet periodically for a group foot bath. Each of us brings a towel and a small kitchen pan for our feet. We simmer up a brew of different soothing herbs — chamomile, lavender, sage, valerian, calendula, and rose petals — for 20 minutes. Then mixing the hot herbal brew with cool water until it is a comfortable temperature, we put our feet in and relax.

You might reflect on your Moon while doing this. How well do you take time to nurture yourself? Get a massage? Linger in an herbal bath? Or get a manicure? How well do you receive? How well do you allow others to give to you? How well do you nurture others?

Because the Moon symbolizes both water and nurturing, as a group you might visit your local hot springs or spa. Spending an evening of relaxation and soothing tired muscles is 'being' rather than 'doing' — helping each other to experience the receptive, feminine mode.

## Childhood Photo

Bring a childhood photo of yourself to the group. Divide into pairs and talk about that time of your life. What were the circumstances around the picture? Spend time recalling your memories around this time. Was it a happy or difficult time? Do your memories summon up feelings? If time permits, extend this exploration to include your whole childhood. Was it a happy or difficult time? Can you recall some specific memories? Allow time to let this process unfold as this can be a very intimate, sharing time for both partners.

If you are alone, take out your baby book and reflect on the baby you were. Can you, in your imagination and in your body, experience yourself as that baby again? You might try curling up in a fetal position, or crawling on all fours.

## Mother

Variation: Bring a picture of your mother. What was she like? What are your earliest memories of her? Was she a good mother to you? How good a mother are you to yourself? Can you see a relationship between how you were mothered and the way you mother yourself? Reflect on your own Moon and its natal aspects.

Can you recall specific experiences which parallel the specific aspects? For instance, if you have Moon opposite Jupiter, can you remember your mom making sure you've eaten, always giving you treats or desserts? Or did you experience your Moon opposite Saturn as mother forcing you to sit at the table until you were completely finished, withholding desserts, or maybe not even home to feed you? These reflections can help you understand your Moon relationships.

## Rocking

Rocking can be a very nurturing group exercise when it's used appropriately. Have one person lie prone. Group members each take an area of the body, a leg, the head, upper torso, etc., place their hands underneath and as a group slowly lift the person to waist height. Then gently rock them back and forth, up and back. It is important that there are enough people to do this comfortably. (It works best when one person takes the head, two people the torso.) Also be sure the head is comfortably supported and the rest of the body is kept in alignment. Then after a few minutes slowly lower the person until they are lying back on the ground. Be silent. This is a good closing for an individual's full astrodrama as a means of acknowledging and integrating. It can evoke strong feelings. I have seen this work effectively for everyone who has tried it. Don't start off the group with this one, wait until some level of group trust has been established.

Variation: If you have a back yard with trees, string up a hammock. I have a hammock and most days in the summer I'll take a break and rock myself.

## Childhood Home

Describe your childhood home. If there were many, choose the one you most liked. Extend this to describe the neighborhood, favorite childhood hangouts, etc.

## Where You Grew Up

In a group, take turns briefly describing where you grew up. Extend this to ask, 'Where were you in the summer of 1968?', for example. It's interesting to know where the individuals in the group were at exactly the same time. Were there any parallels of life experience then with anyone in the group?

## Home

Reflect on the home you now live in. Are you happy there? What special features do you like about it? Where is your favorite place? If you are not happy now where you live, what kind of home do you want? Using good Moon transits to either look for a new home, or actually move in, is great use for this energy.

## Childhood Toy

Bring a childhood toy. Divide into pairs and share memories about the toy. Do you know who gave it to you? Do you remember seeing it for the first time? What social experiences did you have with your toy? Can you recall a specific experience in which it comforted you?

Variation: What was your favorite toy? Describe it fully. You might find more 'food for thought' if you have the groups divided according to the particular toy, i.e. all those whose favorite toy was a bear, or dog, or frog. Is there a quality about that animal that they exhibit in their personality?

## This is Your Life!

As a birthday present for a member in an ongoing group, spend an evening of 'This is Your Life.' Get photos, childhood experiences from their mothers, sisters, brothers, and friends.

Variation: Give a group massage as a birthday present to a friend. Treat them to a facial, an herbal bath, etc.

## Feminine Issues

A group discussion about feminine issues can expose the emotional patterns and feelings of the individuals in the group. If your intention is to stir up feelings as part of the group process then choose emotional issues like abortion, women's rights in the workplace, sexual harassment in the workplace, etc. If your intention is to draw the group closer, share your pleasant, funny childhood memories with each other.

## Childbirth

Because the Moon represents the function of childbirth and the nurturing of children, another discussion might be to bring up the topic of having or not having children, or have women share their personal experience with the birth of their own children. In connection with this you might watch a film of a child's birth and spend time sharing your feelings. Or, if you can, witness the birth of a child.

An extension of this may be to facilitate a process through guided imagery to allow the group to return to the moment of their own birth. Or if you want a strong Moon experience you might even bring in a qualified re-birther. (This is a therapeutic method of re-experiencing your birth.)

If you believe in reincarnation, remembering the distant past is also lunar. Perhaps you might use a past life regressionist to guide you through a past life experience.

## Women's Issues

Have a 'women only' group addressing some women's issues. Once everybody's feelings on a particular topic are known look at the group members' charts. Where is the

Moon by sign, house, aspect, and/or transit? Does this reveal something about the kind of feelings, or the manner in which they were expressed?

## Time Line Charts

Making time line charts is a long term project for regularly meeting groups interested in learning more about the Moon. Using posterboard, construction paper, or notebooks, have each person construct a time line, beginning with the year of birth and continuing to the present. Leave room for the future too. (Leave more room than you think you will need.) Then spend some time recalling and writing down the memories in brief. For example, write down 'first rode a bike' under the month during which that occurred for you. You'll be amazed what a wonderful recall tool this is.

One recovered memory will remind you of another, and another — until you have to start squeezing new headlines in. Then bring your time line to the group and share your new memories. Spend group time looking at the transits of major childhood events. (If your group can meet at the house of a member who has a computer, transits can be done quickly.) This look at past transits can be very enlightening. Often a fuller insight is gained about a particular experience. For instance, 'Ah, I learned to ride my bike when Jupiter was conjunct my Mars in Sagittarius!' or 'Saturn was squared my Sun when my fourth grade teacher made me go to summer school!'

## Autobiography

A further extension of making time line charts is to write an autobiography. This is a truly reflective lunar experience helping you to reawaken yourself to your past. So few of us spend time reflecting and digesting our experiences. Writing an autobiography can be a therapeutic and integrating experience.

## Pipe Cleaner Timeline

Buy a packet of long pipe cleaners (hobby shops carry these as well as tobacco shops). Pass one out to each person. Use the pipe cleaner as a symbol of your life. Twist it and bend it to express the progression of your life till now. Use it to express the highs and lows of your life, express major events, etc. Once everyone is finished, share what your life symbol means throughout your life.

## Sand Play

A technique offered by Jungian therapy is sand play. In this therapy, participants stimulate early life feelings and memories by returning to the sandbox complete with toys, etc.

## Motherpeace Tarot Deck

This is a lovely tool created by Vicki Noble and Karen Vogel to bring about inner healing of the feminine.[8] The emphasis on love and compassion, circular shape, and empowering images makes it ideal for tuning into the Moon's energy on a continuing basis.

## Moon/Cancer Films

Fanny and Alexander, On Golden Pond, Ordinary People, A Trip to Bountiful, Let It Be.

## Cancerian Planet Walk

Visualize yourself as a young child having just learned to walk. Feel the tentative, unsure feeling within. Begin to move, exploring your environment. Respond to things around you as if for the first time. Roll, crawl, walk, or fall as you move, being aware of your changing inner feelings from delight, fright, or surprise. This exercise will help you touch the lunar/Cancer part of your psyche.

## Moon Meditation — The Tides

(This is especially strong near a full moon in Water signs.)

An effective way to meditate on the Moon is to play a recording of ocean tides, with nothing but the wash of the waves. First get your tape recorder ready and place it next to you. Now close your eyes. Take some deep breaths. Turn on your recording and slowly begin to imagine that you are lying down in your favorite place near water. Feel the sand beneath you. Feel the sand under your feet, calves, thighs, butt, back, shoulders, arms, hands, head. Breathe deeply and allow yourself to drift. Allow yourself to follow the process and your feelings in any way it unfolds. When the music ends allow yourself some moments of quiet reflection and reorientation.

## Mirror Dancing

Turn on music which is flowing and easy to dance to. Begin in pairs. Loosen up your bodies, then have one of the pair raise their hand. That person is the Sun and will lead. The other dancer is the Moon and follows the Sun as exactly as possible. Follow with your feet, legs, body, arms, facial expression. Feel what the Sun is doing. After a time, switch roles. How does it feel to follow? To lead? Was it hard or easy to 'shadow' the Sun?

A variation is to have one partner pretend to be the mirror that the other is looking into. Add a dramatic element. You are hiding in a room and must keep from being discovered. Someone who is searching for you enters. He is standing right in front of you. You must be his reflection not to be discovered. Dramatic embellishing can add more thrills, concentration, and fun.

## Suggested Music

'Feel Flows' Surf's Up (The Beach Boys), 'Dock of the Bay' Best of Otis Redding

(Otis Redding), 'Hymn to Her' *Get Close* (The Pretenders), 'Woman' *Double Fantasy* (John Lennon), 'Waltzes and Nocturnes' (Chopin), *Clair de Lune* (Debussy), *Violin Concerto* (Beethoven), *Water Music* (Handel), *Blue Danube* (Strauss), 'Stardust' (Nat King Cole), 'The Tide is High' *Autoamerican* (Blondie), 'Here Comes the Rain Again' *Touch* (The Eurythmics).

The conference with the Angel Raphael

# Mercury, Gemini, And Virgo

Mercury is the thinking, analyzing function of the human psyche. It is the way we assimilate our experience through dividing, discriminating, and sorting out data. It is how we form connections, become aware of underlying relationships between things, and exchange ideas with others. Mercury serves the dual function of inner communication and communication with the world around us.

In this respect, Virgo represents Mercury's introverted, analytical inner aspect of thinking, while Gemini is the extroverted, outward-seeking aspect of communication. (Mercury is one planet which has a dual rulership of both Virgo and Gemini.)

Mercury is connected with the Greek Hermes, an androgynous being who possesses the keys of knowledge and carries messages between the Gods and humankind. Mercury is linked to words, the origins of language, all literature, and to all ways and means of communicating and educating through bodies of knowledge.

Individuals with strong Mercury/Gemini energy in their horoscope may have a healthy desire for acquiring knowledge and mental adaptability. If afflicted one can scatter their mental forces and use their social skills as a defense against deep intimacy. Those with less Mercury/Gemini energy may lack sociability.

Those with strong Mercury/Virgo may have excellent analytical skills and are willing to work hard for perfection. If afflicted one can be incessantly critical of self and others. Those with less Mercury/Virgo energy may lack focus and attention to detail or experience feelings of shyness and incompetence in some area of their life.

## Mercury/Gemini Experience

Mercury represents the particular skills and techniques we learn during our lives. Any experience of skill refinement and improvement is a good example of Mercury energy. Ideal for this is a guided imagery called 'Skill Rehearsal with a Master Teacher' which is described in Jean Houston's *The Possible Human*.[1] The exercise allows you to achieve a deeper learning, improve your motor connections between brain and body, and gain new resourcefulness in the use of your skills.

Time: 45 minutes. Directions can be pre-taped or guided by a facilitator.

Chose a skill you wish to improve. Go through the physical motions of the skill where you are, rehearsing with as much attention to detail as possible. Obviously it would be easier to practice a tennis swing than swimming the butterfly stroke. Once you have rehearsed, stop, and imagine in your mind's eye that you are doing this activity. Re-create as full as possible your body's response to this activity. Now go back and forth, acting out the skill, and seeing yourself acting out the skill in your mind/body. Now run around like a three year old, twisting, turning, rolling, jumping until you are exhausted, then lie down.

Listen to these instructions:

Feel yourself lying alone in the bottom of a little rowing boat. You are being carried out into the ocean by gentle waves. You feel relaxed as the waves carry you further and further out. The boat begins going down and around as if you are being carried in a vortex, deeper and deeper into the ocean. The water does not close in on you. The water rises above you and you go deeper into a tunnel of water. You land on the ocean floor. You discover a door handle which you pull. The door opens and you take a stone staircase leading to a realm beneath the ocean floor.

You step down, down, down, deeper and deeper. The stairs end and you are in a great cavern filled with stalactites and stalagmites. You find a stone corridor and walk down it. You come to an oak door over which is written 'The Room of the Skill.' Entering that room you find yourself in a place completely imbued with the presence and spirit of your skill. In this room is the master of the skill. This being is your master teacher and in the time that follows this teacher will give you full and patient instructions to help you improve your skills.

The master teacher may speak in words, or teach you through feelings or muscular sensations. The learning will be effective and deep and give you much more confidence. The skilled person within you is emerging and overcoming inhibitions and blocks, as you are undergoing very intensive training and learning. (Take five minutes, which will be all the time you need to have this rich lesson with the master teacher.)

Now it is time to leave your master teacher. Thank this being and know that you can return here whenever you want. Before you go you see a special light streaming down from the ceiling. Stand in the light. It is the light of confirmation of your skill. Feel the deepening and confirming of your skill throughout your mind and body, letting the skill become a natural part of you. You are being confirmed in your skill. (Allow 30-40 seconds for this.) Leave the room carefully closing the door. Move quickly, through the corridor to the cavern and into your little boat, feeling the skill growing in you. Emerge up and up through the vortex, reversing itself now to bring you up and up to the ocean's surface. You feel your skill continuing to grow within you, permeating your whole being, rooting itself in all your nerves, neurons, cells and synapses.

As your boat is approaching the shore you feel excited and want to get out and try your skill. When you touch the shore you are wide awake and full of your skill, and you get up as soon as possible and try it out. Rehearse your skill physically. Now stop and rehearse it in your mind/body. See the image of you performing the activity perfectly. Go back and forth between doing your skill and seeing yourself do it in your mind's eye. Rehearse until you feel the integrating of the two.

In closing ask yourself:

What do you notice about the improvement of your skill?

What do you remember about your master teacher?

I participated in this experience in one of Jean's workshops. Before we started this journey to the master teacher, Jean asked for a volunteer to demonstrate their skill both before and after the visualization. A woman volunteered to play the piano. She was extremely self-conscious, played hesitantly, and made quite a few mistakes.

After the visualization she sat down with a look of sheer joy on her face and played the same piece smoothly and flawlessly.

## Mercury Movement

Mercury's action is quick, changeable and mischievous. Put on some Mercurial music, for instance music from the Talking Heads. Move your body and mime with your hands the conversational rhythm of the music.

## Dialogue with a Planet

An important technique of interaction that many of us do not consider is to talk with our own unconscious through our planets. The planets are not abstract symbols; they are living energy within us. Sit down with your natal chart and have an exchange with a planet giving you trouble. Ask yourself one of these questions: On a regular basis what planetary energies most affect my life? (Examine your natal chart and list them in order.) What planetary energies are affecting me most right now in my life? (Examine your transits. What strong harmonious/adverse aspects are now most evident?)

This can be done like a meditation. Take a few deep breaths and begin to focus on the planet you want some answers from. Imagine that a living presence or archetype of that planet is before you. (You might imagine Hermes for Mercury, Aphrodite for Venus, a warrior for Mars, the tarot card of the Fool for Uranus, or the High Priestess for the Moon.)

Visualize that image standing before you. Invite it to sit down to talk with you. Continue to deepen your concentration, flooding yourself with the feeling of that planetary energy before you. Ask these questions one at a time:

If this planet brings problems for you ask, 'Why are you giving me such trouble?'

If this planet is clearly helping you, thank it for its help and ask, 'What else do you have to give me?'

Then ask, 'What is it you need from me?'

Allow some quiet time for each answer to emerge. Because you are taking the time to interact with your own unconscious, new insights and answers do come.

## Memory Games

Because Mercury has to do with the function of ordering data it can be stimulated by a game, like the following one, that exercises our power of memory. Take a full deck of cards. Spread them out face down. Select a card and turn it over. Select a second. If the numbers match, start a pile for matched cards and take another turn. If they do not, return them face down in their original place and try to remember what number is where. Time yourself on how long it takes you to remember and match all the pairs. Doing this exercise on a regular basis will show a measure of improvement in your memory.

Another version of the game allows two players using one deck of cards, scoring one point per card. In a group, you might pair up and see what team can pair up all the cards in the shortest time.

To play this game with a group, gather a number of small objects (about 25) on a board and cover them so they cannot be seen. Uncover the board and show the objects to the group for a brief 10 seconds. Cover them again and ask that each person write down as many objects as they can remember.

## Telephone

This well known children's game is a good Gemini exercise, telling us how clearly and accurately we listen and communicate. Form a circle. Someone begins by whispering in the ear of the person next to them a fairly long and descriptive sentence which is challenging for adults. Pass it on around the circle, having the last person speak the sentence they received aloud.

## Conceptualize the Sky

The Zodiac and planets are part of the astrologer's conceptual model, yet many of us do not keep a daily awareness of where the planets are. Stop and think. What degree is the Sun in and where is it in relation to you right now? Where is the Moon? What part of its cycle is it in — first quarter, full moon, etc? Where is Mercury? Mars? Venus? Is it the morning star, or evening star? Where are all the other planets?

At night, go out and find the Zodiac belt and identify what planets are visible. Which ones are about to rise or set? Which are on the other side of the Earth? Making a daily mental or visual observation of the moving planets around you will keep you more in touch.

Some of us do not have a good mental grasp of the astronomical model we use, nor do we have a good understanding of celestial motion. What is the celestial equator, declination, right ascension, azimuth, planetary nodes, for example? If you don't know the answers to these questions, buy a book on astronomy for astrologers. Frequently, there are classes in astronomy at conferences — take one. Or sign up for a few classes at your local planetarium.

## One Week Event Diary

Keep a written log of astrological observations you make of events around you. If you see a pedestrian angrily shaking a finger at a motorist, write it down with the notation (Mercury/Mars), or a heavy-set man buying some éclairs in a bakery (Sun/Jupiter/Venus/Neptune), or a child hugging his teddy bear (Moon/Venus), or a funeral procession passing you on the highway (Saturn/Mercury). Relate what you see to the astrological symbols. You'll learn to use astrology more readily in relation to your day-to-day environment.

## 'Cocktail Party'

In a group, hold a 10 minute 'cocktail party' where each of you is the host. Your goal is to make social/verbal contact with everyone in the room. Was this uncomfortable for you? Did you feel at home in a highly social, communicating environment?

## Miming

Form a pair and take turns miming each other's movements. Try to observe carefully and imitate as perfectly as you can, paying attention to eyes, hands, expressions, etc.

A version of this requires that each pair do something together in front of the group. For instance, mime being a pair of puppies, or objects which work in tandem together (mortar and pestle, hook and eye, two turning pedals on a bike, etc.). Have the group guess what you and your partner are imitating.

Strong Mercury people tend to be excessively verbal. Doing non-verbal exercises in which we express ourselves is helpful. With a partner, make statements about everything you have done since waking up. Instead of repeating the statement, your partner uses his or her hands to express the statement silently. Switch roles.

## Follow the Leader

Ask the group to line up against one wall in a large space. Turn on some good dance music. Take turns leading out with a movement or action which everyone tries to mimic exactly as they move across the room to the other side. Continue until each member has led a movement at least once.

## Learning to Listen

The consciousness it takes to listen is in itself the discipline that sharpens one's ability to communicate. Sit with a partner you do not know. Take turns telling each other about yourselves. Pay attention to what your partner says and how she says it. Now introduce your partner to the group mirroring as closely as possible how your partner introduced herself to you.

## Relaxation

Both Gemini's and Virgo's primary tool is their thinking function. They have strong tendencies to get carried away in their heads, absorbed with their thought processes and out of touch with their feelings and their bodies.

For Mercurial people, any mental relaxation technique is excellent. They should learn to 'dial the mind down', to breathe deeply and return awareness to their body. Learning how to just 'be' is good for Mercurial types.

## My Ideal Trip

Mercury, particularly Gemini, is associated with travel. In your imagination spend 10 minutes creating your ideal trip. Where would you go? How would you get there? How long would you stay? What would you do?

Variations: In a group, have a member lead a guided journey, re-creating their most memorable travel experience.

Get a group together to see slides and photographs of a recent exotic trip taken by someone in the group. Have them tell in vivid detail what the experience was like. Ask each person to imagine as fully as possible what the sights and sounds of the trip were like.

## Language

The process of learning a new language is a Mercury experience. Take a class or course of study.

## Charades

For an experience of communicating without use of your mouth or words, this is a classic game.

## Gibberish

With a partner, spend five minutes in conversation without using any known language. It may be hard to get started but once you have the hang of this you can communicate quite explicitly. It's fun and silly.

## Siblings

Get together with your brothers or sisters and ask each to write three paragraphs about your mutual family. First describe your father, then your mother, and finally your early home life. Compare notes. Do you each see them differently? Can you see, in your brother or sister's chart, why they responded the way they did?

## Dictionary Game

This is a classic game of words, word mastery, and trickery — all a part of Mercury energy. In a group, hand out slips of paper and pencils. Give each person a turn to trick the others by choosing an obscure word from the dictionary. The object of the game is to make up a definition that sounds like it fits. The real definition is written down by the player who has chosen the word, with fake definitions by everyone else. Gather them and read aloud. Each person then guesses which definition is the dictionary's version. A player scores a point for choosing the right definition or when someone chooses his or her faked one. If no one chooses the correct definition the player who chose the word stumps the group and scores additional points by taking one point away from each player. This is a game in which you learn new words and sharpen your ability to organize thoughts. It can be challenging if you play with a group of people with strong Gemini/Virgo energy.

## 'Trivial Pursuit'

The board game 'Trivial Pursuit' is an ideal game made for the Gemini/Virgos among us!

## Health Profile

Virgo is often connected with our health concerns. Make a health profile of your past to help clarify some of your health patterns.

Several months ago I ran across my medical file recorded by my family doctor. It documented every illness, accident, complaint, and immunization I have had since birth. By writing down each illness, and noting the particular transits at that time, some interesting patterns were revealed to me. For instance, I have had three accidents involving cars, motorcycles, or horses, as well as two accidents with kitchen knives under a Mars/Uranus transit, a repeated side effect to a particular drug every time Neptune aspected the ruler of my sixth house, and noticeable weight gain whenever Jupiter squared or opposed my natal Venus over the last nine years. Knowing this I may better safeguard myself with similar future transits.

## Task of Detail

Observe yourself doing some task which needs attention to detail. It could be a handicraft project, sewing, knitting, woodworking, or cleaning and organizing your office junk drawer. How do you feel while doing the task? Do you feel you did it well? Are you satisfied with the results?

## Work Analysis

Spend time examining your current work situation. Are you satisfied with your job? Satisfied with how you are performing? What bothers you about it now? What's pleasant about it? Do you like your fellow workers? Who? Why? If something is bothering you about work or co-workers, can you think of something or someone that may help the situation? Can you develop a strategy and plan to deal with it more successfully?

## Mercury Films

*Absence of Malice, All the President's Men, Altered States, Breathless, Room With A View, House of Games, Diary of Anne Frank.*

## Mercury/Gemini Planet Walk

Visualize yourself as a young curious teenager. Feel the peppy, fresh energy exuding from you. Adjust your walk so it is light and spritely, almost as if you were just barely keeping on the earth. Express curiosity about many things as you walk down the street, keeping your attention flitting from one object of interest to another.

## Mercury/Virgo Planet Walk

Observe yourself walking normally. Can you notice any way in which you can change to make your walk more efficient? Notice the whole process of your walk as minutely and precisely as possible, from small motor responses to where and how your foot carries your weight. How long is your average footstep? Where do you focus your eyes when walking. Walk now in very slow motion. Do you notice anything else about the way you walk?

## Mercury Meditation

Story-telling is a Mercurial form of meditation whether you are the teller or listener. The story-teller weaves words to create stories. Stories are designed to make us think and listen. Curl up with a good story.

## Suggested Music

'Coyote' *Hejira* (Joni Mitchell), 'Cross-eyed and Painless' *Remain in Light* (Talking Heads), 'Once in a Lifetime' *Remain in Light* (Talking Heads), *Speaking in Tongues* (Talking Heads), 'I Feel so Good' (Mose Allison), Songs of Bob Dylan, *Sergeant Pepper's Lonely Hearts Club Band* (The Beatles), 'Mercury, The Winged Messenger' *The Planets* (Holst).

# Venus, Taurus and Libra

Venus is the feminine, balancing and harmonizing function of the psyche. Venus is connected with the more ancient Greek goddess Aphrodite, the goddess of love and beauty. Venus is the urge to unite the opposites, look for similarities and bring equilibrium. She is linked in a magnetic polarity with Mars, the god of war, which expresses the opposite principle of aggressive action and coercion, exposing differences and creating waves that rock equilibrium.

Venus is linked to all forms of behavior that produce solidarity, coherence, sympathy and peace, everything we value, money, possessions, relationships, intimacy, and our aesthetic sense and appreciation of art and beauty.

Venus has sensual and softly erotic attributes, contrary to Mars which is sexual, raw and primitive. The Renaissance painter Titian depicted this sensuality in his painting, *Venus*. Botticelli's *Birth of Venus* is a painting that not only captures her sensual, full nature but paints her arising in a shell born from the sea. This myth of Venus' origin of birth is worth noting since the higher, more refined manifestation of Venus is Neptune, ruler of the sea.

Individuals with strong Venus/Libra energy in their horoscope can be agreeable and co-operative. If afflicted one may be too passive and idealistic, choosing not to confront the difficult part of any relationship. Those with little Libra energy may be unwilling to work at long term committed relationships.

Individuals with strong Venus/Taurus energy can be determined to succeed and have a steadying effect on others. If afflicted one may be acquisitive since their security

Adam and Eve

needs are often directly tied up to possessions, money or sensual pleasure. Those with less Taurus energy may have little urge to enjoy the pleasures of the world. They may not be very sense-oriented.

## Venus — A Sense Experience

Since Venus influence, especially with Taurus, is so sense-oriented, here is a group experience for you to feel it. For a touch experience gather objects such as balloons, clay, slinkys, magnets, whiffle balls, paper clips, etc. Ask the group to sit in a circle and space themselves close enough to easily pass the objects around. Have them take a few deep breaths to relax the body. Rubbing palms together will stimulate the blood and tactile sense.

Because we rely so habitually on our sight, these sense experiences are best done with eyes closed to help focus more acute attention on the other senses. Ask this to be done in silence since spontaneous verbal responses may be distracting for others. Begin by passing each object one at a time in the same direction around the circle.

Encourage each participant to experiment with the object, brushing it across their cheek, neck, wrists, legs or feet. What do you imagine this looks like? Smell it. Taste it. Listen to it. Do you notice any sound it is making? Imagine each object to be a special personal object of yours. What kind of feelings do you have with each one?

After each object has gone around, place it in the center. When an individual has experienced all the objects, have them open their eyes and sit quietly until everyone is finished. This process is interesting to watch as facial expressions reveal a variety of feelings — certain objects elicit similar responses of pleasure and dislike. For many you can observe 'the child' come out. In fact, some of these objects will stimulate early childhood memories, especially objects like slinkys, jacks, chalk, etc. (If stimulating memory is your goal, this experience could be used for a Moon exercise as well.)

If you want to try this on your own, gather your sense objects in front of you, close your eyes, mix up the objects and taking one at a time immerse yourself in touching, smelling, or tasting. Or, for a more sensual experience, choose various fabrics — silk, taffeta, velvet, fur, lace, ribbons, etc.

To experience the sense of smell, gather small bags of different fragrant herbs — chamomile, bay leaf, basil, dill, etc. Or a number of different and distinctive perfumes. To experience the sense of taste gather different flavors and textures of foods — lemon, marshmallows, grapes, cooked pasta noodles, tobacco, etc. Or taste different kinds of nuts.

## Oranges

Bring to the group one orange for each group member. Have each member choose an orange and sit with it for five minutes, noticing special markings, how it feels, etc. Then put all the oranges in the center, mix them up well and have each member find their orange.

## Contact

Our sense of touch is as important to our contact with reality as our sense of sight. For hundreds of years in our culture we have encountered the world primarily through the domination of sight. For many, the world of touch is new territory. Here are ways with which to communicate without words and learn to touch.

## Massage

Massage is a healing art. When practiced between friends or lovers it can be a beautiful way to show love and caring. The essence of massage is the unique way it communicates without words. Most of us are out of touch with our bodies and not paying too much attention to the stresses that build up in us. Massage can be a wonderful gift that helps another get more in touch with their body, release tensions, relax, and receive some nurturing. For more specific information on techniques of massage, try *The Massage Book* by George Downing.[1]

## Contact Games

These are games which bring people into contact through touch. Remember to follow any experience that has to do with touch or intimacy with an adequate amount of process time. This may be stirring for a number of players, stimulating their issues about intimacy, sexuality, or relationships. Be sensitive to this. Contact games in general are better played after a level of trust has been built in the group.

**Contact Dancing** — described under ice-breaking.

**Hug Tag** — described under ice-breaking.

## A Massage Line

Have the group turn in one direction. For five minutes spend time massaging the back, neck, and head of the person in front of you.

## Spoon Touch

One player is blindfolded. He or she takes a wooden spoon in each hand and stands in the center. One player comes and stands in front of the blindfolded player in any position they choose — kneeling, bending, laying down. The blindfolded player tries to identify who the person is through touching them with spoons.

## Sheet Game

Each player puts a sheet over their head. Walk around the room in silence and try to identify each other by feeling through the sheet. How do you recognize people? Perhaps by particular physical features? Afterwards ask the group how they felt about feeling others through the sheet? Hesitant? Aggressive? Embarrassed?

## Contacting Others

Have everyone close their eyes and begin to move, arms extended. When two people make contact square off facing each other keeping your eyes closed. Drop your arms. Focus on your feelings. What do you feel about this person? Spend a minute sensing them. Then move onto making contact with another in the same manner. After four or five contacts sit down, open your eyes and make a list. What words describe the quality of contact with one, two, etc. (You might have met up with the same person twice.) Now can you match up your sense experience with the particular individual?

## Stand Up

This co-operative game is great for drawing a group together. It results in a whole crowd of struggling, giggling folks. Start with two people sitting back to back, knees bent and elbows linked. Now stand up together! With a little practice and co-operation this will work. Now add one more person and try to stand up. Continue to add people until the whole group is attempting to get up together. (The trick for a large group is to stand up quickly and at precisely the same moment.) If you make it past four people, your group has made a genuine accomplishment!

## Pillows

Since Taurus loves comfort, gather a huge amount of pillows together. Take turns piling into them, rolling around, under them, surrounding yourself with their 'squooshy' soft comfort. What words describe this experience? Do you have any planets in Taurus?

## Food Addictions

Venus can represent food addiction, particularly to sugar. Examine your food patterns, especially your use of sugar. How many times a week do you eat dessert? Do you get cravings for it? Do you binge out on a particular food? If so, when? Is this a technique for coping with painful emotion? If change is desirable, read any of the many books now on the market about alcoholic addiction. The same strategies can be applied to sugar addictions.

As a group, eat out together. This could be done with an eye toward just enjoying and sharing the food and company. Or go to a restaurant pretending you are all food critics, evaluating the food, decor, and service.

Spend an evening together discussing food. What's your favorite food, cuisine, most memorable meal, most decadent food experience? See if you can come to a group consensus and choose the best restaurant in your city that has the best malted milks, sushi, hamburgers, desserts, coffee, etc.

For an experience in learning taste discrimination go to a wine tasting session. Many of the larger cities now have classes or one-night tastings of particular wine varieties. (Did you know there are over 80 descriptive categories used by wine connoisseurs to discriminate the subtle tastes in wine?)

## Eating with Mindfulness

With the greater availability of fast foods and eating on the run we are more inclined to eat mindlessly, stuffing in food and being mostly unaware of our experience. This exercise can help to regain the sense of pleasure and enjoyment we can experience from eating. Take a piece of bread or your favorite cheese and feel the texture with your hands and fingers. Notice the appearance and color. Smell it. Now taste it, noticing its texture on your tongue, the explosion of taste sensations in your mouth. Savor the taste. Chew slowly, noting the changing flavor and texture sensations in your mouth. Above all, take the time to really eat.

## Pleasure

Make a list of your pleasures and delights. What are the things you truly enjoy? Windsurfing on the lake? Ice cream bars? Swinging in a hammock in Oaxaca, Mexico? Going to the season première at the symphony? Recalling these memories can heighten your sense of pleasure.

Choose one that is most vivid. Visualize this experience deeply as if it were happening now. Return to that moment. Hear it, smell it, let that experience fill your whole body. If appropriate, reach out and bring it close. Or move with it. Enact that pleasure, allowing it to flood your being. You might sing or draw it. Relish this re-experiencing.

## My Most Attractive Feature

Make a list of your most attractive physical features. Rank them in order. Choose your most attractive feature. (If you are in a group, share this.) Then evaluate this experience. Was it easy for you to come up with features you like? Was it difficult, and if so, why? If this was difficult, do you have either a natal or transiting Saturn in challenging aspect to Venus? Do your feelings mirror any aspect you may have to your natal Venus?

## Clothes Evaluation

People with strong Venus in their horoscopes can be 'clotheshorses.' Take time to go through and evaluate your wardrobe. What don't you like? What no longer fits? What are your basic color themes? Have you had 'your colors' done? Are you spring, winter, summer, or fall? What accessories do you have? What items do you need to look for to give your wardrobe more versatility?

Or make an appointment with a clothes consultant to have them help you overhaul your wardrobe. Jupiter trine/sextile Venus is a wonderful time to buy your spring wardrobe. If you want to shop and find things you like, do it at this time. You may spend more money than you want, but you will love what you buy. This is a classic for beautifying or pampering yourself. Get a new hairstyle, cosmetics, massage, or manicure.

## Parties

Venus/Jupiter transits help to make memorable parties and/or celebrations. Try having one when Venus is in easy aspect to your Jupiter, or better still, Jupiter to your Venus. With good food, wine, company, and pleasant environment, this will be one occasion talked about for a long time!

## Money Assessment

Money and Venus are intimately connected. How do you feel about your money? Do you budget? Or do you have no idea where your money goes? How much money do you need, or want? Have you ever seen a financial planner? Is that a good idea now? Take out a 20, 50, or 100 dollar bill. Talk to your money. (Sounds silly but it can help you get a clearer idea of your relationship to it.) Or if you want to create more money, make a 'money magnet', setting aside a large sum of money which you will not spend. Its purpose is to act as an attractor for more money. Wrap your stash up in a cloth bag, leather pouch, or silk and keep it in a sacred place. Treat it as a ritual or ceremonial object. See what happens.

Jupiter/Venus aspects are superb for ritual, especially rituals to empower your love, wealth or healing ability. It's a powerful time to send healing to self and others.

## Erotica

Venus symbolizes that aspect of our sexuality that is gentle, subtle, inviting, sensual, and feminine. Much of erotic literature (*not* pornography) is Venusian in tone. Erotica dwells on the emotions of relationship, the excitement of romance, and the subtleties of surroundings.

Before Anais Nin's *Little Birds* and *Delta of Venus*,[2] women had little choice but to read Victorian erotica written by men. Because of this, 12 years ago, Anais Nin encouraged women to write their own erotica. Now, over the past few years, women's erotica has blossomed and it is available from large publishers and mainstream book clubs.

If you want to experience Venusian erotica more intimately, here are other good sources of reading — *Ladies Own Erotica*[3] by the Kensington Ladies' Society, or Lonnie Barbach's *Pleasure or Erotic Interludes*.[4] These are sensitive and well written books.

## Relationships

For most of us our first significant relationships are with our parents. Write down a list of people with whom you have formed your most significant relationships from birth until this current time. After seeing them written down, go back one at a time and reflect. What quality of feelings does this relationship have? What is your most pleasant memory with this friend? What quality do you most like or dislike about them? What did and didn't you like about the way you were with them? By doing this re-evaluation, you may see a pattern of the way you relate to others.

## Art

Art as a creative medium is an expression of Venus. Spend a day at your local art gallery or an exhibition. Or take a class in art appreciation. Read a book on how to approach and criticize art. Or spend time reflecting on one of your favorite artists. Take a class exploring a new creative expression such as pottery, still life, photography, dance, or music.

## Art Supply Box

This is an indispensable resource for anyone involved in experiential astrology. The more variety of medium you have at your fingertips, the better for your spontaneity and inspiration. Get large sheets of construction paper, clay, colored paper, Magic Markers, colored pencils, crayons, finger paint, temperas, water color, glitter, feathers, sequins, plaster cast gauze (for impromptu mask-making), and basics such as glue, scissors, tape, etc. Keep them together and accessible in a large cardboard box. Just knowing you have these resources will incline you to want to make use of them.

## 'My Heart Now'

Draw a picture of what your heart looks like now using colors, images, words, whatever feels right. Study this picture. Is there any negative feeling in your heart now? Is this feeling connected to a particular individual? If you want to do something about this, focus on the parts of your heart that are clear, warm, and loving. Imagine that part is expanding slowly into the more negative spaces. Intensify the positive image and feeling. Allow your love to take in the imbalanced energy. Is there something you want to take into your heart now? Imagine it in front of you. Now see your heart suck it up like a vacuum cleaner, absorbing it inside.

## Luxurious Baths

A true manifestation of Venus is to pamper yourself in a special bath. Try a bubble bath. Or an herbal bath. Some herbs are used for relaxing muscles (sassafras bark, mugwort, burdock root), soothing the body (comfrey, chamomile), and others to stimulate and rejuvenate (lavender, peppermint, nettles). Place a handful of herbs in a pot, bring to the boil and simmer for 10 to 20 minutes, or fill a muslin bag or tea brewing ball with herbs and drop it into your tub.

## Jeanne Rose's *Herbal Body Book*[5]

Here is a wealth of ideas for natural beauty care for men and women. Ms Rose includes a glossary of useful herbs both for health and beauty, facial steaming, natural lotions, shampoos, make-up, conditioning packs, herbal hair dyes, and herbal baths. Get together with a small group of friends and spend the afternoon beautifying.

## Lingerie

Nothing makes a woman feel more feminine than lingerie. Just knowing you have pretty lingerie on under your street clothes is psychologically lifting. If you have Saturn aspecting Venus a trip to the lingerie store might give you the psychological boost you need.

## Goddess Worship

When Venus is in good aspect to Jupiter or Pluto by transit, you can strongly empower yourself with the feminine goddess energy. If you have a meditation altar or sacred space, create an altar to the goddess. You might have a statue of Kwan Yin, or mentally envision and embody Ishtar, Inanna, Psyche, Persephone, or Aphrodite. If you have a Jupiter transit that lasts a month, spend that time dwelling on the goddess energy within you, inviting the goddess into your consciousness. Bring her out with you into the world. If you have a good Pluto transit to Venus, this year-long positive transit would be the most powerful time for catharsis and in-depth healing of your heart. Use this magical time to deeply heal your heart's wounds from the past, transforming and creating a change of heart.

Work intensely during this time to deepen your contact with your own heart. Then take the strength of that inner love and send love lines out to those you know. Radiate your love lines up and out of the atmosphere and send them radiating around the earth.

A very cathartic group experience especially at a large conference is to ask each individual to intensify the love in their heart. Consciously send it out to all those who touched you. Then send it to anyone in the room you may have had difficulty with. Let the power of the group love dissolve that difficulty. Let the barriers and separations dissolve. Ask the group to see their hearts linked up to everyone else's. See one big heart. Imagine the group heart expanding and contracting with each of your breaths.

## Venus Films

*E.T., Black Stallion, Out of Africa, Casablanca, South Pacific, Emmanuelle, Splendor in the Grass.*

## Venus Walk

Venus is reflected in flowing, sensual, and soft movements. Think of the moment you first knew you were in love. Recapture that joy in your body, in your step, in your smile. Do this while wearing something wonderful.

## Venus Meditation

Lay down and get yourself comfortable, preferably on a pile of soft pillows. Turn on some Venus music. Take a few deep breaths. Focus your attention on your heart. With each breath expand your heart filling it with love. Expand your heart and your love for a few minutes until your heart feels as big as your body. Now let your heart be a dancing heart. Then, after a few minutes, let your heart be still. Breathe deeply and slowly into it. Mentally chant repeatedly, 'I will build and preserve all that is meaningful in my life.' Spend a few minutes just drifting, absorbing your joy.

Another powerful variation is to ask, as you are expanding your heart, 'How much bliss can I take in?' As you feel your heart resisting, limiting, breathe into that resistance until you can feel it expand. Keep asking yourself this question, reaching a limit, breathing, and opening. (This is wonderful meditative process to use in rituals especially utilizing Venus/Jupiter/Pluto/Neptune transits.)

## Suggested Music

'Icarus' (Various Artists), *Deep Breakfast* (Ray Lynch), 'Sailing' (Christopher Cross), 'Natural Woman' *The Best of Aretha Franklin* (Aretha Franklin), 'Love is All Around' *Greatest Hits* (The Troggs), 'There is Love' (Captain and Tennille), 'Evergreen' (Barbara Streisand), 'Ave Maria' (Schubert), 'Jesu, Joy of Man's Desiring' (J.S. Bach), 'To a Wild Rose' (Liszt), 'Angels of Comfort' (Iasos), 'On Wings of Song' (Mendelssohn), *Canon in D Major* (Pachelbel).

# Mars And Aries

Mars symbolizes the first step in the process of individuation, how we differentiate and separate ourselves from the group and our manner of initiating this process. It is how we act to get things done. Without Mars, little would be accomplished. Mars is the 'primitive' root of our instinctual and biological urges, especially our sexual nature. Mars tells us how we are likely to feel about sex, the type of partners we attract, potential conflicts in relationships, as well as how we approach confrontation.

Individuals with strong Mars/Aries energy in the horoscope have a love of action (athletics) and a pioneering spirit which can act with independence and initiative. If afflicted the frustrated energy can turn to aggression — bad temper, destructiveness, egocentricity, and recklessness. Those with little Martian energy can lack initiative, self-motivation, self-assertion, and the impetus needed to bring things to fruition.

## Mars — NASA Group Adventure Game [1]

This game is ideal to explore the Aries/Libra polarity, observing independent and co-operative group decision making processes in a Martian situation — survival.

Allow one-and-a-half to three hours. If the group is large, break up into smaller groups of five to eight players. Each player should have paper, pencil, and these instructions: You are members of a space team which had originally planned to meet up with a mother spacecraft on the surface of the moon. As a result of technical difficulties, however, your spacecraft has been forced to land about 200 miles away from the meeting place. A lot of equipment on board was damaged during landing. Since your survival depends on reaching the mother ship, you have to choose the most vital of the available equipment for making the 200 mile journey. Below you will find a list of 15 items that were not damaged. Your task is to arrange them in order of their importance for the journey. Write '1' beside the most important item, '2' beside the second most important item, and so on.

Box of matches
Tube of food concentrate
15 yards of nylon rope

30 yards of parachute
Portable heater
Two pistols
Box of powdered milk
Two 10-gallon oxygen cylinders
Astronomical chart
Rubber dinghy, automatically inflatable, with bottles of $CO_2$
Magnetic compass
Five gallons of water
Signal flares (ignitable in vacuum)
First aid box with syringes
Telecommunication receiver and transmitter with solar batteries

In this exercise, we act out our ability to make decisions under pressure, test the most sensible way of making decisions, and see what difficulties arise in the process.

First, as an individual, work out your own solution to the problem. Then gather with your group and arrive at a joint consensus. (This means everyone in the group must agree to the order necessary for survival. Sometimes a full consensus is impossible but try to design a plan that each member can at least partially accept.) Once the group has arrived at a solution, compare the group's plan to that of the NASA experts who gave the following order:

Oxygen cylinders (fills respiration requirements); water (replenishes loss by sweating); astronomical chart (one of the principal means of finding direction); food concentrate (supply daily food required); telecommunication apparatus (distress signal transmitter for possible communication with mother ship); nylon rope (useful in tying an injured individual onto another or for help in climbing); first-aid box (oral pills or injectable medicine valuable); parachute (shelter against sun's rays); rubber dinghy ($CO_2$ cartridge for self-propulsion across chasms); signal flares (distress call when line of sight possible); pistols (self-propulsion devices could be made from them); powdered milk (food, mixed with water for drinking); heater (useful only if party landed on dark side); magnetic compass (probably no magnetized poles, thus useless); matches (little or no use on the moon).

At this point, have the group reflect on their own charts and how they handled both the individual decision-making and the group process. If you are a strong Aries Capricorn type, did you decide quickly or attempt to take control? How soon? Did you hold a strong opinion and force your view on the group? If you are more Libran or Virgo in nature, did you abdicate control, not care about control, withdraw, or find yourself easily swayed?

Recognizing current transits can add another dimension of understanding. For instance, with your transiting Neptune square Mars, did you find difficulty deciding what choices were best? Is this influence now affecting your normal take charge behavior? How did this affect the group and how is it influencing areas of your life now?

If you are facilitating this group, be aware of the evolving group process. Did members work objectively? Emotionally? Was there a power struggle? How was this

The mouth of Hell

handled? How well did the group get along during this process? Who was quiet, verbal, pushy or argumentative? Your observations will serve to help the group further understand its process and experience.

The NASA game opens and stimulates recognition of behavior patterns in everyday life, both as an individual and as a member of a group. Much interaction and insight can result.

## Athletics

An obvious way to feel Martian energy is through sports. Any activity in which you physically exert yourself is Martian. Any sport in which you test yourself and aim toward higher physical achievements, such as weight lifting or body building, is Martian.

If you have good transits involving Mars, plan to take a challenging and physically exerting excursion like a 20 mile roller skate, or a 100 mile bike trip. Or take an obstacle training or survival course.

## Adventure!

Most of us know that when we take risks and expose ourselves to challenge we live fully in each moment. We become more *alive*. Nothing's more exhilarating than traveling to another part of the world and testing yourself physically, mentally, and emotionally with a new experience. Take an adventure! Book a river raft trip down the Colorado. Go scuba diving in Cozumel. Take that long dreamed of trip trekking the Himalayas. Many of us have secret longings like this. Don't just long to begin an adventure, *do it*!

## Competitive Sports

Mars individuals love to challenge themselves against others, especially in individual sports that pit one person's ability against another — wrestling, tennis, golf, downhill racing. Observe this sense of competition when engaged in a sport.

## Professional Football Game

Few sports express pure, brute, raw Martian energy as well as football. Get yourself as close to the action as possible. Spend post-game time in the neighborhood sports bar. See how it feels to get rowdy.

## Amusement Parks

The excitement and thrills of an amusement park are Martian. Observe how you approach going on that first ride. What words describe your process? How do you confront risks and challenges?

## Emergencies

Have you or anyone in the group ever found themselves in an emergency situation? Have you pulled someone from a burning car, or given CPR to someone having a heart attack? Tell about this experience. Did you act without thinking or was your action calculated? Did you at any time feel fear or danger for yourself? Do you recall experiencing any physical sensations while responding? How did you feel afterwards?

## Aries/Libra Pushing

Pair up with someone of comparable physical strength and spend a minute pushing against each other. Then join another pair and take turns being a strength of one pushing against the strength of three. Notice your feelings while you are doing this. Do you like pushing? Do you feel challenged when pushing three others or resigned to losing against them?

For a Libra/Aries version of this get into pairs and take turns being the aggressive one who pushes and the other who submits. Which role feels more familiar? Which didn't you like? (This could reveal something of your male/female elemental split, or about your Libra/Aries contact axis to other planets. It may also reflect current transits).

## Anger

Recall the last time you really got angry. Who were you angry at? How did the process unfold? How did you respond? Did you confront the person explosively? In control but direct? Did you have to think about it first? Did you 'stuff' your anger? Did your responses correspond to the aspects of Mars in your chart? Or was there a fiery square or opposition by transit at the time of your argument?

Observe anger in others and how they express it. What sign do you imagine their Mars is in?

## Observing Your Mars

Make a list of your responses to these questions:
What makes you angry?
When and how did you last take a risk?
When and how have you been courageous?
For what causes would you crusade?
For what causes would you physically fight?

## Martian Images on TV

Television is loaded with examples of aggressive, macho, hard guys. Turn on any channel and there is bound to be a number of hard-hitting good guy-bad guy story lines.

## Mars Films

*Mad Max Beyond Thunderdome, Raging Bull, Pumping Iron, Rambo, Mona Lisa, Fatal Attraction.*

## Mars Planetary Walk

Assertive, aggressive, and direct. Have you recently pushed your way onto a subway? Or hurried to beat someone in line? What feelings are associated with this act — uncaring, childish, embarassed, triumphant? Is this the way you frequently are? Rarely are? Examine Mars in your natal chart.

## Mars Meditation

Since Mars relates to action, a moving meditation would be appropriate. To experience Mars in Libra try a T'ai Chi class. T'ai Chi has been practiced for over 600 years as a meditational technique, health practice, martial art, and is essentially a sacred dance for evoking the life force. The practice of a T'ai Chi form is a series of movement patterns intended to be executed with no excess muscular activity or tension in the center of gravity so that all parts of the body are properly balanced. When done correctly, it generates the life force throughout the entire body and revitalizes one's energy.

## Suggested Music

'Mars' from *The Planets* (Holst), 'Birds of Fire' (John McLaughlin), *Dynamic Meditation* (Music of Shree Rajneesh Ashram), *Flashdance* soundtrack, 'Immigrant Song' *Led Zeppelin III* (Led Zeppelin), 'The Ride of the Valkyries' (Wagner), 'Pull up to the Bumper' *Nightclubbing* (Grace Jones), 'Music for Bouzouki and Orchestra' (Theodorakis), *Marche Slave* (Tchaikovsky), 'African Sanctus' (David Fanshawe), 'Marches' (John Phillip Sousa), *Chariots of Fire* soundtrack, *The Empire Strikes Back* soundtrack, *Oklahoma* soundtrack, 'Missionary Man' *Revenge* (The Eurythmics), 'I Need a Man' *Savage* (The Eurythmics), *Toccata and Fugue in D* (J.S. Bach).

# Jupiter and Sagittarius

With Jupiter we leave behind the forces of the personal realm, our social drives and impulses experienced through the Sun, Moon, Mercury, Venus, and Mars. Jupiter and Saturn are the guardians at the gate of the personal sphere that take us outside the boundaries of our ego and within the influence of the outer planets, the collective unconscious.

Jupiter symbolizes the force that drives us beyond our individual concerns, the hunger for more encompassing states of consciousness. It is the urge to bring the chaos of the unconscious into the light of greater perspective, recognition, and acknowledgement. In so doing we perceive and understand the meaning of life's experience from a more expansive vantage point. Jupiter is the spiritual urge within ourselves and our society that sustains hope and meaning. Its force arises from an inherent faith in the essential 'goodness' of humankind.

Jupiter is linked to our philosophies, belief systems, our sense of justice, and our instincts to heal. It is associated with the father archetype who inspires his children through his warmth and acceptance. Individuals with strong Jupiter/Sagittarius energy will be philosophical, generous and helpful. If afflicted, particularly to the Sun or Moon by sign, house or aspect, one can overrate their own abilities, be an unrealistic 'pollyanna,' easily become self-righteous, or hold on blindly to dogma and misconception. Those with little Jupiter/Sagittarius energy in the horoscope may not feel motivated to refine their more base instincts or to reflect upon their lives.

The spirits in Jupiter

## Jupiter — An Acknowledgment Experience

The greatest of human potentials is our power to acknowledge each other. Our society has concentrated so much on 'appearing' successful that those appearances hide the starvation of our inner world in which meaning wanes and essence is denied. To be acknowledged by another, especially in times of confusion and discouragement, is to be given some sunshine. By simply saying, 'I see you', we prime the circuits of others and provide the stimulus for renewed hope.

In a group, take turns sitting in pairs for five minutes. What about this person can you truly acknowledge? Variation — each group member takes a turn sitting in the middle to spend a few minutes being acknowledged by others. This can be very uplifting and healing.

Learning to acknowledge oneself can be an even more difficult task. We are so conditioned as a culture, through media and other sources, to recognize what's not working, inefficient, ineffective, and inept that we don't see how this pervasive Saturn state permeates our everyday life. If each of us were to make a list right now of our qualities and characteristics I would guess that many of us would list a fault or two near the top. Try making a Jupiter list. Only list positive qualities you can acknowledge in yourself. This is a fine exercise to balance against challenging Saturn transits, which is precisely the time you need to validate yourself. Or if you know someone who is currently experiencing Saturn, make a point to acknowledge them now. Reflect over the last week. Who in your life helped to make your life more pleasant, whether it was the postal clerk, the cashier at the grocery store, your neighbor, or your spouse. Did you acknowledge their kindness?

## Beliefs

Most of us might be amazed at the many unconscious beliefs we hold about ourselves and others. Our beliefs can be like fences preventing clear judgement and obstructing our vision. Spend time reflecting and listing what you believe about yourself, your life, and about life in general. What beliefs feel most comfortable? Which of these do you believe most deeply? Do you sense that any of these beliefs are limiting you in any way? If you are doing this with a group, spend time sharing your thoughts.

## The Mountains

What better way to feel the expanse of Jupiter than cantering on a good horse in the mountains. Under good Jupiter aspects, try taking a two day pack trip. Under the influence of Jupiter you'll return more inspired, motivated, and envisioning your life from a 'higher' perspective.

## Friends

Some of us do not distinguish between the acquaintance and one who is truly a friend. What does the word 'friend' really mean to you? What qualities do you most value in others? Who around you has those qualities you admire?

## Surprise Trip!

Here is a terrific way to manifest Jupiter. Ask a group of close friends, in couples, to a Friday afternoon party. Prior to the party day you have collected $50 from each couple. Ask that everyone come to the party packed for a weekend trip. Once your party gets rolling, hold a drawing for a surprise getaway. Hand the winning couple plane tickets to some exotic locale and send them off! Win or lose, participating in this event is great Jupiterian fun.

## Theme Party

Organize a theme party for your friends. Perhaps a group slumber party or a Southern 'Dixie' dinner complete with country ham, corn pudding, and videos of *Gone With the Wind* or *Cat on a Hot Tin Roof*. Ask your guests to come as Rhett Butler and Scarlett O'Hara.

## Exaggeration

In a group, or even with just two or three others, select an episode in your recent life to talk about. Instead of relating this experience in a normal manner, really embellish your tale. Exaggerate. Stretch your story to its limit. See how grand a story you can create.

## Famous People

Imagine you are giving a splendid party in a beautiful mansion, complete with opulence, elegance and style. What 10 individuals who have existed in history would you invite for an evening of repartee? Why?

## The Philosophies of the World

Jupiter symbolizes the spiritual basis, codes of conduct, and values that are adapted by a society to hold the group together. These are the creative forces which merge to form the great religions of the world. Spend time studying one of the holy books of the great world religions — the Bible, the Talmud, the Bhagavad Gita, the Upanishads. Study one that is not from your own religious background.

## People of Other Cultures

To stimulate Jupiter, go to dinner with one of your foreign friends. Hang out at your local university. Or spend the afternoon at an art gallery or museum. Write down how many different nationalities of people you see.

## Foreign Films

Foreign film festivals can give you the flavor of Jupiter. Read reviews of the particular directors and screen-writers to more fully appreciate their style and methods.

## Foreign Journeys

Along with the spiritual thirst to exprience our inner horizons, Jupiter represents the need for a richer life, an enlargement of perspective, a longing to know and participate in the world beyond the horizon. Journeying to foreign countries and exposing ourselves to the different philosophical or religious contexts of other cultures allows us to understand our world from a wider point of view.

## Travelogues

Traveling to a foreign country would be the number one choice on many of our lists, but time and money may make it impossible. The next best thing might be to have a second-hand experience of someone else's trip. I recently spent an evening saturated with images, descriptions, and stories of my friend's six-week trek in Nepal. The group probed her with endless questions. By the end of the evening we all experienced a vicarious adventure in the Himalayas.

## Give Aways

Here is a native American tradition that is pure Jupiterian. At the year's end gather together a small group of your special friends. Each brings something which has been important to them and that they want to pass on. It may be a special crystal, a book, good luck piece, etc. The gifts are spread on a blanket. Take turns telling the story of why your gift is special to you. Then one by one select a gift. The process is interesting. Observe yourself choosing what gift you will give. How willingly can you part with something meaningful? How meaningful is your gift? Do you experience a subtle bond with the one who takes your gift?

## Stretch

So many of us sit in chairs for long periods. Sometimes you can feel your vertebrae squashed down on top of each other. To remedy this constricted state do a full body stretch. Lie down and imagine your body getting longer. Start from your toes. Stretch every part of your body, then let your body move as it tells you to.

## Fingerpaint

No other art medium offers a Jupiter experience quite like finger painting. Get yourself a package of large paper with a shiny non-porous finish and bright blue finger paint. Lay your paper down on top of newspapers to protect your floor. Open the blue jar, turn on some Jupiterian music, and swirl away. Really feel the sensuous quality of your hands sweeping in large circles on the paper. Imagine that each circle represents a situation in your life that you are feeling good about. Express it and feel it.

## Jupiter Films

*Ghandi, And Justice for All, A Thousand Clowns, The Sound of Music, The Robe, The Ten Commandments, Song of the South, Chariots of Fire, Cry Freedom.*

## Jupiter Walk

Wear loose fitting clothing that allows your movement to be fluid and flowing.

Visualize your body. Imagine it is growing, expanding out from every pore. Feel your body to be a giant helium balloon. You are barely able to keep your feet on the ground. Try walking down the street, your steps longer and lighter with this expansive feeling.

## Jupiter Meditation

Lay down with some ethereal music in the background. Stretch and relax your body. Take a few deep breaths and begin to imagine your breath visually expanding outward. Envision inhaling more space with each breath. Continue your visualization until you are breathing in the sky. Imagine it has become night. Breathe in the planets in the solar system, the stars in our galaxy, and all the stars in the universe. Breathe in this Jupiter state of awareness.

## Abundance/Healing Meditation

An excellent affirmation to neutralize a Saturn state of consciousness is: 'Every day, in every way, I am becoming lighter, more confident, more empowered, more inspired.' Use it daily, even hourly, if necessary.

## Suggested Music

'Fanfare for the Common Man' (Copeland), 'Jupiter' from *The Planets* (Holst), *Shadowdance* (Shadowfax), 'Journey to the Center of the Earth' (John McLaughlin), 'Sailing' (Christopher Cross), 'Tell All the People' *The Soft Parade* (The Doors), 'Wedding March' (Mendelssohn), 'Climb Every Mountain' (Rodgers/Hammerstein), 'Halleluja Chorus' from *The Messiah* (Handel), *Symphony No 5* (Beethoven), *Sound of Music* (Rodgers/Hammerstein), *Piano Concerto No 1* (Brahms), *Prelude to the Afternoon of a Faun* (Debussy), *Symphony No 41* 'Jupiter' (Mozart), 'Whistle While You Work', 'Zipitty-Do-Dah.'

# Saturn and Capricorn

Saturn (ego) is the gatekeeper between the realms of the personal and the collective realms of the psyche. Saturn symbolizes basic form: the structure of the psyche or the body (bones), boundaries, responsibilities, abandonment of old forms (death), and the principle of contraction. Through the force of contraction, one learns to work with limitations, communal values, standards of conduct, and rules, to create a stable ground to conduct life with greater security, self-knowledge and wisdom.

Saturn is associated with the Father/God Yahweh from the Old Testament whose inaccessible, cold, and harsh disciplinarian nature demands obedience to his commandments.

Individuals with strong Saturn/Capricorn energy in their horoscope may exhibit self-control, perseverance, and a methodical, steady approach to life. If afflicted one can be inaccessible, skeptical, or even heartless. Those with little Saturn/Capricorn

The vision of the valley of dry bones

may not possess staying power, be easily discouraged and controlled by others, and lack a sense of life direction.

## Saturn/Capricorn Experience

Since Saturn symbolizes the death of form an interesting experience for Saturn is enacting the struggle of the chick breaking out of its eggshell. Turn on some appropriate laboring music such as 'Saturn' from *The Planets* (Gustav Holst). Alone, or with a group, allow yourself to relax and begin to feel the music. Imagine you are a baby chick safely curled up in your comfortable and cozy shell. Enjoy the safety of your contained, nurturing environment. Now slowly imagine with the intake of nourishment, you are growing bigger. With each breath you grow. You begin to feel the sides of the shell. As you grow bigger the shell feels more confining. With each breath the shell brings a stronger feeling of confinement. Pay attention to how you are feeling as you meet these limits. Does it feel like any current situation in your life? Focus on that situation. Keeping in contact with your breath, feel the shell (the situation) become unbearable. You strain, pushing out, struggling to break the boundaries. Somewhere you break through. From that point allow yourself to wiggle, straining to get out a foot, leg, your head. Stay in contact with your feelings as you break through the shell, which shatters into pieces around you. You are free but the effort has exhausted you. Rest. Take time to reflect.

Is there some new feeling or awareness? Has this experience helped move you through your 'stuck' place? After reflecting, write down what this was like, or pair up with another group member and share what happened. Discuss these feelings with the entire group.

## Boundaries

Experiences of boundaries and limitation elicit a Saturn feeling. If a group member is undergoing a Saturn transit, or was born with a difficult natal Saturn that they want to explore more fully, ask him to stand in the center of the group with his arms at his sides. Direct him to begin to take slow deep breaths, bringing awareness to his body. Ask the group to move *slowly* in toward the center, encircling the individual. As the circle tightens, remind the individual to keep breathing and to focus on the feelings in the body. Is there constriction anywhere? Are there fears coming up now? Keep him in contact with his emerging feelings. Allow the process to unfold as it needs to, keeping alert and sensitive to his responses. Ask, 'Does this feel like a specific circumstance in your life now?' Keep up the group 'pressure' as long as the individual feels it appropriate. Ask, 'Do you want more pressure?' If you can keep him focused on his breathing and feelings, some important awarenesses may emerge.

A group I was working with in Phoenix did this exercise for a woman who wanted to better understand her natal Saturn in the seventh house. In this case, we added another Saturn element — a body brace which confined her from her hips to her head. The work elicited strong suffocation feelings and early childhood memories of anger and sadness. This experience was a catalyst for her to break through into new realizations about her seventh house Saturn. (Remember to tread softly with sensitivity and alertness for the individual's process. That is the most important element of this experience.)

Variation: Instead of a circle, have the individual get down on all fours. Another member exerts pressure by draping over the individual's back. Ask if the individual wants the weight of another person. Have them identify each new weight with a specific individual or life situation in which they are feeling restriction. Then process the experience.

If you want to do this on your own, use weights of two, five and 10 pounds. Place a number of weights in front of you. Identify each with a difficulty you are now having. Pick one and walk back and forth with it. Without letting go of the first weight, carry another one around, and then pick up the next, and so on. Pay close attention to how you feel as you add more weights. Can you arrange the weights to make them easier to carry? Is there anything you can let go of? Express feelings to the group either by talking or non-verbally by drawing a picture.

## Life Cycles

Most people are aware of the rhythmic process of natural events such as the daily cycle of night and day, the moon's cycle from new to full and back again, but few are aware of how extensively cycles permeate our lives. Our bodies have a multitude of cycles — our red blood cells regenerate approximately every 128 days, the ovaries release an egg every 28 days, the stomach contracts about three times a minute, our heart beats 76 times a minute and the brain's various Alpha, Beta, Theta and Delta rhythms pulse nearly 10 cycles per second. These hidden cycles are the life forces of a human being. But we also can observe broader, longer rhythms in life.

Typically we see our lives in phases, as a baby, a child, a teenager, a young adult, an adult, middle aged, and elderly. Using these categories go back in your life and look at each of these periods as a distinct unit of time. How was your babyhood? What key events can you remember that marked it? What words come to mind when assessing it? Do the same for each of the other periods. Compare them. Which phases were most difficult, easier or more fulfilling? Examining our life in its cycles can bring us more conscious clarity.

## Foundations

Either individually, or as a group, draw a picture of your current foundation. Does it feel firm and strong or is it weak in an area? If so, where? What does that weakness look like? What aspect of your life does it symbolize? Is this situation demanding major reconstruction? Do you have the means to 'shore up' this weakness? Ask each person to do this exercise individually, then share what was discovered.

If your intention is for group members not only to clarify, but to work through a Saturn issue, ask them to identify what resources they possess that could possibly help them improve the limiting situation in their lives. Each participant should then draw up a strategic plan to execute in the coming months.

## Clay

Playing with a soft clay is a superb antidote for Saturn transits. Because we feel so stuck, so encased under difficult Saturn transits, feeling and working with soft clay unconsciously reminds us about flexibility and the fresh, pliable phase that follows the breaking up of dry old forms. This is particularly effective with a Saturn return chart in which the clay becomes a symbol of the new foundation and structure you are starting to build.

## History Around Your Birth

We know that babies, like soft clay, are impressionable. We each absorb the psychic energy around us before and after birth. What series of events were going on in the world for the nine month period before your birth? Or at your birth? During your first year of life? What feelings did you unconsciously absorb? Can you relate any of these world events to the ways you feel about life?

## Saturn Return

Because the Saturn return represents the culmination of a 30 year cycle it is obviously an important transit. Try this experience when Saturn returns to its natal position for you, a friend, or a client.

Many long term transits can be more easily understood in metaphor. One of the better images I have found for the Saturn return is hiking down a railroad track tunneled into the mountains. The six to nine months preceding the exact Saturn return is symbolized by the conditions approaching the tunnel; the one year period of the exact transit is symbolized by the journey through it, and the six to nine months immediately after the return is symbolized by the new vista and the conditions on the other side of the tunnel. Use this metaphor in guided imagery for your group. Modify the experience to focus on particular phases of the life cycle. Working with this metaphor over a period of time will help to crystalize understanding of this transit.

To guide your client through this 'tunnel' ask some of the following questions. Have you ever backpacked in the mountains? If not, imagine what this is like. Envision carrying all your gear — tent, poles, food, pack. As you begin to approach the tunnel create a picture that represents your life now. Identify each piece of gear you are carrying with specific situations in your life. Venture into the dark tunnel carrying all the gear. What are you getting tired of carrying? What feelings do you associate with the burden? What can you drop off? Let go of the items you don't need. What does it feel like to be free of the excess baggage? Look ahead of you. Can you see some light at the end of the tunnel? Walk through the tunnel until you are standing at the other end. What do you see? What new visions and unexplored vistas open up? Create a final picture of what you envision in this new phase of your life.

In my experience, this process helps people to vividly express their feelings about this often troublesome period, to restore clarity of purpose, to redirect their focus on the future, and to renew hope and anticipation.

Variation: Let the vista before the tunnel represent the 30 year cycle. What do the first 30 years look like? What features, qualities and experiences mark the time period? Can you represent them symbolically in a drawing? What successes, disappointments, challenges, completions took place? What colors or tones dominate the different stages of the 30 years? Or draw the vista after the tunnel to represent the next 30 year cycle. What features, qualities and experiences are you hoping for?

## Saturn Retrograde

Any time that Saturn is retrograded by transit and has eased off a difficult aspect to your natal chart is a 'grace' period, giving you a potentially valuable chance to assess your responses to the first transit of Saturn. Some of us waste this time, feeling so relieved the pressure is off we slip back into our old ways or think we have solved our problem. Use this reprieve to look at your life. Have you approached a recent problem in a constructive way? What new methods can you continue to employ to meet the challenge that will likely resurface as Saturn goes direct and aspects your natal planet once again?

## Asteroid Belt

Under difficult Saturn transits this exercise is helpful to crystalize what is limiting in your life. Envision yourself traveling through the asteroid belt between the planets. Draw a picture of your surroundings. Include big and little asteroids. Mark each asteroid with a limitation you are now feeling. Identify your biggest obstacle with the biggest asteroid. Giving a name to difficult Saturn influences can be therapeutic.

Which of these obstacles can you most easily get rid of? What is the biggest obstacle? What resources do you have to help you around this obstacle? Do you have any upcoming positive Saturn transits you can use? Initiate a strategy to implement when you have the help of a good transit.

## Draw Your Current Problem

This exercise can be done alone but is most effective when done in an ongoing therapeutic group. Ask each participant to draw a picture of their biggest current problem. Take turns showing the drawings. As a group, assess each picture for vividness of image. Note its strengths and weaknesses. How well are the components integrated? What is the degree of symbolism?

Discuss these questions — How well is the person coping with the problem? Is its seriousness being denied? Who's winning? Who or what does this person feel is responsible for the problem, and for the healing? How indicative is the drawing of a good outcome? What resources, defenses and supports can help them solve the problem? Are there any supporting transits?

## The Shadow

Recognizing our own darkness seems to be the prerequisite for self-knowledge. List the personality traits you have the most difficulty dealing with in others. Once this is done you will have produced an accurate description of the repressed characteristics in your own unconscious! You have described your own shadow. Precisely what bothers us about others are the key unintegrated elements of our own psyche that we project out onto the world. This exercise may stir some uncomfortable feelings but offers plenty of 'food for thought.'

## Old Age

In a group, discuss the role of the elderly in our society. How are the elderly treated in other cultures by comparison? Because of the advancing age of the 'baby boomers,' within 20 years our culture will experience an enormous demographic change. There will be far more older people than we have now. What are the potential problems and results from the growing numbers of elderly in our society? What creative solutions can the group devise?

## An Old Person I Remember as a Child

Either alone or with a group member lie down and get comfortable. Let your mind drift back into your past and recall an older person close to you when you were a child. Focus on visualizing that person. Describe them as fully as possible. What were they like? What kind of feelings did you have toward them? What gifts of wisdom did they give you?

## The Old Wise One

In many cultures elders are respected and revered. Saturn is time, and time teaches through experience. Many of us have known one or two elders who have taught much.

A rewarding experience is to sit with an older person and ask them about their life, their memories, joys, pains, lessons, accomplishments. Through them we glimpse our own lives. Record the personal history of this elder. Include their significant moments: meeting their spouse, their first home, his leaving for the war, her taking a bus alone to the hospital to deliver her first child, etc. My husband's mother sent us an audiotape of just such information. We realized how important it is to have some record from our family elders, some memento of the history of our personal lineage. You might ask your parents to do this. Or perhaps interview them on video tape. Down the road, you may find it a treasured possession.

## Strengthening Your Foundation

A harmonious Saturn transit is an auspicious time to strengthen your base. What aspect of your life could use more discipline? What part of your foundation needs reinforcement? Once you've identified that area develop a strategy to strengthen it. Corrections made now with diligence and hard work will solidify your base and advance your goal.

For example, there are several productive ways to make good use of a Saturn trine to your Sun. This is the time life runs more smoothly, when you can accomplish much and make your position in the world strong. Spend a few minutes a day trying to consciously impact your psyche with positive Saturn energy. See your body and your life force getting stronger. If you have a weak part in your body, imagine it is receiving vital, life giving energy. Use the daily affirmation. 'Every day in every way, I am getting stronger.' Or decide now to begin some physical regime — quit smoking, start daily exercise, etc. Speak this intention with conviction. By maintaining that conviction and self-discipline you will see successful results. In a group you can further empower your Saturn trine Sun transit by facing each person separately and speaking your intention *with resolve*

Variation: Being positively recognized can strengthen your psyche. Let the group compliment you about your accomplishments and successes. Write them down to read again when Saturn is squaring your Sun, or when you are having a difficult Saturn day.

Being acknowledged by others is important for each of us. Start a file of appreciative notes and letters you receive from clients or friends. This can be a useful psychological resource when dealing with the discouragement or lack of appreciation you might experience when Saturn squares or opposes your Sun.

## Goals

Planning and developing concrete strategies can be most realistically assessed and effectively implemented under good Saturn transits. What goals have you set for this next year? The next five years? If you haven't got concrete future plans take the time to do it now!

## Role Playing Difficult Saturn Transits

What if you have transiting Saturn opposite your Uranus and you want to use an experiential method to bring it to conscious expression? Remember, the more you deny the existence of a problem, or resist facing it, the more likely your problem will surface suddenly or explosively. This experience can be effectively done with one other friend or in a group. What specific problem is causing you a sense of uneasiness? Whose authority are you resisting? What do you want to break away from?

A metaphor for this transit is a wild stallion in a corral, restless and straining against the rope that is feeling restrictive. Breaking out may be your impulse but you need to watch how to go about it. Uranian energy is so unpredictable, you might impulsively jump the fence and get snagged on the barbed wire, or escape the confines only to find you are unprepared to fend totally for yourself.

Role play with someone what it feels like to be in a tug-of-war between yourself and an authority figure or issue. You might literally get a rope and act out a tug-of-war. First breathe deeply and get focused on your feelings. Now have someone representing the 'other side' pull against you, testing you and challenging your validity or position. Keep your focus on your inner process. Keep breathing. Express these feelings aloud. Do you feel tension in your body? Specifically where? Act out this tension by kicking on a mattress or pounding on a pillow. The point of this exercise is to help you release and diffuse some of the unconscious tension and bring more awareness to a potentially explosive situation.

If after releasing some of the tension you still feel stirred up, you might evoke Jupiter within. Visualize a beam of healing light intervening, bringing you insight, understanding, and a higher perspective about this situation. Who in your life can provide Jupiter support and perspective now?

## Near Death Experiences

Have you ever experienced a moment in your life when you thought you might die? Recall and reflect about that experience. In a group, share the experience. Did it change you? If so, how? Do you feel differently about death now?

## Death

Consider your feelings about death. Do you think about the possibility of your own death? Does it make you uncomfortable? Has anyone close to you died? In a group, divide into pairs and tell the story of the death of someone close. Let your partner be your Moon and quietly reflect your feelings. Though this exercise may re-stimulate sad or painful feelings we can often find relief and healing just by 'telling our story.'

## Study Of Death

There are several excellent sources for those who want to study death. *Death and Dying in the Tibetan Tradition* (Glenn Mullin) is a survey of nine Tibetan sources.[1] It covers topics such as meditational techniques to prepare for death, inspiring accounts of the deaths of saints and sages, the experience of death and its secret and inner signs, and methods of consciousness transference.

*Who Dies?*[2] (Stephen Levine) is a sensitive and inspiring book to help you and loved ones face the process of death, and *Beyond Death* (Stanislav and Christina Grof )[3] draws illuminating parallels of concepts of the afterlife in different cultures, the accounts of those who survived a clinical death, the death and rebirth episodes by schizophrenic patients, and psychedelic states induced in experimental psychiatry.

## Saturn Films

*Sophie's Choice, Death of a Salesman, Places in the Heart, They Shoot Horses, Don't They? I Never Sang for My Father.*

## Saturn Walk

Saturn's gait is slow, heavy, and laborious. Imagine that your feet weigh 30 pounds each. Better yet, attach wrap-around weights to your ankles and move about.

## Saturn Meditation

I travel the roads of nature until the hour when I shall lie down and be at rest; yielding back my last breath in to the air from which I have drawn it daily, and sinking down upon the earth from which my father derived the seed, my mother the blood, and my nurse the milk of my being.

Emperor Marcus Aurelius: Meditations.[4]

## Suggested Music

'Saturn' from *The Planets* (Holst), 'Dance of Maya' (John McLaughlin), 'I Want You (She's So Heavy)' *Abbey Road* (The Beatles), 'Adagio for Strings' (Theme from *Platoon*) (Samuel Barber). Many Leonard Cohen songs ('Dress Rehearsal Rag', 'Nancy', 'Desolation Row'), 'Goin' Home' (Negro spiritual), *Symphony No 4* (Brahms), 'Point Blank' *The River* (Bruce Springsteen).

# Uranus and Aquarius

The classical planets (those known since ancient times) from the Sun to Mars represent the sphere of personal ego. Jupiter and Saturn together represent the boundary or bridge between the personal ego and the collective unconscious. It is in this realm of the three outer planets, Uranus, Neptune and Pluto, that we can reach an awareness of something more in life than what relates to our ego. A new dimension is added to the psyche, the awareness of energies that travel on the periphery of our everyday consciousness.

Uranus is the 'primordial chaos' whose energy is erratic, unpredictable and sudden. Like a lightning bolt it shocks and disrupts, shaking up old foundations and patterns that have become too rigid. This can create liberating new forms which give the psyche breathing room and new possibilities for future development. If suppressed in the unconscious, this energy can explode, painfully demolishing and destroying hard-won structure. Uranus links to action that is original, creative, inventive, or even bizarre.

Individuals with strong Uranus/Aquarius energy can be highly independent. They experience change as life-restoring and they have an intuitive realization that there is more to the world than the realm of concrete thought bound by facts and the perception of the senses. If afflicted, one can exhibit categorial rejection of the societal structures and explosive, unpredictable behavior. Those with little Uranus/Aquarius energy may express themselves more conservatively, fear change, or criticize those who 'rock the boat.'

## Uranus — An 'Electrifying' Experience

One of the more accessible places to experience Uranus if you're near a big city is on the trading floor of the commodities markets or stock exchanges. Visiting one can be an exciting and unnerving experience. The intense, emotionally demanding, nerve wracking scramble for a piece of the action, where fortunes are made or lost in a matter of seconds, makes this one of the most unpredictable environments imaginable. From the early morning bell, the pits reverberate with frantic ear-crushing screams, chaos, high anxiety, pushing, pulling, and the extremes of human emotion — panic, elation, greed, insecurity, joy. The highly unpredictable

The creation of fish and birds

nature of the pits on a day-to-day basis, the high risks and game playing, attract those high rollers who love the freedom to be their own boss, and who thrive in this environment.

## Movement

Uranian movement is erratic, bizarre, and abruptly changeable. To give yourself a taste of it, turn on heavy metal rock music and start shaking your hands vigorously. Now shake your arms, upper body, whole body. Shake your head. Let yourself get disoriented. That's Uranus.

## Unexpected Events

Expect the unexpected. One of the hardest transits to predict with accuracy is Uranus. Inevitably you can brainstorm 10 different possible ways to anticipate the effect of a particular Uranus transit, and, true to its nature, Uranus will manifest in a way you never thought of. Try this brainstorming approach with your next Uranus transit. Watch closely for any ways Uranus manifests that you hadn't considered.

## Accidents

One of Uranus' favorite ways to manifest suppressed energy is through accidents. Have you had any accidents in recent years? This past year? Can you go back immediately *before* your accident and identify what was going on in your mind? Was there any anger, rebellion, or repression?

## Creativity and Originality

Uranus encourages an appetite for experimentation, creativity, and the creation of new forms. Try these:
    You have just inherited a suspender-making factory from your dear auntie Nell. Because the fashion of suspenders has gone out of style, the factory has lost money. What other uses can you think of for all those suspenders? Brainstorm as many possible alternatives as you can.
    It is well-known that as human beings develop we use less and less of our brain capacity. By the time we are grown most of us use less than 10 per cent of our brain. You have been hired to come up with solutions to this problem. Brainstorm as many possibilities as you can.

## Newspaper Tower

Using two sheets of newsprint and 24 inches of Scotch tape construct the tallest tower that you can in 30 minutes. Cut, fold, or form these materials anyway you like.

## Space Fantasy

You are a crew member of the spaceship 'Intrepid' and you have just entered a previously unknown solar system. Your ship lands on a planet nearest its central star. Draw the environment you are now seeing for the first time.

## Science Fiction

Try reading one of the plethora of science fiction books that are available. Books by Isaac Asimov, Robert Heinlein, and Clifford D. Simak are some of the best written. Stretch your own imagination to include these strange universes, worlds, and beings.

## Bizarre Humor

Two cartoonists with Uranian humor are Gary Larson (*The Far Side*) and Gahan Wilson (*Playboy*). *The Far Side Gallery*[1] by Gary Larson is a collection of cartoons depicting his funny, sometimes strange humor — cigarette smoking dinosaurs, grandmothers in bumper cars, an elephant on crutches in a phone booth. Very funny. Very strange.

## Brainteasers

The last pages of the monthly magazine *Omni* are a good source of Uranian brainteasers and games of mental challenge. Or buy *Classic Puzzles*[2] by Gyles Brandreth which includes 300 classic puzzles involving numbers, words, shapes, and more.

## Planetarium

Visit your local planetarium and see a sky show. Many sky shows create an experience of traveling outside the solar system and beyond by using sophisticated lasers, images, music, and sound effects. In Chicago, the sky show at the planetarium changes every two months so there is always something new to see and learn about.

## Uranian Art

The creative geniuses who have helped us perceive the world in new ways are examples of Uranian/Aquarian expression: the art of Pablo Picasso and Mark Chagall, or the architecture and vision of Paolo Soleri and Buckminster Fuller. If an art gallery is near, spend time experiencing their art, or get books about them from your local library. Spend an evening being absorbed into their unique world of creative images and ideas.

## Genius

Read biographies of the lives of individuals whose minds demonstrate creative Uranian thought process, such as *Einstein, The Life and Times*,[3] by Ronald Clark; *The Unknown Leonardo*,[4] edited by Ladislao Reti; or *Prodigal Genius: The Life of Nikola Tesla*,[5] by John O'Neil. Or treat yourself to the ideas in Thomas Kuhn's *The Structure of Scientific Revolution*[6] or James Gleick's *Chaos, Making a New Science*.[7]

## Aliens

The phenomena of UFOs and alien abduction experiences are Uranian. Try reading books like *Communion*,[8] by Whitley Strieber, who recounts his abduction experiences, and *Intruders*,[9] by Bud Hopkins whose book presents the results of his investigation of 135 subjects claiming abductions by aliens. These books invite us to examine our notions of reality.

## Space Programs

What do you think is the future of our role in space? Should we plan trips to Mars or beyond? The fields of science and space have most successfully engaged the spirit of co-operation between nations. Should nations work together on joint projects in space? How do you envision this? This makes a good discussion for a group.

## Electronics

Any computer or video games are Uranian. Spend the afternoon in a video arcade. Play an adventure game on your computer. If you have a modem, plug yourself into a computer conversation.

## Uranian Weekend

Here is a helpful strategy for any time you are feeling bored and at the mercy of habit. Take one weekend to do as many things that vary from your normal routine as possible. Go to new places, do new things, eat foods you have never tried, wear your clothes in new combinations, hang out in Uranian environments, even brush your teeth with the other hand. It's a playful challenge to try to think of as much variety as you can. My husband and I usually do this in February when winter sets in. We've had some great fun and pretty bizarre experiences being this spontaneous!

## Future Transits

Speculate or predict what you think we'll see manifesting as Pluto begins to transit through Sagittarius in 1995, Uranus into Aquarius in 1996, or Neptune and Jupiter into Aquarius in 1997. How will these transits affect the field of astrology? In what new ways will astrology be a part of our culture? Can you envision astrology's potential with these particular transits? Get a group of your astrology friends together. As a group what can you envision? Brainstorm. Let yourself imagine.

## The Year 2020

What do you imagine the year 2020 will be like? What advances do you think we will have made as a species? Draw a series of sketches to depict what you guess your daily routine might be like?

## Uranus Films

Mondo Cane, Clockwork Orange, Blade Runner, F/X, Mad Max Beyond Thunderdome, The Man Who Fell to Earth, The Last Days of Man on Earth, Slaughterhouse Five, 2001: A Space Odyssey, Star Wars.

## Uranus Walk

Walk quickly and erratically as if someone is zapping you with an electrical shock — spin, jump, do whatever comes into your mind. Don't censor, just do!

## Uranus Meditation

Take a trip in your imagination out of the solar system and galaxy, out of our local group of galaxies, past the galactic center to the furthest reaches of the universe. (There are some guided imagery tapes that do this.)

There is a fine film short called *Powers of Ten*,[10] which dramatically illustrates relative distances that are so hard for us to visualize. It begins with a couple on a picnic blanket in Lincoln Park in Chicago and sequentially magnifies to images above the targeted area, past our solar system, past the galaxy, then rapidly returns through images to the couple on the picnic blanket. Though just a short 10 minute film it puts space into perspective and gives us a direct experience of the enormity of the universe in which we live. There is also a book by the same title describing the process of the filming, but by all means, if you get the opportunity, see the film.

## Uranian Music

The music of most electronic, heavy metal, or progressive jazz artists. Much New Age music, especially Kitaro. 'Hard Rock' and 'One Word' (John Mclaughlin), 'Sheena is a Punk Rocker', 'We're a Happy Family' and 'I Don't Care' *Rocket to Russia* (The Ramones), 'We Want the Airwaves' *Pleasant Dreams* (The Ramones), 'Choke on This' and 'Can't Change the World' *Choke on This* (Rhythm Pigs), 'Rated X' from *Get Up With It* (Miles Davis), 'Uranus, the Magician' from *The Planets* (Holst).

# Neptune And Pisces

Neptune is the most difficult planetary energy to understand because, by its nature, it symbolizes phenomena that are vague, subtle, illusory, and unclear. The urge of Saturn is to build a psychic foundation, an ego from which to operate. Neptune is a contrary force in the psyche which is ego-denying and ego-dissolving; it grants us an awareness that the ego is not ultimately what one is.

Neptune is epitomized by the principle of entropy. A given amount of energy, when released into the environment, gradually becomes diluted or diffused until it appears to be dissolved into it surroundings. The amount of energy remains the same but is so diffuse that it can no longer be restored to its original form.

Neptune is a feminine force which allows us to sacrifice the goals of the ego and

The heavenly choir

to immerse ourselves in the whole, in the void of the cosmic womb, returning with richer imagination, inspiration, greater sensitivity, receptivity, and human dedication. Neptune is linked to dreams, intuition, imagination, illumination and true mysticism.

    Individuals with strong Neptune/Pisces energy in their horoscope can be sensitive, idealistic, spiritual, romantic and compassionate. If afflicted Neptune can produce fears and phobias, cloudy misunderstanding, dependence and escapism especially through alcohol and drugs. Neptune is particularly difficult in a weak ego for it can open the individual to these powerful unconscious energies with sometimes drastic consequences. Those with little Neptune/Pisces energy may not be at all aware of the subtle dimensions of spirit. They may be intolerant, rigid, and have little human compassion.

## Neptune — An Experience

(This is best facilitated by a guide.)

Imagine you are a one-celled organism living in a tiny puddle of water. This puddle is the totality of the world you know. Focus your attention on the one cell of your body. See it clearly. Now see the puddle you live in. It begins to rain again. Your puddle gets bigger. It merges with a smaller puddle on the ground next to you. Focus on your one-celled body. It continues to rain. The many little puddles around you merge into a small rivulet. Now see the rivulet you live in. You begin to float, flowing down, in more and more water. Focus on your one-celled body. The rivulet becomes a stream. See the stream you live in. You are moving with the flow of water, down into a creek. You are being propelled faster by the cumulative force of the water. Focus on your one-celled body. Now the creek joins a small river. See the river you now live in. The river gains more momentum, more volume. It winds its way into a bay and into the open ocean. Focus on your one-celled body. A wave carries you along, further and further from the shore, moving you out into its great body, propelling you with its full force into its huge dimension. Feel yourself free floating, moved by the rhythm of the waters.

(The guide brings you back into the bay, river, stream, rivulet and puddle, continuing to remind you to focus on the one cell of your body.)

## Movement

Neptune's movement is best to visualize in water. Imagine you are a fish moving freely, fluidly. Your spine is supple, bendable, and you turn easily. You can ride the currents up and down like a roller coaster, or surface and be moved along by the wave.

## Float Tank

If you live in a major metropolis you might have access to a 'samadhi tank,' or float tank. Invented by dolphin researcher John Lilly, it is a large, enclosed, 'bathtub' which you enter by stepping through a door. Closing the door you are in total warm darkness. The tub is filled with a saline solution so it is easy to lay down and float. The sensory deprivation and warm floating sensation feels like a return to the womb. For some at first this may be scary. Others may adapt to it quickly and find it a nurturing, blissful experience.

## Blind Walk

Neptune deals with difficulty in seeing the subsequent feelings of being out of control and the response of surrender. Here is an effective experience to get more deeply in touch with these feelings within ourselves. This is an ideal exercise for anyone with a strong Neptune either natally or by transit. It can be done with one friend or in a group. (You'll need a large handkerchief or scarf for this.)

First find a partner. One of you covers his eyes with the blindfold. The other leads the blindfolded parner preferably outside and around the block, or if time permits, to a grocery or other public setting. Whether you are the guide or the blindfolded one, keep in touch with the different feelings you experience. Afterwards share your feelings. How does it feel to not be able to see or know where you are? How do you feel being dependent? Does this stir up feelings about current dependence or control issues? How did the guide feel? How did it feel to be depended upon?

Now switch roles and repeat the exercise. Examine your natal charts. Check for current transits. Does this reveal more to you about this experience?

## Neptune/Saturn Variation

This is a good exercise for someone with a difficult Neptune/Saturn combination. It is better done indoors in a house. Ask the individual to take particular notice of the room she is in. How big is it? Where is the furniture? The doorways? The walls? Walk around with them into other rooms helping them get familiar with the layout of the house and the relationship of the rooms to each other. Come back to the original room. Now have them cover their eyes with the blindfold. Once blindfolded, lead them into another room of the house. Give them six to eight books to carry, heavy enough to make it difficult. With you as a guide to keep them from falling into furniture, ask them to find their way back to their position in the original room. (As a guide you want to help them only when they might hurt themselves, or if they appear at a high point of frustration.) This experience of feeling blind and burdened replicates what one feels like with this combination in a difficult natal or transiting aspect. Process these feelings.

## Group Healing

Form a circle, sitting down. Get comfortable, loosen tight clothing, take off your shoes, relax. Join hands and begin to breathe deeply. Become aware of a point of healing light between your eyebrows. Let it slowly grow and intensify. Let it fill your whole head. Now expand it to include your whole body. When you've done this envision going around the circle to every person, bathing them with your healing light. Now take turns, one at a time, sitting in the center of the circle. With each new person focus your full attention on them. Send them healing. Repeat their name silently, asking that your healing light be received. Those in the center should try to be as receptive as possible to the subtle spiritual energy being generated on their behalf.

## Variation

Sit in a circle and begin to chant as a group. A most effective chant is the universal cosmic sound, 'Aum' (pronounced 'ah-omm.') Repeat it at your own rhythm and soon there will be a beautiful vocal symphony all around you. Let it stop of its own accord.

## Vocables

I am a part of a ritual group in Chicago that (among other things) chants vocables. We begin with the 'Aum' chant, then we each express ourselves allowing whatever sound feels appropriate to move through us. It produces haunting group sounds which linger into the silence.

## Subtle Healing Forms

Neptune is symbolized by holistic subtle healing forms such as the Bach flower remedies, healing with gems and crystals, and Reiki energy balancing. Learn more about them. Have healing work done on you. Do you feel its effects?

## A Contemplative Retreat

From time to time we all seek solitude and withdrawal from the world. Take a week or weekend retreat to a Zen Buddhist monastery or participate in a weekend intensive at a spiritual community.

## Drugs and Addictions

If you want to learn more about the subtle, sometimes insidious, process of Neptune attend an open meeting of Alcoholics Anonymous or Adult Children of Alcoholics. Get a copy of the *Twelve Steps Toward Recovery*. Listen to what the group members have to say about their lives.

Are you the child of an alcoholic? Or an alcoholic or drug abuser yourself? Many of us have addictions of a different sort — sugar, smoking, sex, relationships or work and success. They are still addictions none the less. Do the characteristics of one affected by alcohol fit you? Do you need help? Does your chart show a tendency toward addiction? If so, be very attentive to yourself under difficult Neptune transits.

## Activities of Neptune

Go to Neptune's world by swimming at your local pool or scuba diving on your next vacation. How do you feel in water? In a swimming pool versus the ocean? Have your fears ever gotten the best of you? Or do you feel no fear at all? Is this reflective of your natal chart?

## Photography

Neptune is associated with the realm of images. Gather a group of photographs.

Include personal ones and those you find in magazines. Is your Neptune in Virgo? Examine these photos for detail. Analyze what you see. Is your Neptune in Libra? Look for the sense of balance in the photos. How is it composed? Is there a balance of contrast or color? Is your Neptune in Scorpio? What sense of feeling is expressed in the photo? What was the mood of the photographer who took the picture?

## Visionary Art

There are increasing numbers of visionary artists. A stunning series of paintings depicting the sun, moon, planets and stars is *Visions of the Universe* painted by Kazuaki Iwasaki.[1] It is published by the Cosmos Store, a division of Carl Sagan Productions. Any astrologer working with experiential methods will appreciate the beautiful images in this book.

## Neptune Films

Any animated film, especially the animated spoof of Disney's *Fantasia*, by Bruno Bozzetto, *Allegro Non Troppo*, *Lady Sings the Blues*, *Days of Wine and Roses*, *One Flew Over the Cuckoo's Nest*, *The Heart is a Lonely Hunter*.

## Neptune Walk

Walk as you might the moment after you have just met your soulmate. Move in a dreamy, flowing light-hearted manner feeling blissful and at peace.

## Your Aura

In Eastern tradition, the subtle energy field that surrounds all living things is known as the aura. The aura is a constantly shifting pattern, color, and intensity much like what happens in the phenomena of the aurora borealis. From time to time our auras will be more porous, sucking up psychic energy from anyone around us. Sometimes you will feel this by experiencing inexplicable moods, feelings of inner fuzziness or confusion, or a clingy, dependent feeling. To resolve these feelings, first cleanse your aura by physically exercising and/or taking a shower. Allow the water to run over you from your head to your toes. Imagine the disturbing vibrations washing right off you. Dry yourself off, get dressed, sit down and immediately try this meditation. Its purpose is to create the inner strength to protect your aura.

Take a few deep breaths and quiet your mind. Focus your attention on the ajna chakra, the point between your eyebrows. See a silver thread coming out of it circling you and creating a protective silver cocoon. Now see a golden thread coming out, circling you and creating a protective golden cocoon. Feel the safety of being encircled in this lunar/solar cocoon.

See yourself engulfed in this totally protective energy. Mentally say to yourself, 'I will only take in energy of light.' Do this as long as it takes to feel a return of balance. If you believe you are absorbing negative energy from an individual and still have to be around them, reinforce this visualization for a few minutes before being in their company. You can strengthen your aura consciously this way.

## Suggested Music

*Music for Zen Meditation* (Tony Scott, Shinicki Yuize, Hozan Yamamoto), 'Cape Cod Ocean Surf' (Mood Recordings), 'Sailboat Voyage' (Mood Recordings), 'Sanctuary' (John McLaughlin), *Discrete Music* (Brian Eno), 'Tibetan Bells' (Henry Wolff/Nancy Hennings), 'Ancient Echoes' (Steve Halperin/Georgia Kelly), *Music for Airports* (Brian Eno), 'Lucy in the Sky With Diamonds' *Magical Mystery Tour* (The Beatles), 'Lullaby' (Brahms), 'Song of the Seashore' (James Galway), 'Hosanna' (Berlioz), 'Inside the Taj Mahal' (Paul Horn), 'When You Wish Upon a Star', Gregorian Chants.

# Pluto And Scorpio

As the planet farthest out in the solar system, Pluto symbolizes the deepest, most profound level of change possible in the human psyche. It is the primordial feminine power that intrudes on consciousness and cannot be placated by will or reason. Pluto, mythologically, is the ancient Sumerian goddess of the underworld, Ereshigal, whose origins predate that of the Greek god Hades and the Roman god Pluto. She symbolizes the deep inward journey that each of us embarks upon after losing something precious. For most of us, this is not done consciously or willingly, but by inner forces that compel us to enter the purifying fire that separates us from one level of existence to another.

Pluto sounds like a grim unwelcome process. Yet when seen from the full light of the soul it is a necessary process that returns balance to the deep psyche. In responding to this urge to penetrate our own depths and to know 'the self' fully, we confront the 'demons' of an unbalanced ego (*hubris*), desire and power. By sustaining our courage and tenacity, we release our particular demons, integrate this raw power, and emerge with the gift of wholeness that contains within it a storehouse of psychic and spiritual riches.

Individuals with strong Pluto/Scorpio energy exhibit great intensity and forcefulness, sexual magnetism and charisma, a capacity for relentless effort, and in-depth healing. If afflicted one may be power hungry, egocentric, jealous, possessive, coercive or cruel. Those with little Pluto/Scorpio energy may fall victim to the onslaught of their own repressed energy by chronically ignoring what needs to be changed, or they may fall victim to someone else's abuse of power.

Because Pluto is likely to express itself through intensity and complexity many Pluto experiences require competent guides. We need to be aware of the possibility that an individual will feel overwhelmed by the unconscious forces they have unleashed. Dealing with Pluto energies effectively requires two prerequisites — expertise in dealing with deep, sometimes scary, realms and adequate time to fully process the resulting stimulated unconscious material.

Dante and the eagle

## Shamanic Wounding

Shamanism is a phenomenon that spans millennia and has been a part of almost every culture on the planet. A shaman is a priest or priestess who acts as mediator between the worlds of the conscious and the unconscious. They are healers of the psyche who use systems of coded symbols and images, providing a language for the unconscious and a means to express otherwise inexpressible psychic states.

In ancient days the astrologers were the shaman-priests. Now with Pluto in Scorpio, more astrologers are returning to the vital healing role of 'midwife' to the psyche, creating the means and methods to help ourselves and others effectively deal with Pluto energy.

The concept of the wounded healer is significant for astrologers working in a healing capacity today. Carl Jung considered the true healer to be one who has been wounded, who has experienced both the wound and the healing process. As astrologers we can only accompany others as far as we have gone ourselves. To lead another beyond the threshold of the unconscious we must have traveled there ourselves.

Pluto transits often activate spiritual, physical or emotional trauma that catapults us into the inner workings of this wounding crisis. Once these experiences of suffering, dying and rebirth are integrated, we can use the special knowledge of these powerful states for healing ourselves and others. By guiding those who are facing Plutonian forces, some for the first time, we can help to release and relieve the unconscious pressures within and assist our friend or client toward understanding, transforming and integrating Pluto's energy.

There is an excellent experience of the wounding of Pluto devised by Jean Houston called the 'Sacred Wound'. It is a three-hour process done alone, with a guide, or with a group. You are asked a series of questions to stimulate a retelling of the story of your wound and then to repeat it in its mythic proportions. The exercise can be found in *Magical Blend* magazine (Issue 17, p. 56) or in Jean's book, *The Search for the Beloved* published by Jeremy P. Tarcher (Los Angeles).

Other good general sources for reading about the world of the shaman is the series of books by Carlos Castaneda, relating his experiences with the sorcerer Don Juan;[1] see also *Medicine Woman*[2] Lynne Andrews; *Lame Deer: Seeker of Visions*[3] (John Lame Deer and Richard Erdoes); or *Shamanic Voices*[4] (Joan Halifax).

## Shamanic Journeying

Shamanic journeying is a system of psychological and physical techniques to alter states of consciousness without drugs and to enter the 'nonordinary' realm of the shaman. Journeys are deep imagistic trips to the 'underworld' and the 'upperworld'. By utilizing trance, drumming and guided imagery, one enters through the crack in consciousness into shamanic territory.

One of the best and most available resources for shamanic journeying is *Way of the Shaman* (Michael Harner). Harner offers a basic introduction of techniques gathered from his research as an anthropologist and from his experience with South and North American shamans.

## Powerline

This is an exercise to do with a group that has interacted at least several times before. It will not work well with a new group.

First ask the group to form a line. Designate what direction represents the 'front' and 'back' of the line. Pay particular attention to each individual's changing responses as the exercise proceeds. (Participants pay attention to your own responses.) As a group arrange yourselves in order of the most powerful group member standing at the front of the line to the least powerful who stands at the back. Do this silently. Any member can move any other to the position they feel is appropriate for that person. Let the line keep changing until there is a consensus. (This may not happen.) As a facilitator, watch the process carefully. Does anyone immediately go the back or front, or stay noncommittal between the two? Who moves people? Who waits for others to decide their position? This is remarkably revealing of how each feels about their power among others, as well as being captive of feelings about power. After the exercise, allow the group plenty of time to express their feelings and to process what came up. Share your observations. Have each individual examine the Pluto both in their natal chart and by transit. Does this clarify their particular reactions?

Variation:

Here is an exercise you can do on your own. Analyze a current situation in which you are involved with others. Determine and observe the lines of power. Who has most power by title? Who actually has more power? Who aligns with who? Draw up a chart showing these lines of power. Where do you fit in? Are you one of the most powerful, or one of the least? Are you satisfied with your position in the line of power?

## Secrets

This is an interesting way to activate your feelings about secrets. In a group, pass out identical paper and pens. Each person writes down a secret they have never told anyone. Put the secrets in a hat or bowl placed in the center. Each person takes a turn drawing out a secret. Read this secret aloud to the group as if it were your own. If you draw your own, read it anyway. Elaborate about the secret. Fill in its details. During this process keep aware of your feelings. How do you feel about others' secrets? Did any secrets shock you? In your opinion are there some 'worse' secrets than yours? Can you sympathize with the writer of each particular secret? How does it feel to reveal a private part of yourself?

## Body Therapies

Body therapies such as Reichian release work, bioenergetics, and rolfing deal with releasing blocked energy within the body. From the premise that repressed, unintegrated emotional and traumatic experiences get locked in the body as a form of body armor, these techniques focus on building and releasing these traumas through specific sustained body positions or deep tissue massage. *Rediscovery of the Body* by Charles Garfield is a useful overview of the body therapies.

## Parts of Myself I Do Not Like to See

Pluto will put us in touch with aspects of ourselves we don't want to acknowledge.

It is this repressed, dissociated energy that presses up from the unconscious in order to be seen and integrated. What parts of your psyche have you seen glimpses of within you that you haven't really looked at or reflected upon? If these parts continue to be pushed aside you could expect your next Pluto transit to stir them up. What can you do now to begin to come to terms with these repressed energies?

## Resentments

Make a list of resentments. Do you resent anyone in your life now? If so, why? Have similar feelings of resentment been stimulated before? Can you recognize an unconscious repetitive pattern at work? If you are in a group, break into pairs. Talk about your resentful feelings.

Do you feel resentment toward a particular person? Symbolically, place that person in front of you in your mind's eye. As directly and unemotionally as possible tell them why you feel resentment toward them. Be specific. Try to surround that person and yourself in a circle of love to dissipate the Mars/Pluto energy. Say 'I forgive you. I forgive myself.' Repeat this.

Variation:

Pair up with a partner. One person chooses to be their own Pluto. The other becomes that person's Moon. The Moon's function is to silently sit, witness and reflect the feelings shared by Pluto. Those playing their Plutos tell the Moon about their desires, resentments, hurts, ambitions, etc. When Pluto has exhausted their feelings about these areas, switch roles. (Source: Jeff Jawer.)

## Ceremonial Ritual

Ceremonial ritual is done worldwide in all healthy cultures. These deeply symbolical, often annual rites, allow an individual and the community a pause from daily activities to reintegrate and commune with the primal, archetypal undercurrents of the psyche. The annual summer solstice sun dance of native American and other ceremonial communities is an example. Typically, the native American ritual is four days and nights of continuous dancing, drumming and praying. Some of these are open to the public and offer an opportunity to observe these special ceremonial rituals.

## Living 'On the Edge'

Take a trip into Pluto's realm on a challenging and demanding wilderness river rafting trip. There are a number of groups for men, women, or both that offer this type of river rafting or canoeing trip. A week trip on a fast river has all the characteristics of Pluto. It is totally absorbing, demanding and filled with physical and emotional highs and lows. There are points of pure exhilaration when you successfully navigate a difficult rapid, or heart-stopping moments of fear as a boat flips and you see your friend tumbling and totally at the mercy of the turbulent water. Worse yet is the prospect that you yourself might be thrown from the boat, or your boat sucked into a hole. Anything is possible as you face life on a challenging stretch of river. Experiences like these can offer a wonderful feeling of satisfaction.

## Sexuality

Mars and the more intense Pluto are both associated with our sexuality. Either alone or in a group, spend time recalling your most exciting sexual experience! (Obviously, this would not work well with a new group, or in a group where trust has not been established.) When was your last exciting sexual experience? Can you describe it to one individual or to the group?

Variations:

What part of your body don't you like? When you go to bed with someone for the first time, what part of your body are you embarrassed by? What turns you on sexually? What parts of your body are most erotic?

## Tantra

The ancient yogic practice of tantra is a Plutonian pathway to higher states of consciousness and control. By beginning with the most accessible energy, sexual attraction, a springboard is created to more subtle realms. The practice cultivates sexuality by integrating the subtle forces in the human body with the goal of achieving a dynamic balance between the dual and opposing energies called yin and yang. Here are some recommended books on tantra: *Tantrism: Its Secret Principles and Practices* (Benjamin Walker), *Tantra in Tibet* (H.H. Dalai Lama, Tsong-ka-pa and Jeffrey Hopkins), *Tools for Tantra* (Harish Gohari), *Tantra for the West* (Marcus Allen) and *Sexual Secrets* (Nick Douglas and Penny Slinger).

## Taboos

Taboos, whether personal or societal, are usually instituted on grounds of morality. What societal taboos can you think of? What are your personal taboos? Have you ever violated a societal taboo? A personal one? If you are addressing this in a group, can you tell the others about it?

## Nuclear Annihilation

In a group discuss what you think the odds are of a nuclar war in your lifetime. Spend time processing the feelings summoned up by this discussion.

## AIDS

This complex issue is facing all of us. How do we deal with AIDS on an individual level, as a culture, as a world community? How do we protect the rights of those carrying the virus and the rights of those that are not? How do we pay for the enormous medical expense for such a large group? How do we deal with issues of testing, confidentiality, and prejudice? Do you know anyone who has AIDS? Do you know anyone who has died of AIDS?

## Magic

Magic and magical operations fall under the category of Pluto. Many of us unconsciously work magic daily. On the simplest level, magic is the ability to influence the world by psychic means. It is the power to influence and ultimately control one's own space-time reality and eventually to control the space-time reality of others. An excellent source to learn more about magic is *Natural Magic, the Magical State of Being* by Barry Saxe.[5] It is particularly lucid, well-documented, and fascinating reading. A respected and well known series of five books on magic was written by Melita Denning and Osborne Phillips called *The Magical Philosophy*.[6] *The Practice of Magical Evocation*[7] by Franz Bardon and numerous books by occultist Dion Fortune[8] are other resources for specific use and technique.

## One Hour To Live

You have seen the future and know now you have but 60 minutes left of your life on earth. What would you need to say to those around you? Who do you have unfinished business with?

## 'Scruples'

The board game 'Scruples' couldn't be more Scorpionic. It is a game of self-evaluation in which you knowingly make a decision to tell the truth or an untruth. This game puts you and your friends in a number of provocative ethical situations to which you must, after some soul-searching, respond. Would you pose nude for a national magazine for $10,000? You and a stranger hail a cab at the same time. As the cab pulls up do you insist the cab is yours? You witness a car accident in which one party is clearly to blame. Do you come forward to testify? Sometimes you answer truthfully. Or anticipating what your friends think you'll respond, you give the opposite reply. Then you must convince the group of the sincerity of your reply. Very Scorpionic and thought provoking.

## Pluto Films

*Testament, Aliens, Bang the Drum Slowly, Deliverance, Shoah, My Fair Lady, The Godfather, The Lion in Winter, The Burning Bed.*

## Pluto Walk

Pluto's walk is intense and intimidating. Walk with power, strength, and passion. Pretend you are Hades coming out of the bowels of the earth to capture Persephone.

## Suggested Music

*Hearing Solar Winds* (The Harmonic Choir/David Hykes), *Tantric Songs* (Popul Vuh),

*Totem* (Gabrielle Roth), *Chaotic Meditation* (Music of the Shree Rajneesh Ashram), *Dark Side of the Moon* (Pink Floyd), 'I'm Not in Love' (10 cc), 'Prelude to Lohengrin' (Wagner) and much of the work of Wagner, *Apocalypse Now* soundtrack, *Te Deum* (Berlioz), 'Battle of the Huns' (Liszt), *Night on Bald Mountain* (Mussorgsky), *Gloria* (Vivaldi), *Cho-ga: Tantric and Ritual Music of Tibet*.

## Pluto Story

Before the advent of writing all our ancestors relied on story-telling to transmit themes and ideas that are universal and timeless. There will always be stories about where we came from, how the world was created, how light became divided and about love, tests of power, failure, and victory.

Stories and story-tellers are vehicles for keeping the tradition and wisdom of a culture alive. I asked my friend, story-teller Marcie Telander, to tell us a story to help us understand Pluto. Appendix A contains the enchanting story she has written. I hope you will read it with pleasure.

# APPENDIX A

# THE STORY OF
# MARGARET AND TAMLAINE

The tale of Tamlaine, the Tamlin, or Tam, as he is also known,
comes from Scottish and Irish folk tradition, and in particular from
Scottish and Irish word-of-mouth stories and ballads. There are
many versions of this beloved faerie romance. The story which
follows is a personal interpretation of the original tale by writer
and story-teller Marcie Telander. 'Margaret and Tamlaine' is one of
the stories collected in Telander's work-in-progress
*Forbidden Fruit: Adult Romances and Gothic Tales*

Lady Margaret lived in a country far to the north on the Brittanic Isles. Her father,
an aged and wise king, had lost his wife (Margaret's mother) at Margaret's birth.
His fondness for his only child was famous. The king's love was so great that it
seemed he could deny her nothing. He made of her but one request — never would
she enter the Carterhaugh Wood. Thus, Margaret grew to maidenhood choosing
her pleasure, some said, as if she were in truth a man, and the old king's only son
and feudal heir.

Margaret was held to be unnaturally courageous and bold for she rode out with
the men whenever she chose. She flew a fine Merlin hawk she had raised from
a fledgling and kept a great red stallion which she rode astride like any knight or
man-at-arms.

However, it was not that Lady Margaret was cut of such courageous cloth, but
rather that her keen sense of curiosity pushed her always from the castle walls. What
Margaret feared most was boredom. This she could not bear.

The celebration of Litha and the Dance of the Summer Fires was in the air, kindling
the spirits of every woman, man, and child, within the hold and without. Margaret
paced around the castle pitched for adventure like a reed torch. Outside the pantry
in the still room where the beer and mead were brewed and where her childhood
nurse prepared healing herbal draughts, Margaret paused to listen to the old woman
talking with one of the cooks.

'The maidens will go to the well and stand there gawping at that he-creature.
And him not even a mortal but Faerie Fhain.' 'Aye, they will,' her sister replied. 'And
woe be to the father's daughter who tarries too long in the Carterhaugh Wood.

The stag viewing himself in the stream

She will lose more than her wits, I venture, to that sweet Faerie Prince!' The old women chuckled at their secret. But Margaret had heard all she needed. Curiosity had her in its thrall and she was away for the Carterhaugh Wood!

Over the ripe rich fields of summer she rose, bearing ever toward her destination. Soon she saw the shimmering green of the great wood and at its leigh she tied her horse and entered the forest alone. She followed what seemed to be a faint deer path until it joined and ran along a bubbling stream. Deeper and deeper into the oaken wood she walked, until at the very heart of the forest, hidden in a dappled and mysterious shade, she came upon the brook's source, a lovely grotto of stones and a deep pool made by a small stream issuing forth from the depths of the earth.

Here then was the well of which the old women had spoken. Suddenly a terrible crash echoed on the other side of the stream. There, quivering with fear, was a great stag gathering itself to spring across the brook when its wild amber eyes fell on Margaret. All in a moment she saw the long gash bleeding across the hart's left shoulder and heard the evil sound of wild dogs snarling and baying after their quarry. They had tasted blood and were on for the kill. The stag lowered its great rack and, trapped between Margaret and the snarling beasts, could do nothing but prepare to defend itself as best it could.

Without knowing how she found the courage Margaret held out her arms to the bleeding stag. Its amber eyes rested on her for a long heartbeat and then it was across the stream, and fell crumpled from fear and exhaustion behind her at the edge of the well.

The dogs sprang through the underbrush and stopped suddenly when they saw Margaret facing them across the stream. She picked up a sturdy piece of wood and held it in front of her body as she stood between the stag and the dogs. Quietly, but with ever-building force, a voice rose within her as she directed all of her energy at the snarling beasts.

'Vine and grain, Vine and grain,
All that falls shall rise again.'

She sang the ancient chant again and again. Her voice rose, full of force and determination. But she did not move, nor take her eyes from the fierce eyes of the dogs. Suddenly, as if she had hurled burning pitch at them, the dogs whirled, tails between their legs, and were gone in the direction from which they had come. Margaret fell to her knees. For some time she could not think or move. And then slowly she turned to see if the wounded stag was still alive.

But there, standing at the edge of the pool, was a naked young man. His back was turned to her as he ducked his head in the water. She could see what was now an ugly scar carved across his left shoulder. As he lifted his head from the pool and tossed it back, droplets of water flew from his curly brown hair, crowning him in strange light, like the antlers of a stag. Then he turned toward her for the first time. Neither spoke as they looked at one another. Surely he was the most beautiful man Margaret had ever seen. Again, she held out her arms and, as if in a dream, he came to her.

How long had they lay together Margaret could not say. All that had been real to her was no more. And in its place lay the exquisite young man now sleeping in her arms.

When at last he awoke Margaret questioned him about his mysterious appearance. But he only laughed and playfully caught at her hair. 'Well, then,' she said. 'I am Margaret. And I would know *your* name.'

Suddenly the young man's face grew dark as if he had just remembered a terrible dream.

'Ask no more!' he cried. 'For surely there is no more sorrowful man than I.'

'Come now,' said Margaret. 'Have we not lain together? All I would have is your name, my lord.'

'I am Sorrow and Loss. I am the loneliest of men. I belong to no mortal, but must do ever as She bids.' His voice made Margaret shiver, but she laughed and pursued. 'All this, and just for asking a name? But, if there is another woman, I am not afraid. Let me meet her and I know I will match her . . . or better her if it come to that.'

'I am Tamlaine. And now you must know and fear for your own life. For by the Three-fold Goddess, I love you Margaret. Yet the Mistress who claims me is more powerful than all mortals. She is the Great Mother, the Earth, the Morrighan. She is the Faerie's ruler, the Queen of Elphane!'

As he told his sad story, Margaret's heart felt as if it were growing as heavy as a piece of lead. Tamlaine had ridden off to war on the great celebration of Samhain, what some had now begun to call Hallow's Eve, but on his path he had met a beautiful maiden and had lain with her all the night long. Little did he know that it was the Faerie Queen in her maidenly guise with whom he spent that night of nights when the Faerie may enter the world of mortals. Now he was in her thrall and doomed to leave the mortal realm to be her eternal consort. All of this would come to pass when the worlds separated once again on the next Samhain. He ended his story by saying fiercely, 'You must leave me, my Margaret. Leave and never turn back or think of me again. For soon I am gone, and not even a ghost will remain. Now GO!'

What could she do? Margaret bent to gather her cloak that had been her bed. As she turned she saw that the once smooth waters of the well were disturbed. Then she saw the stag where the man Tamlaine had stood. It leapt across the stream and paused for a moment capturing her with its great amber eyes, then sprang through the undergrowth and was gone.

Margaret made her way out of the forest and her horse bore her swiftly home. But she remembered nothing of this. It was as if all her thoughts had fallen deep down into the waters of the well at the heart of Carterhaugh Wood.

She lived through the next months in a cloud of emptiness. She continued her life at the castle like a dumb puppet or corn dolly made by the midwives of the village — a lifeless image of a living being. And then the dreams came. Such dreams: each night she would see the great mist rolling across a barren field and hear the sound of distant thunder. But just as she was about to see what moved relentlessly toward her, the image would dissolve.

Now she knew that she was with child. Tamlaine's child. Her sorrow had sharpened to anger at her lover's betrayal and fear. She would have this child and make it her own. No father, faerie, or foolish love would ever claim her or the child again.

Yet at the time of Leaf-fall and the dark festival of Samhain approached, Margaret felt her anger subsiding. And in its place grew the need to look on Tamlaine's face once again. She wished to stand before him and look into his heart. Was he truly nothing more than a thoughtless sprite who had shared his body with her, and no more? He *must* respond to her like a man!

She remembered Tamlaine's mysterious story of Samhain and she was determined to ride to the Carterhaugh Wood once more and be there when the moon rose on Samhain Eve.

The wind blew cold as she tethered her stallion at the forest's leigh and entered the wood. Following the brook she came to the edge of the well just before moonrise. She wrapped her cloak about her and hid behind a thicket to await, she knew not what. Then, just as in her dream, she heard the strange rumbling as if something huge were being torn asunder. And issuing forth, rolling toward her like a flood, was the unearthly fog. It was the *fith-fath*, the faerie magic which concealed all movement until the world of mortal and spirit opened and the Faerie Rhain rode forth.

Out of the mist stepped 13 great white horses followed by 13 black horses. And then she saw him, her Tamlaine. He was slumped and pale, riding a grey palfrey and dressed all in faerie green. Margaret cried out without thinking at the sight of her love, forgetting her anger, forgetting her fear. She ran toward him. At the sight of her, Tamlaine's deathly face brightened for a moment and then, as if in a faint, he slumped forward. She caught him in her arms as he slid from the horse and fell to her knees holding him.

'So! You have come to see Tamlaine off!' said a rich and powerful voice. Margaret raised her head and saw a magnificent woman gazing down at her from the back of a wild-looking white mare. The woman, if woman she was, was neither young nor old, she was both. She was small and dark and her silver hair fell down her back like moonlight. The blue mark of the horned moon shone in the center of her forehead. Margaret was terrified beyond words. She could not speak, she could not even look at this creature, Earth Goddess and Faerie Spirit — the Queen of Elphane.

'Lady Margaret, look at me. I see your mortal love for this Tamlaine. And the boy-child you carry in your womb. I see all of this. But this night Tamlaine will join me in the great faerie ride and be mine forever!'

Margaret still could not speak. She could only hold the lifeless body of Tamlaine.

'I love a wager, my sister Margaret,' the Queen continued. 'And so I will riddle you three riddles. If your mortal love can withstand these tests then I shall make you a faerie gift of this pretty lad.' As the Queen of Elphane spoke, the mist of the fith-fath gathered around them. 'Can you endure the first stage of mortal love?' cried the Queen. 'Mortal woman, save your man. Raise your power if you can!'

Margaret looked down and what had once been her sweet Tamlaine was slowly transforming into a terrible beast. His hands had become claws, his hair a wild mane and his face the ferocious mask of a savage lion! As she held him the beast's claws sank into her breast and it roared and tore at her. But still she held on; held on to her dear Tamlaine.

At last the Queen laughed and spoke out, 'You have more of the spirit than I thought, Maid Margaret. You have given the devouring beast of Lust, the first stage of human love, all of your tenderness. And look. Your boy lies there again in your arms. But now, prepare. The second test is upon you. Mortal woman, save your man. Sister match my power if you can!' And with that, the fith-fath gathered around them.

As Margaret watched in horror, Tamlaine's strong body began to wriggle and coil. His skin grew scaly and cold and his face became the head of a great serpent whose green eyes shot out a venomous flame. It was a flame of such piercing cold that it cut Margaret to the bone with its icy fire. It burned within her until she thought she would surely die, but still she held the serpent, her Tamlaine, in her arms. At last she heard the Queen's voice.

'So. You have the strength to hold your love with a woman's understanding, even in the throes of the greedy serpent, Envy and Jealousy. And again, your beloved Tamlaine is returned to your arms. But now my Lady Margaret, if ever your mortal love and womanhood have served you, gather them to you here. The third and last stage of human love is the most painful of all. Lose this wager, and the boy sheds his human heart. He shall be mine!'

As the mists gathered around them Margaret shuddered. She felt she had no more strength to give. But she must hold firm.

'Mortal woman save your man. Sister, *quell* my power if you can!'

As the Queen's final challenge rang out it grew deathly still. At first Margaret prayed that somehow the spell had been broken. But then, as if a huge wave of the sea had washed across the land, Margaret saw towering over them the billowing mists. And out of their depths came a howling and keening like no sound Margaret had ever heard. It was the faerie death wail of the Morrighan come to claim Tamlaine for its own. And as she held Tamlaine with the last of her strength her terror rose. Even as she watched, human death was upon him. His young body began to shrivel and age. His beautiful face grinned back at her in the sardonic smile of the grave. What had once been the tender young body of the youth she loved was now a reeking skeleton. Margaret could hear the Faerie Queen's voice through the wailing cry of the Bahn Sidhe.

'This my dear mortal sister, is the final stage. See you how time and age will be the death of your human love? Give him to me so that he shall never face these things but shall be young forever in the Land of Faerie. HE IS MINE!'

Margaret looked down at the clattering bones in her arms. What was she? Only a mortal. All she had to give Tamlaine, the father of the child within her, was her woman's love. Slowly she walked to the side of the well. Into the womb of the earth she would send her love. She must have the courage to plunge him from her, this one last time, into the depths. She released the bones into the still water and began to chant the ancient song:

'Oats and corn, oats and corn, All that dies shall be reborn.'

With all of her mortal courage and faith she willed what had once been Tamlaine to rekindle with her love.

Suddenly, deep within the well the water began to bubble and swirl. As the churning rose toward the surface she saw her own reflection struck by a golden light. And there stood Tamlaine, naked and healed, whole as the first moment she had looked on him. It was as if he had simply risen from bathing in the pool.

She held out her arms to him and held him, feeling his heart beating next to hers. As swiftly as it had come, the rumbling sound and great secret mists rolled off toward the Western Sea. Now Margaret heard it, like a last gentle breath of wind:

'Bless you daughter. Bless you and your mortal love. Bless you.'

Margaret looked into Tamlaine's face. Now she knew that in their life together she would again be called upon to save him and the boychild she would soon bear. And this time she knew also that the power would come to her as suddenly as magic — the only magic she knew. It would come as the power of a mortal woman's love.

# APPENDIX B

# FACILITATING GROUPS: TIPS, TECHNIQUES, AND SKILL BUILDING

G.I. Gurdjieff reminds us that each of us has a definite repertoire of roles which we play in our day to day lives, with a particular role for each circumstance we normally find ourselves in — sometimes one or two for our family, another one or two at work, and another role with our friends. We are not one person, but six, seven or more. At different times we find ourselves so enmeshed in one of the roles we play that we completely identify with it. [1]

When we create an environment which puts us in slightly different circumstances, like a group, we have difficulty finding suitable roles and momentarily become ourselves. Outside our repertoire we feel uncomfortable. Gurdjieff believed that only by experiencing this discomfort can we truly experience ourselves. A group setting helps to eliminate the oppression of our 'dominant perceptions' and allows us to experience other possibilities within us.

Being with others in a group exposes us to other points of view, helping us to see that we all have similar problems and experiences. We see in each other's situations something of our own — some attitude, response, behavior, or reaction we share. By contacting, acknowledging, and accepting another's humanity, we are encouraged to accept our own.

Working together in a group helps individuals achieve a new sense of participation and ability to act in their lives. By participating in the moment we experience ourselves outside our usual roles, and in so doing come to see that we are capable of being as self-initiating and dynamic as we want to be.

## Starting a Group: The Preliminaries

If you want to form a group to try out experiential methods, whether it be for an afternoon, a full day or ongoing, some basic considerations will help you to design a more effective group experience. First, consider logistics. How large will the group be? Do members know each other? If they do, less time will be needed for 'ice-breaking.' Is the workspace for the group adequate? This can be critical. The more comfortable the environment, the more conducive it will be to active participation. A large, well-lighted room, part carpeted and part finished floor, with mirrors and cushions will give you the most flexibility. Movement and expression can't be encouraged in a crowded room.

How long will the group meet? If you are planning a one day group, know that group energy will be highest two to three hours into the process and lowest in the period right after lunch. Plan the key activity of the day in the peak period and choose quiet time or physical activity after lunch.

Find out what enriching resources you have available (costumes, art supplies, participants with acting or group experience, or counselling, music, or dance skills). These can add enormously to the group's experience.

What is the group's astrological skill level (basic, intermediate, or advanced)? Initially you will find it better not to mix all three levels into a single group. Too much difference in skill level can make it more difficult to satisfy everyone's needs. Intermediate and advanced students work well together, but beginners often feel overwhelmed. Once when I inadvertently make this mistake, I found myself overcompensating for those who were just getting started, while not really giving more advanced students the detail they needed — and they let me know it!

## Getting Started

Once you have considered the logistics, clarify your own goals for the group. Is it most important that the process encourage a meditative inner focus, sharing, emotional catharsis, play? Your goals will determine the particular quality and tone the group will have. (A goal of encouraging catharsis will create a very different group experience from one aimed at having fun with astrology.) Schedule your group whenever the transits most support your intention. For example, if a meditative experience is your goal, schedule the group when there's a Mercury trine Neptune. A cathartic goal might call for a Pluto station, or full moon in Scorpio. If your goal is fun, do it with a Jupiter sextile Mercury/Mars.

An overall goal should be that the experience for participants be a positive one, especially in a serious astrodrama. I suggest you begin by giving a positive outlook. This will provide a helpful sense of security when approaching more painful insights. Indicate the resources that the director has to balance out in more difficult aspects. Having explored them, then move to more tender parts of the psyche. Once you have created an atmosphere of possibility it is safe to turn to the more painful issues. From the beginning aim toward a conclusion of the experience that will leave the director with a sense of positive accomplishment.

In any group, be flexible and ready to modify your objectives. Because you can't know the exact response any group will have to these experiences, suspend your own expectations and be open to changing your plan. By adjusting the event to suit the situation, you can better respond to the particular energies of your group.

Be clear in your instructions. Confusion on anyone's part will dampen the effect and even undermine the exercise. If the exercise does not proceed in the way you planned, or the group missed the point, admit it. There's no shame in repeating instructions. The group will appreciate the clarification.

Have the group wear comfortable, unrestricted clothing to encourage movement and a relaxed tone. And by all means be innovative! Use these ideas as a springboard for your own creating!

## Making it Safe

By far the single most critical task for the facilitator of a successful group experience is creating a safe environment. Group members must feel as though they can safely share their feelings without fear of judgment or criticism. If this neutrality doesn't exist there will be conscious or unconscious resistance to the process and your goals will probably not be realized. To be successful you must first create an environment of trust. One of the best ways to accomplish this is to begin slowly. Ease the group into feeling comfortable with each other. Start with warm-ups, ice-breaking exercises and some simple body stretches. Then, as people begin to loosen up, add more movement. When you invite people to stretch their bodies you are inviting them to stretch their discomforts and resistances too. Some groups will require more time to move through this warm-up phase, so have a number of fun, stimulating exercises ready to use if you need them. To maintain trust and group rapport, always ensure that participants can decline any particular exercise without being made to feel uncomfortable.

Experience has shown that if a person approaches what is for them a danger point they will instinctively stop, absorb what they have learned, and reconstruct their defenses. If this is respected, you shouldn't have a problem. Especially important: don't forget to take risks yourself. It gives them permission to do so as well. Your attitude can set the tone. You should also give attention to deciding what role you want to play in relation to the group. Leading a group using the traditional teaching format of one active, 20 passive members is usually less successful than 'facilitating' or guiding the group to create for itself. In this way, the focus shifts from you to the group.

# Group Dynamics

Throughout the 1970s, groups came into special prominence as a means to allow more people to have access to psychological help at lower cost than individual therapy. Thus it became recognized that group members are a great resource to one another as 'psychological helpers,' and a wealth of knowledge began to accumulate on ways of maximizing that help. By drawing on that body of knowledge you can make your own groups effective and can encourage the supportive, nurturing energies that give this kind of experience impact. Much of what follows is taken from my training and experience in group facilitation.

## Feelings

Experiential groups should provide a direct encounter with feelings. Through direct experience we get more deeply in touch with these important emotional responses. Much neurotic behavior stems from a desperate desire to avoid the emotions. For some of us the intellect has provided a kind of 'interference' which separates us from our feelings. I am not discounting the value of reasoning and discussion, but rather emphasizing the value of our neglected feeling life. By evening out the disparity between the two modes of experience we are able to view our world from a more three-dimensional perspective.

Since the emotions released in experiential processes can be powerful, it is important to maintain the pace of events in a group activity. Keep talk to a minimum immediately after an experience to prevent the diffusion of energy. If group members immediately begin talking it may be because they have touched an area which is sensitive for them. Changing the subject just pushes it back into the unconscious where it needn't be expressed.

Also after an experience, it is important to allow the group to 'come down' gradually. Because each experience stimulates us in different ways, you'll want to allow time for digesting and quiet reflecting. By establishing a rhythm between action and reflection you honor the natural interchange between inner and outer experience. This produces a more complete healing event.

If the group is strong in the Air element, focusing on feelings will be even more important. A group like this will tend to stay in their heads and want to 'talk about' feelings rather than express them. Several years ago I had an experience like this with a strong 'Air' group. To help them gain access to their right brain feeling sides, I asked them to perform their astrodramas non-verbally. Although this was very difficult for them it proved to be a valuable intervention.

## Structure and Timing

Too much or too little structure will stifle group creativity. If a group is too structured it will feel repressed and controlled, unable to be spontaneous and expressive. If there is too little structure a group might suffer from dissipated energy. Or it can get bogged down in a competitive bid for control among members. Learning and keeping this balance is something experience will teach you.

The average attention span for adults is 20 minutes, so be sure to change the rhythm of your processes. Mixing individual exercises with a large group exercise, dyads, and small group exercises, keeps the group interested. For example, alternate a left brain exercise with a right brain one, or utilize the four modes of consciousness referred to by Jung, alternating a sensing experience with a mental, or intuitive one.

## Feedback

Throughout the group, teach and model the giving of accurate feedback. The information recorded and shared by others can be as enlightening as one's own living out of a powerful moment, adding shape to the experience. Many of us do not give adequate information to one another about the impact of the other's behavior on us. We are either too 'polite' and give no feedback or give it in a way that's too general or too accusatory. 'You never say anything,' we complain, or, 'You're just as bossy as your mother.' Neither of these gets good results! Learn to be direct and specific, labeling the particular behavior that affected you, the feeling it elicited, and the interpretations you made: 'When you didn't stop and listen to me, I felt angry and hurt, because it seemed that my needs weren't important to you.' In an experiential group, as anywhere in life, bruised feelings can surely occur; they can best be dealt with by accurate, caring, mutual feedback.

*Primum non nocere:* (First, do no harm.)

Among therapists there is a rule of thumb: Do not tear down what you are not ready and able to rebuild. As a facilitator, know clearly what your capabilities and your limits are. Experiential astrology sometimes stirs up powerful unconscious energies so if you do not feel qualified or confident to take the therapist role, don't. If you're sensing that you have approached your limit, move slowly, or better yet, back off. Be especially careful when you recognize 'resistance.' Behind resistance is some kind of fear. Jung might say resistance signals contact with an unconscious 'complex.' Here, symbolically, is where the volcano lies. If you are skilled you can probe it further. If not, do not force the issue. Doing so may have serious consequences.

Working deeply with others takes sensitivity and skill. In my experience you will only be able to take a group as deeply as you have gone yourself. If you are really serious about working at this level of intensity with others, get into therapy about your own issues. Or join a class in group facilitation, psychodrama, psychosynthesis, or *Gestalt.* By traveling through your own depths you will develop the experience necessary to work deeply with others.

If you are already qualified to work in this way, your skills will allow the group to go deep beneath the surface and transform troublesome psychic and emotial energies. But, again, know your limits. Particularly in a group that meets only once or twice, if someone wants to work deeply make sure they have a follow-up resource to go to in the event that feelings continue to unfold. If a participant is currently seeing a therapist, insist that they have his or her permission before proceeding. Refer back to chapter three of this book. The woman described there was in therapy, so she had a place to take her feelings. The result of that one hour session was a two and a half month exploration in which she confronted many of her repressed feelings toward both her mother and father. Though this experience had a positive outcome, it also sobered me to just how profoundly this process can stir others.

# Outline For Experiential Groups

Here is a basic outline I sometimes use for experiential groups. Use it as a starting point, then amend it to suit your situation.

## I. Introductions

Tell the group about yourself, your interest in experiential methods, and some of your experiences with them. Remember, the first 10 minutes of any encounter, whether one to one or in a group, are the most critical; they 'set the tone' for all that follows.

A. Ask the group to take turns introducing themselves. Have each give their Sun, Moon, and ascendant. Do they have experience in this kind of group? What drew them to participate? What do they expect? (This is important. There will always be hidden agendas but it's helpful to know what the conscious expectations are.) Do they have any skills they would be willing to share which may be an asset to the group? (Acting, dancing, extensive group experience, counselling, massage, etc.)

B. Group mix — As group members introduce themselves, ask one person to record the Sun, Moon, and ascendant of each individual. After introductions, tally up the results and discuss the 'group mix.' (Astrologers will recognize this as characterizing only the general tone of the group, since other chart variables are not considered.) This helps groups recognize what characteristics they have as a group and how they are likely to respond.

Knowing and acknowledging the elemental mix of a group allows you to tailor a creative group experience for a particular group of individuals. For instance, if a group is strong in Fire you might add more physical exercises to stimulate their enthusiasm. Or it may be appropriate to monitor that energy and, at some point, ground them with some sensing experiences. If the group has a predominance of Air, be sure they don't habitually 'talk about.' Non-verbal or highly physical exercises and astrodramas may be helpful.

If the group is strong in Water they will tend to be more accessible to their feelings. If this group is scheduled near a full moon in Water, expect much emotional releasing. To break up this emotional atmosphere try some energetic Martian dancing.

C. After introductions let the group know what you have planned for the day so they understand what to expect. For example, 'We'll be doing improvisation dyads until noon, with one 10 minute break in between. Then we'll take one hour for lunch, followed by an afternoon session with two full astrodramas. We'll end the day with 30 minutes for group feedback and sharing, closing at 5 p.m.'

## II. Stretching, Warm-ups, and Ice-breaking

Begin with slow stretches, movement and dancing. Follow this with several ice-breaking exercises that slowly build comfort and trust in you and the rest of the group. Increase the level of interaction from experience to experience, moving from one-to-one to small groups of three or four and, finally, to exercises involving the entire group.

## III. Process

What process you use depends upon your goal and the particular group you are working with. If your goal is to teach the basics to a group of beginners you might begin by focusing on the four elements, describing their differences. Then add an exercise for each element like the ones described in chapter three. Or you might spend one evening covering the five personal planets, complete with an experience of each planet's appropriate music and movement. For variety you might have the group cut pictures out of magazines to make imageboards of the planets.

Or introduce the concept of duality by teaching the dual planets — the Sun/Moon,

Venus/Mars, Jupiter/Saturn. A friend who teaches astrology in Chicago spends one class on each planet. She's so excited about experiental astrology that she dresses in the costume of the 'planet of the week', and conducts the entire class in planetary character! For Mars she's boisterous and energetic, for Venus, soft and sweet!

If the group is more experienced, schedule a Jupiter night where everyone comes dressed as Jupiter and spends the evening sharing insights on the aspects and transits of each individual's Jupiter. Plan the event when Jupiter is strong by transit. For an evening of activity schedule the group during a transit of Jupiter conjunct Mars. An evening of art might coincide with a Jupiter trine Venus. For meditating on Jupiter, try when it is in harmonious aspect to Neptune. Your options with experiential astrology are endless!

## IV. Closure

It's important to allow time at the end of the session for the group to share feelings, give feedback, and say goodbye. Without closure some may walk away still feeling the effect of the experiences of the day. A closing exercise helps the group to end in a focused manner.

Learning how to skilfully facilitate astrodrama groups will take some time to learn. Hopefully this chapter has given you a good running start.

# Astrodrama: Interventions

In chapter five, I mentioned that you'll often want to intervene in group astrodramas. Here are some of the ways I have found useful.

## Freeze!

Sometimes the spontaneous unfolding of astrodramas stimulates the planets to interact and talk with each other all at once. When chaos ensues shout, 'Freeze!' Everyone will stop suddenly and be silent. While the action is stopped, ask the director what they'd most like to see at the moment. Or as facilitator you might make the suggestion, 'Why doesn't everyone be quiet except the T-square. Let's start there and move into its contact with Jupiter.'

'Freeze!' can also be useful to stop the action if you see the director is being overly affected by what is going on. This gives you a way to check in with them to see if they need to do something or if the action is stimulating something and the focus needs to be shifted.

## Doubling

This technique is borrowed directly from psychodrama. A double is a person who walks beside the director and adds ideas or feelings that the director may not be expressing. There are usually two doubles, one to support, the other to tear down. For example, suppose the director is under the simultaneous influence of a square from both Saturn and Uranus. He knows that staying in his current job is killing him but feels paralyzed to move. Here is where the double comes in. Have one person double as his Saturn in this situation, the other doubles as his Uranus. Place an imaginary straight line outside the chart circle and ask the director to walk back and forth along it. The doubles walk with him. One voices the perspective of the Saturn square, 'Stay safe. Stay with what you know. Yeah, it's boring but it is secure.' Then have the Uranus voice his opinion, 'You can't stay any longer. If you do I'll scream. You'll die in this job if you don't move now.' The director then responds to each of these as if they were his inner voices. Is there a way to work with both of these energies now? Have the director walk again and this time let each double interact with the director to help him find solutions to their parts of the problem.

Another example: let's consider another director who has concerns about his upcoming Pluto opposite the Moon. Have one person double the negative quality of Pluto in opposition while the other expresses the positive outcomes and possibilities of the opposition. By playing out the opposition in advance, the director not only touches his fear of this transit but gets a preview of the possible opportunities that await him as well. Frequent use of these doubles can allow him to consciously use and attune himself to the positive side of Pluto.

The last intervention to mention here is an astrological version of Fritz Perls' *Gestalt* intervention of the Top Dog/Underdog which is helpful when a conflict of polarity appears.[2] It is important to remember that polarities not only oppose one another; they also seek out and attract each other. These inner polar conflicts must be integrated in order to give the psyche a sense of wholeness. Perls equated the Top Dog with the Freudian super-ego and characterized it as the dictator and judge who tells us what to do, criticizes and belittles us. The other role, Underdog, is the little, seemingly less powerful, passive one. Perls held that the Underdog usually won through sabotage, postponement, and evasion. To find a resolution between the two halves a dialogue can be set up between them. To use this technique, move two chairs into the chart circle. (Let's say the director has recognized a conflict in her Saturn/Venus natal square which has manifested as a desire to get married. In spite of this desire, she always sabotages and rejects relationships as soon as she knows she has met 'Mr Right.') To begin the process the director assumes both roles and takes turns sitting in the Top Dog then Underdog chair. A typical dialogue might run like this: Top Dog (Saturn) says all men are weak and irresponsible, with a fatal flaw. Underdog (Venus) recognizes her dependency, wanting a man to take care of her, but is surprised by her coolness when she meets a suitable partner. The facilitator asks if Top Dog reminds her of someone. She discovers it is her father. The dialogue shifts to one between her father and herself. Through this exchange she comes to realize that although her father always treated her like a princess he managed to undermine relationships with her boyfriends by degrading them. She sees how she subconsciously agreed with him and that his interfering attitude lives within her.

Resolution to conflict can also be approached without the metaphor of Top Dog and Underdog. Simply ask the director confronted with an inner conflict to sit down and express both sides of his feelings. Have him move back and forth, from one chair to the other, until something begins to break through and make itself known. Then develop the dialogue according to what is revealed.

# NOTES AND REFERENCES

## Introduction

1. Gregory Bateson and Mary Catherine Bateson, *Angels Fear*, New York: Macmillan, 1987, p. 18.
2. Manilius, *Astronomics*, vol. 5, paraphrased in Franz Cumont, *Astrology and Religion Among the Greeks and Romans*, New York: Dover, 1960, p. 79.
3. Ptolemy, *Anthol. Palat.*, ix, 577, quoted in Franz Cumont, *Astrology and Religion Among the Greeks and Romans*, New York: Dover, 1960, p. 81.
4. Sally P. Springer and George Deutsch, *Left Brain, Right Brain* (Revised Edition), New York: Freeman, 1985.
5. Jean Houston, *The Possible Human*, Los Angeles: Jeremy Tarcher, 1982, p. 11.
6. Ibid., pp. 134-145.
7. For Erickson, see Jay Haley, *Uncommon Therapy*, New York: W.W. Norton, 1973. See also:
   Milton Erickson and Earnest Rossi, *Hypnotic Realities*, New York: John Wiley and Sons, 1976.
   For Neurolinguistic Programming, see Richard Bandler and John Grinder, *Frogs into Princes*, Moab, Utah: Real People Press, 1979.
   Steve Lankton, *Practical Magic*, Cupertino, California: Meta Publications, 1980.
8. Stephen Arroyo, *Astrology, Psychology and The Four Elements*, Davis, California: CRCS Publications, 1975, p. xiii.
9. Harvey Cox, cited in Doris LaChapelle and Janet Bourque, *Earth Festivals*, Silverton, Colorado: Finn Hill Arts, 1976, p. 63.

## Chapter 1

1. 'Living the Drama of the Horoscope', *Astrology Now*, Vol. 22, 1979, pp. 12-15, 55-58.
2. Jamake Highwater cites the '95,140 combined body movements which have been laboriously calculated' for ancient Greek dance in his *Dance: Rituals of Experience*, Methuen, Toronto, 1985, p. 42.
3. Aristophanes, *Frogs*, vv. 340-350, tr. B.B. Rogers, cited in George E. Mylonas, *Eleusis and the Eleusinian Mysteries*, Princeton University Press, Princeton NJ, 1961, pp. 254-255.

4. Lucian, on dancing, 15, cited in S. Angus, *The Mystery Religions*, p. 90.
5. Themistios, preserved in Stobaios, IV, p. 107 (Meineke), cited in Mylonas, *Eleusis and the Eleusinian Mysteries*, pp. 264-265.
6. Pindar., *Fragm.* 102 (Oxford), cited in Mylonas, *Eleusis and the Eleusinian Mysteries*, 1961, p. 285.
7. George E. Mylonas, *Eleusis and the Eleusinian Mysteries*, Princeton NJ: Princeton University Press, 1961, p. 284.

## Chapter 2

1. Dane Rudhyar, *Astrology and the Modern Psyche*, Vancouver WA: CRCS Publications, 1976, pp. 2-34.
2. Ibid., p. 5.
3. Ibid., p. vii.
4. Carl Jung, cited in Dane Rudhyar, *Astrology and the Modern Psyche*, 1976, p. 24.
5. Carl Jung, *Memories, Dreams, Reflections.* New York: Vintage Books, 1965, p. 158.
6. Joseph Campbell, *The Portable Jung*, New York: Penguin Books, 1976, p. xxii.
7. Carl Jung, 'Archetypes of the Collective Unconscious', in *The Archetypes and the Collective Unconscious*, Second Edition, Princeton NJ: Princeton University Press, 1968, pp. 3-4.
8. Ibid., p. 5.
9. Carl Jung, 'Psychological Aspects of the Mother Archetype', in *The Archetypes and the Collective Unconscious*, p. 79.
10. Joseph Moreno, *Psychodrama*, vol. I, Beacon House, Beacon NY, 1946.
11. Dane Rudhyar, *Astrology and the Modern Psyche*, p. 69.
12. Michael P. Nichols and Melvin Zax, *Catharsis in Psychotherapy*, New York: Gardner Press, 1977, p. 73.
13. M.H. Klein, P.L. Mathieu, E.T. Gendlin, and D.J. Kiesler, *The Experiencing Scale: A Research and Training Manual*, Bureau of Audio-Visual Instruction, University of Wisconsin Extension, 1970.
14. Claudio Naranjo, 'I and Thou, Here and Now: Contributions of Gestalt Therapy', Chapter III in F. Douglas Stephenson, ed., *Gestalt Therapy Primer*, New York: Jason Aronson, 1978, p. 38.
15. Wilhelm Reich, *The Function of the Orgasm*, New York: World Publishing, 1971. See also:
Alexander Lowen, *The Language of the Body*, New York: Collier Books, 1971.
Stanley Keleman, *Your Body Speaks Its Mind*, New York: Simon & Schuster, 1981.
16. Paramahansa Yogananada, *Autobiography of a Yogi*, Los Angeles: Self-Realization Fellowship, 1974, p. 279.
17. Ken Wilber, *Up From Eden*, Shambala, Boulder, Colorado, 1983. See also:
Stanislav Grof, *Beyond the Brain*, Albany NY, State University of New York, 1985.
Robert N. Walsh and Frances Vaughan, (Eds.), *Beyond Ego*, J.P. Tarcher, Los Angeles, 1980.

## Chapter 3

1. Carl Fitzpatrick. Personal communication, 1986.

## Chapter 4

1. Jose and Miriam Arguelles, *Mandala*, Berkeley and London: Shambhala, 1972, p. 12.
2. This is a useful oversimplification of ideas found in Wilhelm Reich, *The Function of the Orgasm*.
3. Ida P. Rolf, *Rolfing*, New York: Harper & Row, 1977.
4. Barbara Brown, *New Mind, New Body*, New York: Harper & Row, 1975.
5. Lucerne Valley CA: Geetam Rajneesh Sannyas Ashram, 1979.

## Chapter 6

1. Albert Einstein, quoted in Robert H. McKim, *Experiences in Visual Thinking*, Boston MA: PWS Engineering, 1980, p. 11.
2. Carl Jung, *Memories, Dreams, Reflections*, pp. 158-159.
3. Friedrich von Kekulé, quoted in Robert H. McKim, *Experiences in Visual Thinking*, p. 11.
4. Carlos Castaneda, *Journey to Ixtlan*, New York: Pocket Books, 1972, p. 98.

## Chapter 7

1. Jean Achterberg, *Imagery In Healing*, p. 7.
2. G. Prince, 'Putting the Other Half of the Brain to Work,' *Training: The Magazine of Human Resources Development*, 15 (1978): 57-61, cited in Sally P. Springer and George Deutsch *Left Brain, Right Brain*, p. 247.
3. David Galin, cited in Sally P. Springer and George Deutsch *Left Brain, Right Brain*, p. 261.

## Chapter 8

1. Jung, *Memories, Dreams, Reflections*, p. 346.
2. Ibid, p. 345.
3. Edward Rice, *Eastern Definitions*, Garden City NY: Anchor Doubleday, 1980, p. 409.
4. Ibid., p. 408.
5. Swami Satyeswarananda Giri, *Lahiri Mahasay*, by the Author, 1983, p. 92.
6. Paramahansa Yogananada, *Autobiography of a Yogi*, San Rafael, California: Self-Realization Fellowship, 1974, p. 275-276.
7. Ibid., p. 278.
8. Ibid., p. 278.
9. Ibid., p. 275.
10. Mohandas K. Gandhi, cited in Robert T. Jones' background article included with the libretto for the Chicago Lyric Opera performance of Phillip Glass'

*Satyagraha*, New York: CBS Masterworks, 1987.
11. Ibid.
12. Anagarika Govinda, *The Way of the White Clouds*, Boulder, Colorado: Shambala, 1970.
13. Peter Matthiessen, *The Snow Leopard*, New York: Bantam Books, 1978.
14. John G. Neihardt, *Black Elk Speaks*, New York: Pocket Books, 1972.
15. Stanislav Grof, *The Adventure of Self-Discovery*, Albany, NY: State University of New York Press, 1988, p. 30.
16. A.A. Milne, *Winnie the Pooh*, New York: Dell Publishing Company, 1982.

## Chapter 9

1. Ray A. Williamson, *Living The Sky*, Boston: Houghton Mifflin, 1984, p. 220.
2. Chief Letakots-Lesa of the Pawnee Tribe to Natalie Curtis, c. 1904, cited in Joseph Campbell, *Way of the Animal Powers*, San Francisco: Harper & Row, 1983, pp. 8, 18.
3. Franz Cumont, *Astrology and Religion Among the Greeks and Romans*, New York: Dover, 1960, p. 15.
4. S. Angus, *The Mystery Religions*, New York: Dover, 1975, p. 167.
5. Ibid., p. 195.
6. Frances Yates, *The Art of Memory*, Chicago: University of Chicago Press, 1966, p. 39.
7. Ibid., p. 129ff.
8. Ibid., p. 224.
9. Ibid., p. 254.
10. David Conway, *Magic: An Occult Primer*, New York: E.P. Dutton, 1973, p. 104.

# Book II: Resource Workbook

## Introduction

1. Imogen Holst, *Holst*, London, Faber & Faber Ltd, 1974, p. 48.

## The Moon In Cancer

1. Edward C. Whitmont, *The Return of the Goddess*, Crossroad, NY: Garber Communications, 1984.
2. Sylvia Brinton Perara, *Descent to the Goddess*, Toronto: Inner City Books, 1981.
3. Robert A. Johnson, *She*, New York: Harper & Row, 1976.
4. M. Ester Harding, *Woman's Mysteries*, New York: Harper & Row, 1971.
5. Shakti Gawain, *Creative Visualization*, New York: Bantam, 1982.
6. Jean Houston, *The Possible Human*, Los Angeles: J.P. Tarcher, 1982, p. 102-110.
7. Ibid., p. 91-94.
8. Motherpeace Tarot Deck, New York: US Games Systems, Inc., 1981.

## Mercury, Gemini And Virgo

1. Jean Houston, *The Possible Human*, Los Angeles: J.P. Tarcher, 1982, p. 177.

## Venus, Taurus And Libra

1. George Downing, *The Massage Book*, New York: Random, 1972.
2. Anais Nin, *Little Birds*, New York: Bantam, 1980, and *Delta of Venus*, New York: Bantam, 1985.
3. Kensington Ladies Society, *Ladies Own Erotica*, Berkeley, Ca: Ten Speed Press, 1984.
4. Lonnis Barbach, *Pleasures*, New York: Harper & Row, 1985, and *Erotic Interludes*, New York: Harper & Row, 1985.
5. Jean Rose, *Herbal Body Book*, New York: Perigee (Putnam), 1982.

## Mars And Aries

1. NASA Adventure Game, School of Public Administration 786, University of Southern California.

## Jupiter And Sagittarius

1. Glenn Mullin, *Death and Dying in the Tibetan Tradition*, London: Routledge & Kegan Paul, Inc., 1986.
2. Stephen Levine, *Who Dies?* Garden City, NY: Anchor Books, 1982.
3. Stanislav Grof and Christian Grof, *Beyond Death*, London: Thames & Hudson, Ltd., 1980.
4. Emperor Marcus Aurelius, *Meditations*, cited in Mullin, *Death and Dying: The Tibetan Tradition*, p. 192.

## Uranus And Aquarius

1. Gary Larsen, *The Far Side Gallery*, Kansas City: Andrews, McMeel and Parker, 1985.
2. Gyles Brendreth, *Classic Puzzles*, New York: Harper & Row, 1985.
3. Ronald Clark, *Einstein: The Life and Times*, New York: Avon Books, 1971.
4. Ladislao Reti, *The Unknown Leonardo*, New York: McGraw-Hill Books, 1974.
5. John O'Neil, *Prodigal Genius: The Life of Nikola Tesla*, New York: McKay (Tartan Books).
6. Thomas Kuhn, *The Structure of Scientific Revolutions*, Chicago: University of Chicago Press, 1970.
7. James Gleick, *Chaos*, New York: Viking, 1988.
8. Whitley Strieber, *Communion: A True Story*, New York: Morrow, 1987.
9. Budd Hopkins, *Intruders: The Incredible Visitations at Copley Woods*, New York: Random, 1987.
10. Film Short called the Power of Ten from Phillip Morrison's *Powers of Ten, a Book*

of the Relative Size of Things in the Universe and the Effect of Adding Another Zero, Redding, Cn: Scientific American Library, 1982.

## Neptune And Pisces

1. Kazuaki Iwasaki and Isaac Asimov, Visions of the Universe, Montrose, Ca: The Cosmos Store, 1981.

## Pluto And Scorpio

1. Carlos Castaneda, The Teachings of Don Juan: A Yaqui Way of Knowledge, New York: Simon & Schuster, 1968.
See also:
Carlos Castaneda, A Separate Reality, New York: Simon & Schuster, 1971.
Carlos Castaneda, Journey to Ixtlan, New York: Simon & Schuster, 1974.
2. Lynn Andrews, Medicine Woman, New York: Harper & Row, 1981.
3. John Lame Deer and Richard Erdoes, Lame Deer: Seeker of Visions, New York: Simon & Schuster, 1976.
4. Joan Halifax, Shamanic Voices, New York: E.P. Dutton, 1979.
5. Barry Saxe, The Magical State of Being, New York: Arbor House, 1977.
6. Melita Denning and Osborne Phillips, The Llewellyn Inner Guide to Magickal States of Consciousness: Working the Path of the Tree of Life, Minneapolis, Mn: Llewellyn Publications, 1985, and Mysteria Magica, 2nd, revised and extended edition, Minneapolis, Mn: Llewellyn Publications, 1986.
7. Franz Bardon, The Practice of Magical Evocation, Wuppertal, W. Germany: Dieter Ruggeberg, 1975.
8. For example: Dion Fortune, Psychic Self-Defence, and Sane Occultism, Wellingborough, Northamptonshire: Aquarian Press, 1985.

## Appendix B

1. G.I. Gurdjieff, as reported by P.D. Ouspensky, in In Search of the Miraculous, cited in 'ARCS', Parabola, Vol. 3, August, 1981, p. 42.
2. Frederick S. Perls, 'Gestalt Therapy and Human Potentials,' Chapter V in Stephenson, Gestalt Therapy Primer, p. 77.

# BIBLIOGRAPHY

Achterberg, Jeanne, *Imagery in Healing*, New Science Library (Shambhala), Boston, 1985.

Andrews, Lynn, *Medicine Woman*, Harper & Row, New York, 1981.

Angus, S., *The Mystery Religions*, Dover, New York, 1975.

Arguelles, Jose and Miriam, *Mandala*, Shambhala, Berkeley and London, 1972.

Arroyo, Stephen, *Astrology, Karma, and Transformation*, CRCS Publications, Davis, California: 1978.

—— *Astrology, Psychology and The Four Elements*, CRCS Publications, Davis, California, 1975.

Barbach, Lonnis, *Pleasures*, Harper & Row, New York, 1985.

—— *Erotic Interludes: Tales Told by Women*, Harper & Row, New York, 1985.

Bardon, Franz, *The Practice of Magical Evocation*, Dieter Ruggeberg, Wuppertal, W. Germany, 1975.

Bandler, Richard and Grinder, John, *Frogs into Princes*, Real People Press, Moab, Utah, 1979.

Bateson, Gregory and Bateson, Mary Catherine, *Angels Fear*, Macmillan, New York, 1987.

Bettelheim, Bruno, *The Uses of Enchantment*, Arthur A. Knopf, New York, 1977.

Bolen, Jean Shinoda, *Goddesses in Everywoman*, Harper & Row, New York, 1984.

Brandreth, Gyles, *Classic Puzzles*, Harper & Row, New York, 1985.

Brown, Barbara, *New Mind, New Body*, Harper & Row, New York, 1975.

Campbell, Joseph, *The Hero With a Thousand Faces*, Princeton University Press, Princeton, NJ, 1973.

—— *The Portable Jung*, Penguin Books, New York, 1976.

—— *The Mythic Image*, Princeton University Press, Princeton, NJ, 1981.

—— *Way of the Animal Powers*, Harper & Row, San Francisco, 1983.

Castaneda, Carlos, *The Teachings of Don Juan: A Yaqui Way of Knowledge*, Simon & Schuster, New York, 1968.

—— *A Separate Reality*, Simon & Schuster, New York, 1971.

—— *Journey to Ixtlan*, Pocket Books, New York, 1972.

Clark, Ronald, *Einstein: The Life and Times*, Avon Books, New York, 1971.

Collin, Rodney, *The Theory of Celestial Influence*, Shambhala Publications, Boulder, Colorado, 1984.

Conway, David, *Magic: An Occult Primer*, E.P. Dutton, New York, 1973.

Coward, Harold, *Jung and Eastern Thought*, State University of New York Press, New York, 1985.

Cumont, Franz, *Astrology and Religion Among the Greeks and Romans*, Dover, New York, 1960.

Cunningham, Donna, *Healing Pluto Problems*, Samuel Weiser, Inc., York Beach, Maine, 1986.

Denning, Melita and Phillips, Osborne, *The Llewellyn Inner Guide to Magickal States of Consciousness: Working the Paths of the Tree of Life*, Llewellyn Publications, Minneapolis, Minnesota, 1985.

—— *Mysteria Magica*, second, revised and extended edition, Llewellyn Publications, Minneapolis, Minnesota, 1986.

Downing, George, *The Massage Book*, Random, New York, 1972.

Erickson, Milton and Rossi, Earnest, *Hypnotic Realities*, John Wiley and Sons, New York, 1976.

Feder, Elaine and Bernard, *The Expressive Arts Therapies*, Prentice-Hall, Inc., Engelwood Cliffs, NJ, 1981.

Fleugelman, Andrew, *The New Games Book*, Doubleday, New York, 1976.

Fortune, Dion, *Psychic Self-Defence*, Aquarian Press, Wellingborough, Northamptonshire, 1985.

—— *Sane Occultism*, Aquarian Press, Wellingborough, Northamptonshire, 1985.

Gawain, Shakti, *Creative Visualization*, Bantam, New York, 1972.

Gleick, James, *Chaos*, Viking Penguin Inc., New York, 1988.

Govinda, Lama Anagarika, *The Way of the White Clouds*, Shambhala, Boulder, Colorado, 1970.

Grof, Stanislav and Grof, Christian, *Beyond Death*, Thames & Hudson, Ltd., London, 1980.

Grof, Stanislav, *Beyond the Brain*, State University of New York Press, Albany, NY, 1985.

—— *The Adventure of Self-Discovery*, State University of New York Press, Albany, NY, 1988.

Grossinger, Richard, *The Night Sky*, Sierra Club Books, San Francisco, Ca, 1981.

Growtowski, Jerzy, *Towards a Poor Theatre*, Simon & Schuster, New York, 1968.

Haley, Jay, *Uncommon Therapy*, W.W. Norton, New York, 1973.

Halifax, Joan, *Shamanic Voices*, E.P. Dutton, New York, 1979.

Hamaker-Zondag, Karen, *Astro-Psychology*, The Aquarian Press, Wellingborough, Northampton, 1980.

Harding, M. Esther, *Woman's Mysteries*, Harper & Row, New York, 1971.

Highwater, Jamake, *Dance: Rituals of Experience*, Methuen, Toronto, 1985.

Hillman, James, *Revisioning Psychology*, Harper & Row, New York, 1975.

Holst, Imogen, *Holst*, Faber and Faber, Ltd., London, 1974.

Hopkins, Budd, *Intruders: The Incredible Visitations at Copley Woods*, Random, New York, 1987.

Howell, Alice, *Jungian Symbolism in Astrology*, The Theosophical Publishing House, Wheaton, Illinois, 1987.

Houston, Jean, *The Possible Human*, Jeremy Tarcher, Los Angeles, 1982.

Jawer, Jeff, 'Living the Drama of the Horoscope', *Astrology Now*, Vol. 22, 1979, pp. 12-15, 55-58.

Johnson, Robert A., *She*, Harper & Row, New York, 1976.

Jung, Carl, *Man and His Symbols*, Doubleday, New York, 1964.

—— *Memories, Dreams, Reflections*, Vintage Books, New York, 1965.

—— *The Archetypes and the Collective Unconscious*, Second Edition, Princeton University Press, Princeton, NJ, 1968.

Iwasaki, Kazuaki and Asimov, Isaac, *Visions of the Universe*, The Cosmos Store, Montrose, California, 1981.

Kensington Ladies Society, *Ladies Own Erotica*, Ten Speed Press, Berkeley, Ca, 1984.

Klein, M.H., Mathieu, P.L., Gendlin, E.T., and Kiesler, D.J., *The Experiencing Scale: A Research and Training Manual*, Bureau of Audio-Visual Instruction, University of Wisconsin Extension, 1970.

Keleman, Stanley, *Your Body Speaks Its Mind*, Simon & Schuster, New York, 1981.

Kriyananda, Swami, *The Spiritual Science of Kriya Yoga*, The Temple of Kriya Yoga Press, Chicago, 1985.

Kuhn, Thomas, *The Structure of Scientific Revolutions*, University of Chicago Press, Chicago, 1970.

LaChapelle, Doris and Bourque, Janet, *Earth Festivals*, Finn Hill Arts, Silverton, Colorado, 1976.

Lame Deer, John and Erdoes, Richard, *Lame Deer: Seeker of Visions*, Simon & Schuster, New York, 1976.

Lankton, Steve, *Practical Magic*, Meta Publications, Cupertino, California, 1980.

Larsen, Gary, *The Far Side Gallery*, Andrews, McMeel and Parker, Kansas City, 1985.

Levine, Stephen, *Who Dies?* Anchor Books, Garden City, NY, 1982.

Lewis, Howard R., *Growth Games*, Bantam Books, New York, 1972.

Lingerman, Hal A., *The Healing Energies of Music*, The Theosophical Publishing House, Wheaton, Illinois, 1983.

Lowen, Alexander, *The Language of the Body*, Collier Books, New York, 1971.

Marieschild, Diane, *Motherwit*, The Crossing Press, Trumansburg, NY, 1981.

Matthiessen, Peter, *The Snow Leopard*, Bantam Books, New York, 1978.

McEvers, Joan, *Metaphysical, Spiritual and New Trends in Modern Astrology*, Llewellyn Publications, Minneapolis, Minnesota, 1988.

McKim, Robert H., *Experiences in Visual Thinking*, PWS Engineering, Boston, Massachusetts, 1980.

Milne, A.A., *Winnie the Pooh*, Dell Publishing Company, New York, 1982.

Moreno, Joseph, *Psychodrama*, Vol. I, Beacon House, Beacon, New York, 1946.

Morrison, Phillip, *Powers of Ten, A Book of the Relative Size of Things in the Universe and the Effect of Adding Another Zero*, Redding, Cn: Scientific American Library, 1982.

'Motherpeace Tarot Deck,' US Games Systems, Inc., New York, 1981.

Mullin, Glenn, *Death and Dying in the Tibetan Tradition*, Routledge & Kegan Paul, London, 1986.

Mylonas, George E., *Eleusis and the Eleusinian Mysteries*, Princeton University Press, Princeton, New Jersey, 1961.

NASA Adventure Game, School of Public Administration 786, University of Southern California.

Neihardt, John G., *Black Elk Speaks*, Pocket Books, New York, 1972.

Nichols, Michael P., and Zax, Melvin, *Catharsis in Psychotherapy*, Gardner Press, New York, 1977.

Nin, Anais, *Little Birds*, Bantam, New York, 1980.

—— *Delta of Venus*, Bantam, New York, 1985.

O'Neil, John, *Prodigal Genius: The Life of Nikola Tesla*, McKay (Tartan Books) New York.

Perara, Sylvia Brinton, *Descent to the Goddess*, Inner City Books, Toronto, Canada, 1981.

Reich, Wilhelm, *The Function of the Orgasm*, World Publishing, New York, 1971.

Reti, Ladislao, *The Unknown Leonardo*, McGraw-Hill, New York, 1974.

Rice, Edward, *Eastern Definitions*, Anchor Doubleday, Garden City, NY, 1980.

Rolf, Ida P., *Rolfing*, Harper & Row, New York, 1977.

Rose, Jeanne, *Jeanne Rose's Herbal Body Book*, Putnam Publishing Group, New York, 1976.

Rudhyar, Dane, *Astrology and the Modern Psyche*, CRCS Publications, Vancouver, Washington, 1976.

—— *Person Centered Astrology*, Aurora Press, New York, 1980.

Satyeswarananda Giri, Swami, *Lahiri Mahasay*, By the Author, 1983.

Saxe, Barry, *The Magical State of Being*, Arbor House, New York, 1977.

Spolin, Viola, *Improvisation for the Theater*, Northwestern University Press, Evanston, Illinois, 1963.

Springer, Sally P., and Deutsch, George, *Left Brain, Right Brain* (Revised Edition), Freeman, New York, 1985.

Starhawk, *The Spiral Dance*, Harper & Row, New York, 1979.

Stephenson, F. Douglas, *Gestalt Therapy Primer*, Jason Aronson, New York, 1975.

Strieber, Whitley, *Communion: A True Story*, Morrow, New York, 1987.

Walsh, Robert, N., and Vaughan, Frances, (Eds.), *Beyond Ego*, J.P. Tarcher, Los Angeles, 1980.

Whitmont, Edward C., *The Return of the Goddess*, Garber Communications, Blauvelt, NY, 1984.

Wilber, Ken, *Up from Eden*, Shambhala, Boulder Co, 1983.

—— *A Sociable God*, McGraw, New York, 1982.

Williamson, Ray A., *Living The Sky*, Houghton Mifflin, Boston, 1984.

Yates, Frances, *The Art of Memory*, University of Chicago Press, Chicago, 1966.

Yogananda, Paramahansa, *Autobiography of a Yogi*, Self-Realization Fellowship, Los Angeles, 1974.

# INDEX